Design Management

Quantifying and assessing the value of an organisation's design department can be problematic. The tools traditionally used by auditors are usually insufficient to 'measure' either the value of design projects or their influence within an organisation. This book aims to demystify the design development and design management process, scrutinising it against a new set of auditing principles which illuminate its true value in a contemporary context.

Featuring a series of international case studies, *Design Management: Exploring fieldwork and applications* argues that assessment of the design function within any organisation must incorporate both qualitative and quantitative research methods. The book explores a number of key themes, such as new product development, risk in design and corporate identity. Moreover, by drawing on a range of techniques from the social sciences, the authors rigorously develop means by which design may be understood accurately.

This book represents an important and timely contribution to our knowledge of the management of product and service innovation. It will be an invaluable text for students and researchers working in design and management.

Robert Jerrard is Research Professor in Design and Director of the Research Centre for Design and the Creative Industries at the Institute of Art and Design, University of Central England.

David Hands is Award Leader for the MA Design Management course within the Faculty of Arts, Media and Design, Staffordshire University.

Design
Management

Exploring fieldwork and applications

Edited by

Robert Jerrard and

David Hands

LONDON AND NEW YORK

First published 2008
by Routledge
2 Park Square, Milton Park, Abingdon, Oxon OX14 4RN

Simultaneously published in the USA and Canada
by Routledge
270 Madison Ave, New York, NY 10016

Routledge is an imprint of the Taylor & Francis Group, an informa business

Typeset in Perpetua and Bell Gothic by
RefineCatch Limited, Bungay, Suffolk
Printed and bound in Great Britain by
TJ International Ltd, Padstow

British Library Cataloguing in Publication Data
A catalogue record for this book is available from the British Library

Library of Congress Cataloging-in-Publication Data
A catalog record for this book has been requested

ISBN10: 0–415–39333–7 (hbk)
ISBN10: 0–415–39334–5 (pbk)
ISBN10: 0–203–08954–5 (ebk)

ISBN13: 978–0–415–39333–1 (hbk)
ISBN13: 978–0–415–39334–8 (pbk)
ISBN13: 978–0–203–08954–5 (ebk)

Contents

CONTENTS

vi

Figures

Tables

Notes on contributors

Nicholas Barnes is a Post-Doctoral Researcher at the Research Centre for Design and the Creative Industries at Birmingham Institute of Art and Design, University of Central England, UK. He is working primarily on an AHRC-funded project entitled Risk Taking in Design – An Investigation of Critical Decision Points in New Product Development. Nick's Ph.D. was in environmental management and he has since worked on several post-doctoral research projects, including a large EU-funded project examining risk and innovation in the development of new products and technologies in the biotechnology sector. Nick has academic work published in the fields of environmental management and innovation policy.

David Hands is Award Leader for the MA Design Management course, within the Faculty of Arts, Media and Design, Staffordshire University. His areas of expertise include: design policy analysis; implementing technology transfer systems through design. He has recently completed doctoral research into embedding 'crime resistant' thinking and tools into the briefing process for both product and spatial designers. David has written and published over 60 international academic papers and articles on a variety of design management topics. He was also the co-organiser for the successful D2B Design Management conference, held in Shanghai in March 2006.

Ray Holland directs the Master's Design Strategy programmes at Brunel University, UK, multidisciplinary design management courses attracting students from all over the world. His personal research reflects his conviction that design can find its direction through systems thinking and human / cultural issues. He was one of the pioneers of design management education and assists many overseas universities to develop master's and Ph.D. programmes in design and branding. Ray spent his early career as a company lawyer and accountant until he found his home in design. As consultant, he has helped to implement large computer-based information systems and design-led change management programmes.

Lisbeth Svengren Holm is Assistant Professor at Stockholm University School of Business. Together with Ulla Johansson (Göteborg University) she has been project co-leader of the research programme Relations in the Design Process. She has participated in a multidisciplinary research programme, Design in the Niche Society (Dennis), led by the Royal Institute of Technology and University College of Arts, Crafts and Design; and an international research programme, Design Drivers, and Design against Crime, headed by Manchester University and Salford University, UK, respectively. Her primary teaching and research interests are in strategic design management, product development, marketing and innovation. Between 1993 and 1997 she was working on research and development at Swedish Industrial Design Foundation in Stockholm, where she was the editor of *Design-journalen* until 2004. In 2000 she served as secretary of the National Agency for Higher Education's evaluation of the Swedish design educational programmes.

Robert Jerrard is Research Professor in Design and Director of the Research Centre for Design and the Creative Industries at the University of Central England, Institute of Art and Design. His Ph.D. and early work as a Research Fellow at the Royal College of Art centred on the specific problems faced by technology users in the creative industries. He has published widely on theoretical and social aspects of design and technology. He is a Fellow and a council member of the Design Research Society, an associate editor of the *Design Journal*, a member of the Universities Association for Continuing Education and a member of the Arts and Humanities Peer Review College. Bob is currently principal investigator of a major AHRC research project concerning Risk, Risk Perception and Design. He has directed major research into fashion culture and consumption and work-based learning in art and design. He has supervised 15 doctoral studies in a variety of areas of design research and examined more than 30. He is a research consultant for a number of international publishing groups and several UK and overseas universities.

Ulla Johansson is Associate Professor at the School of Business, Economics and Law at Göteborg University, where she is leading the Viktoria Project, a platform for research and other activities on the subject of design management/strategic design and other related subjects. With Lisbeth Svengren Holm of Stockholm University, she has been project co-leader of the research programme Relations in the Design Process. She teaches design management at the undergraduate, graduate and doctoral level. Prior to this in Göteborg at Växjö University she led a visual merchandising and interior decoration programme. In her research, she focuses on design and its relation to management and entrepreneurship. She has done an evaluation of the Swedish government's investment in design and the result is published in a book. She is co-editor, with Sacred Heart University's Jill Woodilla, of a 2005 book, *Irony and Organizations: Epistemological Claims and Supporting Field Stories*.

Gabriella Lojacono is Assistant Professor of Business Administration and Strategy at Bocconi University, Milan. In 1998, she was visiting Scholar at Copenhagen Business School, Department of Industrial Economics and Strategy and at the Centre of Design Development, Copenhagen. Her research areas are the competitive models in the furniture industry and design management.

Shengfeng Qin is a Lecturer in the School of Engineering and Design, Brunel University. He obtained his B.Sc. and M.Sc. degrees in China and his Ph.D. degree in the UK. He was an academic visiting scholar in 1996–97 within the Geometric Modelling group of the University of Birmingham, UK, after working in the East China Jiaotong University, China. Following the visiting research role, he took a Research Assistant post in 1998 at UWIC and subsequently joined the Manufacturing Systems Integration Research Institute (MSI), Loughborough University, as a Post-Doctoral Research Associate in 2000. His research interests include conceptual design, CAD, sketch-based modelling and interface, design computing and design management.

Adele Reid is a Researcher at the Research Centre for Design and Creative Industries at Birmingham Institute of Art and Design, University of Central England. She has been working in the field of ergonomics and design as a researcher for the last eight years. Her main areas of research have been in product design and health and safety. She has been involved in projects for the Ministry of Defence, the Health and Safety Executive and the European Standards Agency and research for the European Union's Fifth Framework Programme.

Mark Smith is responsible for supporting design research within Birmingham Institute of Art and Design. His research background is in sustainable design, eco-preneurship, environmental regulation and design, and environmental policy. He has contributed to various eco-design projects, including the DEMI online education resource, and was an adviser for the first International Eco-Design awards, Sheffield, in April 2001. Other experience includes managing the Sustainable Design Network, and working on a European project on Complexity and Business Strategy. He has held research posts at Cardiff University (BRASS) and the Open University, Department of Design and Innovation, where he completed a Ph.D. on 'Eco-Design Innovation in Small and Medium Sized Enterprises'. He holds a Master's degree in European Environmental Policy and Regulation from Lancaster University, and a B.Sc. in Biological Sciences from Plymouth Polytechnic.

Jonathan Vickery is Programme Director of the MA in International Design and Communication in the Centre for Cultural Policy Studies at the University of Warwick. He trained as a designer, working in London and Rome. He is a Founding Editor and Design Manager of *Aesthesis: International Journal of Art and Aesthetics in Management and Organizational Life*. He has published on art theory, public art and contemporary sculpture, and writes regularly for the *Art and Architecture Journal*. He is Editor (with Diarmuid Costello) of *Art: Key Contemporary Thinkers* (Berg, Oxford, 2007).

Yuanyuan Yin is a Ph.D. researcher in the School of Engineering and Design, Brunel University. She gained an MA degree in Design Strategy and Innovation at Brunel University, UK, and a B.Eng. (Hons) degree in Industrial Design in Xi'an University of Technology, China. Her Ph.D. study research is about design performance measurement.

Preface

The chapters offered in this book present a wide and rich description of how design management theory and, importantly, its practice can contribute to organisational success – not success in its narrowest definition, but success in the way that tacit knowledge, improved communication and the adoption of a more user-centred consciousness have enriched a deeper understanding of the impact and contribution that design can offer. Each case study has been carefully selected, drawn from an international array of guest contributors, providing their unique insights and commentary on the diverse range of design management applications. The first chapter, on design management fieldwork, has been developed by the authors, raising, illuminating and discussing many attendant issues raised in subsequent chapters.

Following on from the first book by the authors, *Design Management Case Studies* (Routledge, 2002), this subsequent book displays a strong international perspective, with contemporary examples taken from a multitude of sectoral contexts. The carefully chosen selection of cases has been the subject of intense academic scrutiny, forming the basis for numerous academic papers and conference presentations.

The book welcomes a contribution on Lenovo (Chapter 8), a case study drawn from China, where the very definition and practice of design management are still under considerable debate by both industry and academia. It advocates the role and importance of an effective and comprehensive design policy whereby the organisation created a fluid and dynamic new product development strategy in the quest to penetrate new overseas markets in Europe. The chapter poses one key question: how can Lenovo use customer 'experience' design as a basis for creating an effective brand strategy that would be successful in the UK?

To complement and further illustrate the changing nature and application of design management provision, case studies drawn from the UK, Italy and Scandinavia view the multifaceted role and diverse benefits that design management offers to key stakeholders both within and outside the organisation. Furthermore, they discuss how, with the impact of new technologies, rapidly changing demographic audiences and their inherent value systems, design management is becoming a strategic asset that can 'imagine' new routes to commercial success in uncertain business environments.

Acknowledgements

The authors wish to thank all those who have contributed to the production of this volume and in particular the numerous companies and individuals who have helped the main contributors develop their particular chapters. This includes the Kartell Group (Italy), IBM and the Lenovo Group (China), Cityspace/Adshel and Parksafe (Derby, UK), Rummey Design Associates, MacCormac Jamieson Prichard and Whitbybird with Alexander Beleschenko, Jochen Gerz, Françoise Schein and Susanna Heron (UK), Nicknax, Kidstuff and Falco (Birmingham, UK), and Stoneridge Electronics, which formed the basis of the sub-supplier chapter.

We would also like to thank Routledge for their patience and encouragement in the development of the original manuscript. Also, both authors would like to thank everyone who has offered critical insights and input, knowingly or unwittingly, to the development of this book. Finally, David would like to thank Anna Vowles for her unwavering help and support throughout this project.

Abbreviations

AIGA	American Institute of Graphic Arts
AMDS	Ashgate Management Development Services
CAD	computer-aided design
CPSC	Consumer Product Safety Commission
CPTED	crime prevention through environmental design
DCF	discounted cash flow
EC	European Commission
EEOC	Equal Employment Opportunity Commission
EMAS	European Eco-Management and Audit Scheme
EPA	Environmental Protection Agency
EPSRC	Engineering and Physical Sciences Research Council
IAA	Internationale Automobil Ausstellung
ICPC	International Centre for the Prevention of Crime
IPR	intellectual property rights
KTP	knowledge transfer partnership
MJP	MacCormac Jamieson Prichard
MO	Modus Operandi
MOMA	Museum of Modern Art
NPD	new product development
NPV	net present value
NYSE	New York Stock Exchange
OSHA	Occupational Safety and Health Administration
PC	personal computer
PCD	Personal Computing Division
R&D	research and development
RDA	Robert Rummey Design Associates
ROI	return on investment
RP	rapid prototyping

ABBREVIATIONS

SBD	Secured by Design
SCP	situational crime prevention
SMEs	small and medium-sized enterprises
SQW	Segal Quince Wicksteed

Introduction

How to use this book

This book follows on from *Design Management Case Studies* by Robert Jerrard, Jack Ingram and David Hands, published by Routledge in 2002. Both books contribute to a paucity of texts in design management but this one departs from previous approaches in its promotion of qualitative research processes. The review questions at the end of each chapter are intended to deepen the reading experience; the project questions are intended to both deepen and practically extend it.

Design is an everyday experience for us all, but researching the diversity of its processes and numerous business applications is sometimes difficult because of its complexity and often contradictory nature. The insider 'knowingness' that designers often enthusiastically admit to in their practice is often a key aspect of the management practice within design-focused companies.

Researching and documenting design have been shown to be varied in both method and result. Whilst the term 'policy' is often used, it is understood to be difficult to research. Indeed 'policy' as a term is often found to be what a company 'does' as opposed to what it 'does not do', and the term 'strategy' is rather more appropriate for the researcher.

'Design in action' therefore for the researcher involves standard methodologies associated with the social sciences, which are then applied in a flexible manner. Even then, focusing on the designer or design department often links to a significant range of information, knowledge and practices. Such a range suggests that evaluating this kind of design research will mean the use of criteria and metrics which could encompass several extant academic disciplines. For example, a design value system within a company may be based on the interrelationships between finance, communication, aesthetics and marketing. How then can a researcher find out about design in companies? From the case studies presented in this book a variety of criteria are used within each example, but in some one aspect is emphasised over another. In this way it is anticipated that the researcher, by selecting the issues thought to be important, will find them to be so, or not.

Selecting to research and then describe the process of design in a reductionist manner is always a danger; however, the detail discussed in some cases is found to be a significant indicator of a holistic view of design, teamwork and differing perceptions. It is recommended, therefore, that the book should be read in its entirety but then studied in parts. Specific chapters will provide general industry-focused insights; others will provide surprises that the researcher should be aware of.

A combination of private study and seminars could be utilised when exploring the book. The methods raised and discussed may be critically viewed; each was individually devised for different purposes. In every case, however, a participatory approach was taken where designers, company archivists and managers were encouraged to provide information in a language known particularly to them and, importantly, meaningful to their peers.

It is anticipated that investigating the management of design will hold more specificity for both practitioners and researchers through the adoption of these approaches. It is hoped that the adoption of these diverse techniques will enable the reader to identify and embrace emergent industry challenges, taking and applying knowledge from less complex industrial cultures.

Chapter 1

Design and the organisation

Robert Jerrard and David Hands

INTRODUCTION

There has been a continual search for a common understanding of the values of design; is there such a thing? Can it be solely the province of creative people to agree on a value system for design? Professional groups are said to be able to be self-referential, that is to establish and maintain a form of 'culture'. However, design is an important part of a variety of business cultures that can lead to positive strategic benefits for companies. For design values to be commercially realised, a framework of organisation and planning is necessary. Design managers (or employees who have traditionally taken on this role) have generally assumed the role of intermediary, to organise the design process and manage relationships between designers and other managers. However, since the business environment has changed, design has become more involved with the goals of other business functions, playing a more significant part in the company's strategy. As an inevitable result, the role of design has broadened, with the responsibilities of the design manager expanding. In many large organisations, ranging from manufacturing to service providers, design managers are being appointed with increasingly greater responsibilities.

WHAT IS GOOD DESIGN MANAGEMENT?

Effective design management involves good communication between different organisational departments. Information appropriate to the design programme needs to be provided by production, finance, marketing and sales, etc. from inception of the project to its successful completion.

The successful outcome of the design project is often dependent upon (Topalian 1994):

- effective management skills
- good relationships with key suppliers and customers
- coordinating design with other tasks, particularly finance, marketing and manufacturing
- senior management support to ensure that adequate resources are allocated to the design project and to gain full commitment.

Borja de Morzota (1998) offers three levels of design management that account for the variety of activities it becomes involved in (Table 1.1).

However, Cooper and Press (1995) argue that the term 'design management' contains a fundamental contradiction. Whereas design is based around exploration and risk taking, management is founded on control and predictability. The outcome of combining the two presents a risk that the management framework might reduce the creative scope of the designer. For those 'managing' design, the danger of restricting the flair and imagination of designers is an important concern, and only the systems that leave space for innovation should be implemented. It is important that design managers truly understand the way designers work so that the project is managed well without inhibiting creativity. Topalian (1994) argues that design management operates on two distinct levels: corporate and project.

A major report submitted to the UK government by Corfield (1979) argued that effective design management is key to companies remaining competitive in increasingly difficult markets. It recommends that product design should be recognised by companies as a key business function specifically identified as a board-level responsibility, on a par with production and finance, for 'failure to adopt a good, strong design policy can only be interpreted as one of the steps on the road to bankruptcy for companies'. Furthermore, the report argues that 'companies should designate an appropriate member of their boards to take on the design function as a prime responsibility where that is not already the case'. Reviewers of the report have criticised Corfield for not making a clear

Table 1.1 Levels of design management

Role	Activity
Operational	Design is involved to improve a system or operation. Marketing/engineering/communications, etc.
Functional	Design as a tool in achieving a competitive advantage. Creation of new products/markets.
Strategic	Design operates at a corporate level by influencing and contributing directly to company vision.

Source: Morzota (1998)

4

recommendation that designers should be appointed to company boards. The Design Council has for some years attempted to promote (although informally) the idea of designers on boards. Topalian (1980) argues in a critique on the Corfield report that 'having designers on company boards may well be a step in the right direction. However, rather than being too keen on transforming designers into design directors, the design professions should concentrate instead on a more sensible approach.' He suggests making designers and managers better at their respective roles whilst increasing the sensitivity and understanding between them.

BS 7000 Part 2 (1997) separates the role of design management into two distinct areas of activity and responsibility: senior management; and project management. Firstly, it argues that senior executives within the organisation should undertake the ultimate responsibility of managing design.

Then, having provided the broader context and role of design management within the organisation, BS 7000 Part 2 details its role at project level. It raises key management issues of what should be addressed concerning the design of manufactured products specific to the project, starting from the concept phase through to termination. Oddly, there is no definition of what constitutes 'design management' in the BS 7000 Part 10 (1995) glossary of terms used in design management. The design management process is generally considered to start with an idea (of which 26 'triggers' – sources for new products or services – are listed in BS 7000 Part 2, 1997) and end with disposal, with all stages in between being part of that process. The standard has been considerably revised and updated since its first incarnation in 1989 (BS 7000 Part 2, 1989), which described design management as 'planning, communication, monitoring and control'. Whilst it was generally accepted that these were all important parts of design management, they were not design management itself.

Pugh (1991) presents a more holistic view of the role of design management, based around a core of design activities within a systematic and disciplined framework. Pugh proposed the 'Total Design' model in which the marketplace is given prior consideration and a thorough specification is developed all before the concept stage of design. This widely accepted model finishes at the commercialisation stage, but the scope of Total Design has been extended to include everything up to and including 'disposal', such as servicing, marketing and redesigns. His 'Total Design' model presents six groups of interactive phases, generic to all kinds of designs; within each phase there is one specific group of knowledge applied. The role of managing the design team within the process, he argues, requires the balancing of both 'static' and 'dynamic' modes of operation.

Oakley (1990) provides a broad and comprehensive overview of design management and in particular the role of design at a strategic level. Through synthesising the work of over 40 leading authorities, Oakley examines the business context of design, and how embracing design throughout many different applications can

5

enable the organisation to secure a competitive advantage. He summarises key points that emerged from the contributors:

- Designers as visionaries: that designers can provide an inspirational role and help to direct the organisation in new directions. 'They alone may provide creative clues to the possibilities which are available to a business.'
- The need for inter-functional collaboration in design work. For success in any design programme, in particular the development of new products, it is vital that commitment and involvement are secured from key participants. 'The dangers of treating design as an isolated, out-of-the-mainstream activity cannot be overstated; at best such an approach leads to disinterest and lack of commitment, and at worst it may give rise to total rejection of design results.'
- The importance of both project and policy aspects of design. There needs to be commitment from top management to embrace the value of design and communicate it throughout the entire organisation. 'There is some tendency for the project aspects of design management to receive the greatest attention and the policy considerations to be largely neglected. In many cases, this is the reversal of what ought to be happening. Too many managers focus their attention on the running of individual design projects and completely fail to consider why the projects have been set up in the first place.'

Peter Gorb (1988) takes a similar perspective in discussing the importance of design management at a strategic level through synthesising a series of papers presented to the Design Management Unit of the London Business School. The contributors discuss a key aspect of design management philosophy, validating the premise that design is a vital and often underutilised resource that adds value to the organisation. Olson *et al.* (2000) take this sentiment further, not only advocating the importance of strategic design management, but providing a five-step framework to successfully incorporating it into the organisation's competitive strategy. The five distinct stages are shown in Figure 1.1.

Hollins (1997, 2000) argues that there is a strong need for organisations to adopt a robust design management strategy in order to remain competitive; but he argues that they should now be planning ahead beyond ten years into the future. 'This must be done through a constant supply of well-designed competitive products. To make sure organisations are moving forward in a logical manner the work on the strategic link with design must also continue.'

Hollins presents a strategic framework that takes into account recommendations from the UK Government White Papers (1993, 1994) that companies should now adopt a ten-year horizon in their planning for new products and services. However, the framework does not clearly illustrate how the organisation can anticipate 'change' in volatile industries, such as information technology, telecommunications and biotechnology.

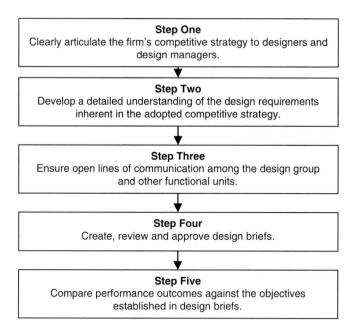

Figure 1.1 *Five-step framework to strategic design management*
Source: Olson *et al.* (2000)

Ahopelto (2002) suggests that design management is a critically important subject for a firm, and a process that creates a connection between the organisation and the customer. The nature of a business primarily determines which functions design management is closely linked with and its relative importance as a competition parameter. A construction of a wide model based on how an organisation aims to compete, the goals that it sets itself and what procedures are needed to achieve these targets is essentially included into the development of a competitive strategy.

WHY INVEST IN DESIGN?

Despite a plethora of indigenous design talent, the UK has been slow to realise the full potential benefits which design could provide in the quest for successful new product introductions and commercial competitiveness. Other countries, in particular Germany, Japan and the USA, have progressed by integrating design at a strategic level rather than employing it solely as a tool to enhance the aesthetic appearance of existing products or surface decoration. In an increasingly competitive marketplace, organisations are continually required to develop and create the 'competitive edge'. The company that does not plan for the future, operating solely on a day-to-day basis, will never unlock its true potential for sustainable growth and commercial success. Design and the many benefits that it has to offer are often misunderstood by many organisations. Design can significantly contribute to:

- a reduction in production and manufacturing costs, and the minimisation of the use of expensive materials
- stronger customer loyalty, often by designing in features that offer real, tangible benefits to customers
- the development of new and innovative products and services that could increase market share in highly competitive markets
- reducing customer complaints through better design of information
- changing the perception of the organisation by embedding features of the way the customer experiences business in line with the brand.

Research undertaken for the Design Council (2001) highlights the many benefits that design can actively contribute to the organisation (Table 1.2). The research provides strong evidence to date that good design can boost companies' operating performance and commercial growth.

As a consequence of the recession in the early 1990s, companies were forced to develop new, often radical, ways of competing in difficult and often tumultuous marketplaces. The vicissitudes of global forces and unrestricted movement of international capital present unforeseen problems for the organisation to face and respond to. Many organisations responded to the effects of 'change' and positively flourished, but for others 'change' caused adverse effects on their ability to compete, survive and prosper. The benefits of design investment at a strategic level to greatly assist innovation are well publicised (Bruce and Bessant 2002;

Table 1.2 *What are the business benefits of design?*

Percentage of firms saying design, innovation and creativity have contributed to the following during the last three years:	
Increased turnover	51%
Improved image of organisation	50%
Increased profits	48%
Increased employment	46%
Improved communication with customers	45%
Improved quality of services/products	44%
Increased market share	40%
Development of new products	40%
Improved internal communication	28%
Reduced costs	25%

Source: Research by PACEC for Design Council (2001)

Cooper and Press 1995; Oakley 1990; Walsh *et al.* 1992), with discussion as to how design can significantly add value to organisations' product or service offerings. Again, research by PACEC for the Design Council (2001) has quantified the benefits of innovative behaviour and product introductions to organisations, identifying the key drivers that force innovation.

Organisations utilise design throughout a variety of different ways, providing many benefits in the way they behave and communicate to their customers. Design can be a powerful tool for managing and coordinating how the business looks and communicates to its customers. Design is also a useful instrument that could be harnessed to help the organisation realise and evaluate potential future business opportunities, in both the service and the manufacturing sectors. At a strategic level, design can help maximise the company's potential to deliver desirable products and services to new markets whilst also defending existing markets against overseas competitors. Table 1.3 illustrates the many different and diverse ways that design has contributed to business performance.

ADDED VALUE

In increasingly competitive marketplaces the ultimate aim of the company is to offer its customers products and services that they want to buy and value in preference to what is on offer from competitors. Therefore, using design effectively will enable the company to increase the perceived value of its product offerings and maintain the competitive advantage. It is widely accepted that the successful organisation will no longer focus on lowest cost but will strive to provide added-value products and services that are distinctive and appealing. Customers are now far more demanding, owing to increased spending power and the proliferation of choice – therefore the company needs to anticipate, respond

Table 1.3 *Percentage of all companies (by employment size) saying design has contributed, at least to some extent, to various issues*

No. of employees	0–19	20–49	50–249	250+
Increased competitiveness	25	75	82	80
Increased profits	22	79	78	76
Better communication with customers	26	80	83	87
Reduced costs	6	62	64	54
Improved quality of products and services	26	69	87	78
Increased market share	16	70	83	83

Source: Design Council (2002)

to and, importantly, exceed the customer's expectations. Companies that fail to adapt and compete will be overtaken by their rivals.

IMAGE

Utilised effectively, design can be an excellent means for managing and co-ordinating how the organisation looks to its customers as well as the way in which it communicates with them. Wally Olins (1990) argues that 'design is a major corporate resource, equal in significance just like other functions'. The organisation is continually producing designed material that conveys clear messages to both internal employees and their customers, so it is vital that a consistent and unambiguous statement of values is reflected in a coherent manner. Failure to coordinate these messages effectively could result in poor company image and limited marketplace recognition. Organisations that have an enlightened understanding of design manage their company image very closely, benefiting from the impact of this positive image in many areas, such as recruitment and increased sales. Olins (1990) comments that design can offer emotional connections between the organisation and its customers as opposed to rational means. Design can be employed in the public service sector equally as much as in the business sector, playing a major role in the way services are developed and delivered more effectively. Design can:

- improve healthcare provision
- improve the quality of education through better environments and systems
- enable more effective and efficient recycling of waste products
- increase the effectiveness and image of public transport.

ENHANCING PROCESS

The importance of a well-defined and executed new product development (NPD) programme is a prerequisite to maintaining the competitive advantage when competing in dynamic global markets. One frequently quoted statistic suggests that 85 per cent of all future product costs are determined by the time a design project reaches the concept stage (Design Council 1998).

Therefore, investing in design at the initial stages of the new product development process is essential to achieving a successful outcome (Cooper and Kleinschmidt 1988a, 1988b; Cooper et al. 1998). Most of products' production costs are already determined by the end of the design stage, even though a small proportion of that is actually spent on design. Achieving this, however, requires an understanding of the discrete stages a project is likely to move through in its journey from idea to product commercialisation. A major report for the Design Council undertaken by the London Business School (Sentence and Clarke 1997) estimated that the manufacturing sector spends £10 billion (1995 prices) a year on design and product development activities – 2.6 per cent of manufacturing turnover, accounting for some 4.5 per cent of the manufacturing sector workforce. A follow-up report (Sentence and Walters 1997) that looked more closely at the link between design and performance concluded that it operated primarily through the impact on export orientation: companies which were more design-intensive were able to grow faster because of their higher sales in overseas markets.

Research by Inns and Hands (1998) investigating design-led Teaching Company Schemes quantified the benefits of in-house design enhancement on organisational activity. In all of the 12 case studies that were investigated, design made a significant impact on NPD activity.

IMPROVING PRODUCTION

Design is also key to enabling the organisation to remain competitive through lowering its production costs. Taking back product design to first principles can significantly increase production efficiency. Through design activity, design can reduce the complexity of component parts in a product, introduce new technology or materials, and reduce production time. Design for Manufacture is 'an approach to closing the gap between the design and manufacture of products, encapsulating the conception, design, production and commercialisation of a product, through such mechanisms' (Wilson 1994).

EMBEDDING DESIGN WITHIN THE ORGANISATION

Often companies fail to recognise the importance of managing design capabilities to their full commercial advantage. A number of possible reasons why companies might neglect design are put forward by Rita Siegel (1982), who argued that short-termism and low-risk management have caused a significant number of US managers to centre corporate strategies on existing markets instead of emerging ones. Such management styles often opt out when it comes down to investing resources into design. Some companies suffer from plain design illiteracy, smaller companies suffer from cost constraints and often larger corporations are prevented by tradition-bound behaviour and internal politics.

11

Table 1.4 Design barriers

Barrier	Characteristics
Design illiteracy	Managers may not know what is involved in design activities and may not have the experience to appreciate the contribution design and the designer's skills can make.
Design segregation	Companies that repeatedly outsource design expertise may have a tunnel view of what the design function does. Design consultancies are brought in with specific deliverables and objectives to complete which often limit the scope or influence on any other aspect of the business beyond the project in hand.
Lack of vision	Some designers blame managers who lack the creative vision to understand how taking risks and developing new markets through design and innovation will separate the global leaders of the future from the rest. Companies that underestimate the value of creativity do not appreciate the strategic consistency of design.
Poor communication	Lack of coordination and shared goals causes a divergence from corporate aims. Departments become self-sufficient and less team-orientated.
Perceived risk	Often companies link design with high risk and fail to acknowledge the potential benefits for strategy and growth.
Sourcing expertise	Less experienced companies may find sourcing and managing design expertise a difficult challenge. Without guidance, mistakes can be made, and such experiences have negative effects on future use.
Cost constraints	Many managers still view design as just a cost instead of weighing up the potential rewards. Efforts are being made to convince such companies, especially SMEs, to adopt a design strategy to aid future growth.
Tradition-bound behaviour	Hierarchical and bureaucratic behaviour. Often a set corporate culture, where strategy is dictated from the top, can inhibit designers and marketers from being creative. Such companies have a clear format and employees are reluctant to stray.
Company politics	Company politics surface at all stages of proposed development. Self-interest from separate business units may prevent the uptake of a new strategy aimed at creating a common corporate goal but which may reduce their individual resource allocation.

Source: Siegel (1982)

MANAGING THE INTEGRATION BETWEEN DESIGN, TECHNOLOGY AND MARKETING

Management may gauge reaction from the employees to consider the most effective way to integrate different functions. For example, should meetings arranged between departments be on a structured periodic basis, or should they only be arranged when a problem occurs? Factors for effective integration between departments will emerge through discussions with representatives from company functions.

If the disciplines to be integrated are not familiar with one another, possible informal meetings may establish contact. Encouragement should be given to departments to interact on an informal basis primarily, which may help integration occur more naturally, as social relationships are established first. Organisations will all differ, owing to varying factors such as company culture and the size of the company. In smaller organisations employees may already be familiar with one another, and may discover that they need more structure to meetings, with prescribed topics of discussion. In contrast, a larger company may find its departments scattered across the globe, thus making it difficult for them to communicate effectively.

> Communication is the cornerstone of both business and social life. The ability to communicate effectively is increasingly important and is a vital factor in the development of an individual's confidence. Good oral communication skills involve the ability to exchange ideas with colleagues, to brief others and to make clear and relevant contributions to discussion.
>
> (Design Council 2007)

Effective communication between disciplines is essential to integration. If employees do not have strong communication skills it may be advisable to build on these skills through training, or develop them through social interaction, before integrating with other departments. In order to coordinate skills and knowledge, managers must first understand the types of skills and project needs, the knowledge that should be made available, and how design and designers can contribute. Gorb and Dumas (1987) contend that design-competent firms have an understanding of how design affects different aspects of a business so they automatically involve it in corporate decision making.

Some projects may not benefit from getting all parties involved. For example, a marketer may not be beneficial to a meeting involving a project at the production phase but may be more crucial at the earlier stages of the product development process. Management will play a large role in deciding who are the most appropriate members to be present at project meetings.

AUDITING DESIGN AND 'MEASURING' DESIGN VALUE

The value of design 'enhancement' on the organisation has been clearly demonstrated. Wide-ranging and detailed surveys across many diverse and different industrial sectors have demonstrated the increase in turnover and profitability which can result from design investment (Roy and Potter 1993). Also, at an individual organisational level, case studies have explained how individual products, product families and indeed services have significantly benefited from consideration of design issues (Thackera 1997). However, very often for an organisation this message can be frustrating; despite the evidence of research and investment into adopting a design-centric approach, it can be difficult to know how to value design within the company, where to start to augment its application and, inevitably, how to effectively manage it. The generally accepted solution to this problem is to engage the services of an external design consultant; although this approach is often successful, evidence suggests that there can be problems with it.

There is still continual debate as to the role and definition of design within an organisational context. Often, design is posited within the context of new product development and attendant development processes; in the company context, design is defined as a process in which products are developed by combining design with other core competencies. While design competence is creative in its basic nature, the role and importance of design management have a strategic character. Design management has emerged into an important stage of corporate recognition, placing greater demands on the skills and competencies of design managers, whereby they have to utilise their innate knowledge, interpersonal skills and forecasting strengths. Design-trained personnel are now in an enhanced position to lead organisations along with their management counterparts in fast-changing commercial environments.

As the impact of internationalisation and the emergence of overseas new markets take on a more strategic importance, design is increasingly regarded as a means to handle knowledge and complexity with the aim of attaining competitive businesses, products and services. To counter these conflicting and often contradictory demands, design managers must adjust their current thinking and understanding of design and the services they offer. A greater attention to the design process and its constituent elements and methods is required as a basis for the integration of knowledge and requirements. Design services must continually adapt and adjust according to client needs. Tacit knowledge must be described, communicated and shared with the client and constituent stakeholders to create a shared basis. Walton (2002) offers a comprehensive definition of both design and design strategy within this context, suggesting that:

> Design is both process and product. It is a way of thinking synthetically, of looking at problems in unexpected and creative ways, and seeking

innovation. It is also about specific outcomes – products, graphics, communications, and business settings. More broadly it is about how consumers and stakeholders experience the outcomes – the design interface must be all these things – a strategy for action, as well as the results of those actions and decisions.

The design process can be considered as the 'immaterial creation' of the product, that is, at the end of this process the product does not yet exist but everything is defined beforehand. As a consequence, design in its current conception incorporates a significant amount of complex information and knowledge that must be properly managed. Therefore, a mature, sophisticated and continuously improving series of processes is becoming increasingly important for organisations. This in turn requires a sound and robust management of the whole development process, integrating the appropriate tools and techniques, with the necessary supporting infrastructure. These problems highlight the need for a set of flexible tools which can help in assessing the whole process, and provide the opportunity to identify specific aspects in order to later focus on them during the improvement phase.

One notable series of guidelines to assist the organisation in the design and development process of new innovative products is BS 7000. The standard offers a comprehensive framework on the management of design, addressing issues of responsibility and consideration throughout all levels of organisational operation. The series includes:

- BS 7000–1: 1999 Guide to managing innovation
- BS 7000–2: 1997 Guide to managing the design of manufactured products
- BS 7000–3: 1994 Guide to managing service design
- BS 7000–4: 1996 Guide to managing design in construction
- BS 7000–5: 2001 Guide to managing obsolescence
- BS 7000–6: 2005 Guide to managing inclusive design
- BS 7000–10: 1995 Glossary of terms used in design management.

One of the key contributors to the series of guidelines, Alan Topalian (Alto Design Management), argues that the 'emphasis is placed on ensuring close coordination during the development process so all disciplines contribute effectively at all stages, before and after introduction to market'. The series of guidelines emphasises the importance of financial planning, key decision pathways, and roles and responsibilities of design and management functions from the boardroom to the designer at project level. Initially, BS 7000 was considered unwieldy and inflexible in operation; however, after a series of modifications and amendments, industry has warmly received the guidelines, commonly adopting their application in practice.

In addition to the BS 7000 series of published guidelines, the Design in Business Organisation in conjunction with the Design Council has produced a three-part framework focusing on how the organisation can develop innovative product and service offerings. The 'Design Atlas: a tool for auditing design capability' (see Roberts 2001) provides straightforward and highly applicable support information that measures design capability, processes and planning considerations in three parts. Part 1 describes the frame of reference covered by the audit tool and outlines how it can be utilised to review design capability within an organisation. Part 2 provides a detailed description of the questions that constitute the entire three-part framework. Lastly, Part 3 provides examples of actions that can be taken to develop and augment organisational design capability in response to the audit.

Although the Design Atlas framework provides a more accessible and easy-to-use approach to understanding design capability within the organisation, its industry acceptance has yet to be fully investigated and understood. However, although anecdotal evidence suggests that its popularity and application are increasing, the benefits of its implementation remain unclear.

Cooper and Press (1995: 187–222) provide a broad account and definition of what constitutes a design audit, offering methods and design auditing techniques to the reader. They offer a flexible framework whereby the organisation could undertake a full strategic design audit, taking into consideration four dimensions of investigation: the wider environmental context in which the organisation operates; physical manifestations of design, focusing upon visual identity and communication material; the internal corporate culture and understanding of design; and, lastly, design management procedures and processes. The authors emphasise and signpost aspects of organisational activity to investigate but do not provide an exhaustive list of considerations to adhere to. They provide a cautionary note that using audits 'will help organisations to define current practice and benchmark themselves against other organisations, but relying on audits to measure practice, stimulate improvements in practice and for overall change is inappropriate'. Predominantly, the audit framework has been, and remains, hugely popular with both design and management postgraduate students negotiating the complexities and nuances of auditing design for the first time.

ORGANISATIONAL KNOWLEDGE

Knowledge of all kinds exists within organisations at a number of management and operational levels; it is often considered intangible and 'unmeasurable'. However, the process by which knowledge is acquired and subsequently used is via individuals in often discrete and tacit ways. In recognition of the interdisciplinarity nature of design in an area like NPD (Jerrard *et al.* 1999), the study of the associated knowledge is important.

Networks formed by individuals are unlikely to provide all of the day-to-day specific knowledge that the organisation requires; informal networks, however, continue to be the lifeblood of small competitive companies. These networks contain social capital and as such often add tremendous value to the life of companies. The successful integration of information from different sources therefore may be said to provide 'informational advantage'. Knowledge has long been thought of as a key commercial resource but one which is so often elusive to many and frequently misunderstood.

For such knowledge to be advantageously retained and embedded by the company, then, a process to evaluate it needs to be developed, refined and embedded within day-to-day practice. However, for a small or medium-sized enterprise it is often extremely difficult for a number of reasons. These include the fact that small companies necessarily have to deal with simultaneous information for complex concurrent working whilst operating on tight deadlines and limited financial and human resources. Also the personal nature of networking often reduces the perceived value of knowledge, as it may appear subjective and may not be shared in full. There often appear to be significant differences between organisations that are easily able to generate and use knowledge and those that find it difficult. This is partly geographical; it is not surprising that national or even global competition is derived from regionally clustered groups of companies. Such networks may be considered in relation to one firm, and employees may see themselves as occupying a more central aspect of knowledge. However, such networks are often viewed to be more dynamic, with third parties relating to fourth parties and so forth. In this way knowledge can produce specific and valuable capacity, which in turn may be generally viewed as 'social capital'. Plainly, assessing social capital poses a problem of scale; networks are often defined through an individual and that individual's efforts. Some observers (see Burt 1992) have attempted to measure the strength and diversity of an individual's network. However, this may only be possible in generic terms; individuals alone may not be able to contextualise what they know through others.

In assessing the knowledge potential of a small organisation, in design, it appears that networks may be particularly important. Membership of professional bodies for designers (for example, the Chartered Society of Designers or the Design Business Association) has always aided business; although many would admit to learning little through membership, this is unlikely to be true.

In a knowledge-creating company there appears to be a strong emphasis on internal entrepreneurism where all may be considered knowledge workers (see Nonaka 1991). This may be perceived as a loan activity, but providing velocity for the knowledge appears linked to a process of sharing. Designers seem to do this all the time; a community of designers may be observed regularly making tacit

17

knowledge explicit, and indeed this may serve as a metaphor for the design process itself. The promotion of design knowledge may be an evangelistic pursuit where such tacit 'behaviour' is regularly reviewed and integrated within day-to-day work. Functional knowledge is often viewed as complementary to design knowledge and may be evidenced by the provision of appropriate business outlets for the complex skills of a designer. Within many design-centred organisations such divisions may not yet be detectable, which may explain why auditing design appears complex and so often contradictory.

Designers possess many types of knowledge, and these can be categorised (Table 1.5).

The examination of skills illustrates the many ways designers and design can influence business decisions. Observation and research from both academics and practitioners agree that sustainability will come from competencies and skills that are nurtured within a framework of organisational learning. Through the development of knowledge and know-how, companies can formulate strategies that afford them a competitive advantage.

In order to coordinate the skills and knowledge, managers must first understand the types of skills a project requires, the knowledge that should be made available, and how design and designers can contribute. Gorb and Dumas (1987) contend that design-competent firms have an understanding of how design affects different aspects of a business, and that consequently they automatically involve it in corporate decision making.

Table 1.5 *Designers' knowledge*

Knowledge	Description
Explicit	A knowledge that is written down embodied as information.
Tacit	A personal slant or intuitive way of doing something.
Declarative	Factual knowledge taking the form of a model or rule which leads to an intended result with certainty.
Procedural	Know-how, how to do something in terms of action, as decision usually comes from practical experience.
Heuristic	'Rule of thumb' information that has a good probability of leading to an acceptable result.
Algorithmic	A set of exact steps that will lead to a solution, if one exists.
Deep	Information given over which is backed up with a rational explanation.
Shallow	Information offered without the back-up of an explanation.

THE ORIGINS OF THE COMPANY AUDIT

The systematic and objective process of approval within organisations flourished with the development of large corporations in North America and Europe in the early part of the twentieth century. However, the Roman Empire used the 'audit' to develop common and sustainable cultural practice throughout its provinces. Such directed social engineering provided for the practice of normative process. Internal audits now confine themselves to the organisation, leaving external viewpoints to be gained through the democratic political process. The legislative audit is still practical, particularly where the results of government policy are indistinct. Auditors therefore have a responsibility, whether operating a small in-company process review or a government review across a nation, that is as agents of constructive consequence. The ultimate centring on outcomes has always been represented by considering a domain of 'problem focus' and a domain of 'impact' together with the relationship between these two. These two features are ever present.

AUDIT EXPLAINED

Auditing refers to a range of activities aimed at improving how an organisation operates. This may be in a strategic area where current and past plans are evaluated against results. Alternatively an audit may apply to a management area where any aspects of an intangible process may be considered. Operations may also be 'performance researched', particularly from a compliance viewpoint where a complex range of goals both precise and imprecise may be located against what actually goes on.

Overall, an audit is concerned with structure, process and their relationship although the effective audit value varies considerably depending on the ability of the auditors to focus on the issues and the ability of the organisations to facilitate the audit process. A cycle classically describes most audits (Figure 1.2), where a process of improvement is used which involves research. However, whilst the hypothesis-stimulated process called research may be concurrently evaluated, audits tend to have greater specificity.

Also, audit is unlike research in that recommendations for change and implementation are involved, together with their monitoring and evaluation. The audit process is linked in formalised areas of work where compliance dominates, which is perhaps most useful when objectivity within the process of change is required. The degree to which audit practice is transferable is difficult to determine, although the process, despite its potential to represent threat through change, is commonly understood where the business process is recorded. Where it is not then the audit criteria used are perhaps as important as the audit itself.

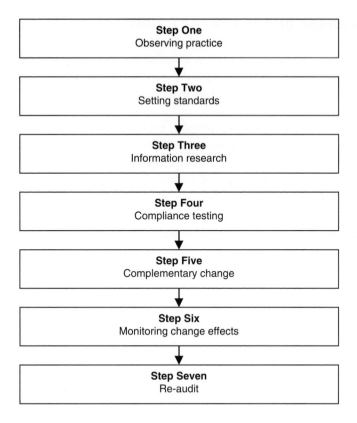

Figure 1.2 *A seven-step audit process*

The general benefits of the audit process are:

- the provision of knowledge of current practice
- the improvements in standards of process
- the highlighting of non-compliance
- the identification of potentially damaging practice
- the rewards which are intrinsically linked to accurate knowledge
- the securing of future cohesion
- the promotion of higher standards
- the facilitation of further planning
- the stimulation of learning.

An audit works best when self-improvement is identified as a goal. This may be achieved by recognising that knowledge is lacking in the day-to-day operations of an organisation. An audit should provide a structure through which change may be identified and implemented. Also, audits encourage the airing and discussion of problems and the shared critical evaluation of practice. The objective position of the audit should promote construction and encourage team debate and decision making rather than management-led change. In this way, change may be self-developed where managers may use the audit process to guide the decision-making process. Therefore, if viewed in an entirely positive light the audit process may become transferable and reusable, so a team may be empowered by the process, effecting change internally.

Audits act to improve or to facilitate self-improvement. This is sometimes described as 'stewardship', which relates to 'capital', i.e. financial capital, human capital, intellectual capital and the responsibilities and power associated with them. The development of this process of stewardship may be attributed to the complexity and density of professional life, particularly where necessary targets are present where they may be imprecise. As a first principle, stakeholder audits may represent the development of standards and quality and, indirectly, their sharing. Certainly the impartiality and 'fact-based' nature of audits ought to elicit both comparisons and exemplars.

The audit process, within the context of design (as with all audits), reflects the nature of the activity. As design is often represented by a variety of activities it is perhaps natural to focus on a qualitative audit methodology. This, as it may relate to people in design, draws upon much activity from social communication and the recognition of cooperative working. In this way a design-led organisation or department may usefully be described as a collaborative enterprise but perhaps regularly celebrating its particular diversity. Collaboration should actually expect surprise, acknowledge the chaotic nature of creativity and avoid a philosophy of predictability, particularly in assessing outcomes. This, from an audit perspective, presents some difficulty; successful collaboration at work will involve the relatively unpredictable contribution of participants. This could be called 'creative collaboration', which in design creativity is encouraged but not entirely measurable through audit. In fact, attempts to adopt audit compliances within creative environments reduce task variety just when its breadth may be a key business success factor. The audit therefore has to acknowledge human conditions and aspirations related to communication, trust, authority and tacit knowledge. The demands for business efficiency if narrowly defined therefore would actually develop predictable activity and produce, through audit, negativity. Social audit therefore proposes trust as a key aspect of control.

Auditors are required to balance their methodology. The nature of autonomous organisations (in particular certain aspects of the design office) is to serve their own local interest. This should not be audited in isolation. The power of individual design and creativity within organisations resided within a reciprocal framework of self-feeding and business delivery. This may be difficult to acknowledge from the perspective of the audit, as detailed processes are often reviewed only with exclusive reference to larger organisational systems. Creative design groups 'self-reference' prior to recognising an organisational system. In

21

relation to this, a first-level audit defines creativity as a value within the context of the overall aims of the organisation. A second-level audit is one which assesses focused operational work referred locally. An auditor therefore is required to perceive both levels at the onset but acknowledge the recursive nature of most organisations. Reinterpretation of larger-scale compliance through audits is often central to the audit task. This is ultimately a qualitative process if one acknowledges the responsibility of creative units in the development of goods and the associated qualities of experience. An audit that centres on control should therefore measure the effect of control at both levels. A bureaucratic organisation will centre on verifying adherence to negotiations; creativity naturally questions such control, and so audits may represent reconciliation between each level.

Western management processes often appear to increase bureaucratic control; 'managing' creative design may subscribe to this perception. However, there is a growing acknowledgement of the need for internal self-control, and responsibility suggests that our competitive future increasingly is reliant on fostering creativity in organisations. The traditional audit view of capacity should increasingly be related to self-control. Intrinsic control (Beer 1966) therefore should be applied, that is control more focused on tacit knowledge and less on normative control. Alternatively the auditor as an extrinsic controller, taking a 'Fordist' view, will adjust systems to exterior performance criteria. This in turn may actually reduce effective control of creative processes, as trust between levels is lost and individual contribution denied. Business pressures naturally increase the control dilemmas focused in hierarchical relations. Furthermore, the increased complexity of the creative process linked to new product development actually calls for more focus on compliance and detail (for example, product safety standards). This compliance naturally attacks the required flexibility to operate creatively in design development. The decision to audit, particularly in recursive environments, should be taken with the expectation of change for all. An effective organisation therefore may be one which is able to apply intellectual activity at all levels and to similarly deal with holistic change. Paradoxically, audits may arrive for new areas like design from a development of 'bureaucracy', which naturally assumes predictable behaviour.

Audits should aim to develop understanding between autonomous units and to reduce the expectation that individuals may have of unchallenged implementation of their personal policies. In this way the first step an organisation may take, particularly involving creative elements like design, is to demystify the complexity surrounding tacit knowledge and its counterparts. Change from a mutual understanding between autonomous groups could therefore be seen as a rather more natural process than one which is brought about by compliance audit, potentially based on organisational norms. Mutual understanding is a product of agreement through communication; therefore audits may be used to:

- form strategic alliances between units
- develop a deeper-level communication
- understand complementary competences.

This dispels the traditional image of auditing as solely concerned with non-compliance. Audits therefore develop knowledge; it is important to work with what you have (designers, managers, salespeople, account handlers, etc.), but a deeper-level audit ought to inform the company of the precise nature of such people and resources.

ENVIRONMENTAL AND SOCIAL AUDITING

Environmental legislation and compliance represent a moral imperative often at odds within the prime focus of the organisation. Therefore particular aspects of environmental auditing are useful to design, as the compliances provide them with a wider acknowledgement of the values of intangibles.

Companies will use audits to assess environment risks, energy consumption or emissions. This is often to a specific level of compliance, for example ISO 14001 or the European Eco-Management and Audit Scheme (EMAS). This implies a level of external honesty by organisations which know that environment compliance is often expensive to develop and maintain; implementation through control may be ineffective. Rather a whole-company mission-based approach seems to work where voluntary action within compliance is used. Unfortunately companies have been known to 'green-wash' their process by undertaking an audit process. However, companies should also realise that the audit may benefit them by public accentuation of the positive elements. Indeed the rise in the consumer lobby and the power invested in it by the media mean that environmental audits take on a completely new and often strategic significance.

The audit therefore has been developed as a continuous process allied to quality assurance, i.e. continuous improvement. This in evident by:

- establishing and implementing environmental policies
- periodic evaluations
- public broadcast.

Thus an audit operated every three years within the EU Environmental Programme sits between the company's environmental management system and regularly (externally) developed environmental objectives. The resultant expected compliances within the business sector have been supported by the International Chamber of Commerce codes of practice aimed at the promotion of such compliances.

The adoption and development of an ethical stance by a company is a complex commitment but, unlike design, relies on a tacit knowledge focus. It has been suggested that such audits are devices for public relations development; however, embracing social responsibility doctrines through (voluntary) audits has in turn developed positive social acceptance. Petroleum companies are known through their advertisements for their social and environmental policies rather than their core business. As with design, assessing social impact through audit is mostly qualitative. Different groups interpret such audits within their own agendas; herein is the company dilemma – whether to voluntarily audit or whether to commission external agencies. Approaches have been categorised by Buchholz (1982):

- inventory – listing and describing the social programmes within the firm
- programme management – cost benefit analysis of traditional audit and social programmes
- process audit – as above, but dealing with history, context and evaluation
- social indicator – the use of social information to clarify community needs and thereby company policies.

Clearly the audit process 'range' reflects the range of potential company policies. A number of UK agencies are able to help a company develop an audit process; these include the Environmental Protection Agency (EPA), the Occupational Safety and Health Administration (OSHA), the Consumer Product Safety Commission (CPSC) and the Equal Employment Opportunity Commission (EEOC). The social audit is an opportunity for the company to consider and reform its value system. This may result in developing new dual targets related to consumers, to protect current business practice and to monitor and evaluate social orientation and reputation.

Social audits can effectively deal with the genuine issue of quality, particularly by opening debate within the company about its perceived and actual values system. Also, the social audit can provide education intervention: change via employees rather than by compliance.

As in design, such values and change are not easily quantifiable, but the social audit remains a unique tool for interdepartmental monitoring in relation to both the objectives of employees and the company mission.

THE DESIGN AUDIT

At the heart of assessing design competence within the firm via an audit is the individual designer. Designers will not see themselves as 'measurable' even though their efforts plainly relate significantly to the operation of the company.

Design groups tend to reference value within themselves; this is typically found in all professional groups. Indeed design solutions which themselves vary from company expectations may be viewed, by designers, as independent. Traditionally the designer is the free 'irreverent' employee who alone appears to have specific personal engagement with his or her work. In directing design, one is aware of the necessity to encourage designers to question and think (unlike many other employees) beyond the current scope to the company. The environment fostering the design and development of new products and services is complex and involves a variety of risks at a number of levels in a wide range of situations. The literature on design management is equally varied, from that which is calculable to that which surrounds the perceptions of adventure in design (Jerrard 2000).

How then can design be audited? Do we take a social audit model or an economic one? Or is design more closely related to the development of alternative solutions, as in ecological or environmental auditing? Are the metrics just too complex? Plainly, aesthetic judgements cannot be 'measured', and the benefits of good design might relate to spiritual benefit (both the designer and the customer) as well as to economic benefit. Designers' motivations therefore are always likely to be partly covert. Consequently a range of assessment criteria for a design audit might include the following broad categorisation at both strategic and operational levels:

- aesthetic policy and achievement
- the working environment
- professional (peer) evaluation
- financial management
- training
- education
- marketing
- design research
- client orientation
- company alliance strength.

These categories may lead to quantitative, 'reductionist' conclusions and thus would move the audit away from the symbolically social issue of design as being intrinsically valuable.

However, assuming that a design department is not assessable would isolate it. One approach has been to socially audit popular product processes, as in the Body Shop and Ben & Jerry's ice cream (Johnson 1996). Also, a 'stakeholder' view (Jackson and Carter 2000) might objectify the view of design departments. This is echoed by the Audit Commission in its expectations in arts auditing (Matarasso 1997). Design in itself may be seen as profit making, and a number of accounts suggest that it is pivotal to the fortunes of many companies (Design Council

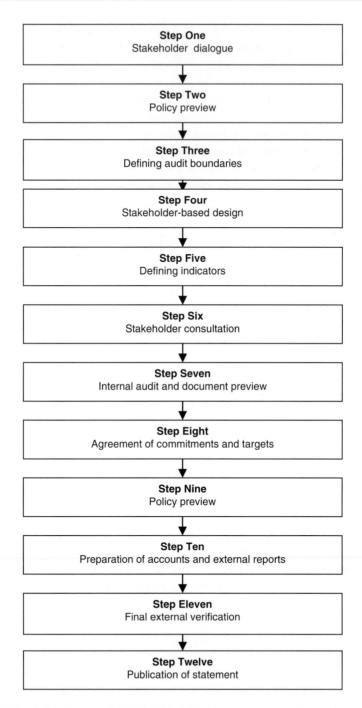

Figure 1.3 *A possible twelve-step design audit*
Source: Pearce *et al.* (1996)

1998). In this context rules to evaluate design are likely to be socially based; for example, focus groups of users, consumers and manufacturers would all contribute significantly to design audits. Involving such stakeholders is well known in social auditing.

Such a process should represent an audit which allows for value assessment based on the full extent of designers' work, i.e. aspects that are important to them. This hopefully avoids a claim that creativity can be measured and that an individual contribution may be similarly quantified in a narrow formulation. However, socially based recognition of design quality should be a commercial currency in order for it to contribute to company evaluation within audit.

MEASUREMENT

Within any organisation, design will involve complex activities and a variety of links to other activities. Furthermore the associated activities within most definitions of design (in the humanities) may even defy description. However, there is a variety of starting points for describing design activities within companies so they may be assessed or even measured. Initially the design department may be viewed as a series of informal and formal networks. Common characteristics of networks include (1) social measures and (2) performance measures. Social measures will include: participation, communication, trust, professional norms and common purpose. Performance measures will include: business contribution and product or service market innovation. Clearly an audit of design (and the design function) is likely to have particularly broad but interrelated measurement criteria. Some common themes from a wide approach include:

- a mixture of qualitative and quantitative data
- an ability to equate formal measurement with assessment and derive accurate 'hybrid' conclusions
- measurements of aspects of value systems (e.g. social capital) with elements of structure (networks inside and outside the company)
- comparison, involving contextual references within the company, between design and other developments and functions.

There are, however, specific problems in attempting to measure design performance. These include:

- an understanding of social *and* economic measures
- a conceptualisation of generic questions to specific situations
- the process of obtaining and categorising diverse information

- difficulties in equating innovation and change with compliance and benchmarking
- the absence of precise performance indicators
- the interpretation of audit results.

The tension involved in promoting the design audit as a specific process is ever present. Design, as with other functions, may be viewed as essential to the company but valueless if viewed through traditional measurement/assessment techniques. What makes a strong or weak design department? Is the design department able to be commonly ranked against departments? Rigorous measurement is one challenge; another related aspect is demystification of design in order to allow for audit results to be understood and potentially acted on. Evaluation of the design function appears to predicate measurement of it even though inputs and outputs may be particularly imprecise in design. What then makes a good design audit, one that provides valuable and accurate 'opportunity cost' results, which may be used as a measure of effectiveness? The required indicators would include:

- specificity – target areas to be measured
- measurability – access to information and people
- reliability – features which are representative but also consistent within the criteria
- rigour – real-life information rather than wholly anecdotal interpretation
- comprehensiveness – the features which represent day-to-day activities in design
- continuity – common, transferable audit techniques.

Design, as well as involving complexity, is internationally diverse throughout a variety of sectors. The ability to universally audit design (see Design Council Atlas) is hampered by sector-specific practices and geographical locations. Plainly, design practice involves common values and common business ideals, but how design effectiveness is measured in one industry or country may be vastly different to how it is measured in another.

AUDITS FROM MODEL DEVELOPMENT

Management models have always provided representation of process success and failure. Whilst many such models exist, their effectiveness in design environments should perhaps be questioned. An examination of a simile seems often typical – companies as machines, human bodies, journeys, etc. Such glib metaphors add little to the analysis of a design management problem. The purpose of all audits is related to the development of an 'accurate' picture as opposed to generic problem representation. However, the day-to-day terminology of management (e.g. performance targets, quality assurance, etc.) appears too general or even inappropriate for design. Modelling design is often viewed as inaccurate and, as with all such systems, usually represents scientific convenience and reductionism. How then can we model design processes 'accurately' as part of a process of problem (or success) diagnosis within an audit? A rather more isomorphic approach is called for – if the process model resembles spaghetti it should be described as such. Therefore isomorphic models are perhaps best for applications in design departments where it is essential to preserve the operational characteristics in the design department within which a novel (specific) process terminology exists. How then can design audits gain currency against audits in other areas of the company?

It is evident that there needs to be a degree of common process and terminology in all management models within the same organisation. Individual departments may be best modelled at an operational level when conceptual models would apply generically. However, this suggests denial of the strategic role design often has within an organisation. The best way to model design is therefore to integrate its isomorphic model with a homomorphic company model. The model of the company will acknowledge design, and the design department will acknowledge the company. This at the level of operations recognises synergy as a component of business success. This account, and indeed the whole book, illustrates that design audits allow for the application of management and process models to areas of the company which are often overlooked.

REVIEW QUESTIONS

1 What might be the constituent parts of 'design knowledge' in a specific industrial sector?
2 Are British Standards an aid to innovation?
3 Does compliance to manufacturing standards increase or decrease market share?
4 What are the measurable characteristics of a managed design process?
5 How do design audits differ from financial ones?
6 What kind of metrics would apply to assessing design value?
7 Within a design consultancy how can design quality be invested in?
8 What is meant by 'measuring' design value?
9 How do design audits differ from financial ones and from ecological ones?
10 Can 'rules of thumb' in design management be modelled?

PROJECT QUESTIONS

1 Discuss the origins of selected types of design knowledge; map the inter-relationship of different knowledge types around the job of a design manager.
2 How is it best for a company to utilise BS 7000 (Part 1 or 3)? Plan a process of adoption over 12 months in a company you know.
3 Discuss the various value systems associated with design within a company – describe them and their contribution to design quality.
4 Within a team, conduct a design audit through three company visits.
5 Construct an investment plan for the development of a small design department within a company you know. Consider, over a two-year period, a financial commitment to employ two designers and the potential pay-offs for the company within five years.

REFERENCES

Ahopelto, J. (2002) Design management as a strategic instrument. *Acta Wasaensia,* 99, Industrial Management 4

Beer, S. (1966) *Decision and control.* (Chichester: Wiley)

Bruce, M. and Bessant, J. (2002) *Design in business: strategic innovation through design.* (Harlow: Pearson Education)

BS 7000 Part 2 (1989) (London: British Standards Institute)

BS 7000 Part 10 (1995) (London: British Standards Institute)

BS 7000 Part 2 (1997) (London: British Standards Institute)

Buchholz, R. (1982) *Business environment and public policy.* (Englewood Cliffs, NJ: Prentice-Hall)

Burt, R. S. (1992) *Structural holes: the social structure of competition.* (Cambridge, MA: Harvard University Press)

Cooper, R. and Press, M. (1995) *The design agenda: a guide to successful design management.* (Chichester: Wiley)

Cooper, R. G. and Kleinschmidt, E. J. (1988a) New products: what separates winners from losers. *Journal of Product Innovation Management,* 4(3): 169–184

Cooper, R. G. and Kleinschmidt, E. J. (1988b) Resource allocation in the new product development process. *Industrial Marketing Management,* 17: 249–262

Cooper, R. G., Edgett, S. J. and Kleinschmidt, E. J. (1998) *Portfolio management for new products.* (Reading, MA: Perseus)

Corfield, K. G. (1979) *Product design.* March. (London: National Economic Development Office)

Design Council (1998) *Design Council Red Paper 1.* April. (London: Design Council)

Design Council (2001) *Facts and figures on design in Britain.* (London: Design Council Publications)

Design Council (2002) *National survey,* http://www.design-council.org/uk

Design Council (2007) *Creative and cultural skills.* Account of the work of the industry-led Design Skills Advisory Panel, 24 April, updated 25 April, http://www.design-council.org.uk/en/Design-Council/3/Press/Design-industry-calls-on-government/ (accessed 7 June 2007)

Gorb, P. (ed.) with Schneider, E. (1988) *Design talks.* London Business School Design Management Seminars. (London: Design Council)

Gorb, P. and Dumas, A. (1987) Silent design. *Design Studies,* 8(3), July: 150–156

Hollins, B. (1997) So tomorrow doesn't come as a surprise: suggestions for dealing with the future. In: Conference proceedings of 'The Second European Academy of Design Conference', Stockholm, Sweden

Hollins, B. (2000) Developing a long term design vision. *Design Management Journal,* 11(3): 44–49

Inns, T. and Hands, D. (1998) Design in-house: 12 case studies describing how the TCS [Teaching Company Scheme] has improved in-house design capability. Brunel University, Design Research Centre. University of Central England in Birmingham, School of Design Research. (Uxbridge: Brunel University)

Jackson, N. and Carter, P. (2000) *Rethinking organisational behaviour.* (Harlow: Pearson Education)

Jerrard, R. (2000) *Researching designing: cycles of design research, foundations for the future – doctoral education in design, La Clusaz, France.* (Stoke-on-Trent: Staffordshire University Press)

Jerrard, R., Trueman, M. and Newport, R. (eds) (1999) *Managing new product innovation.* (London: Taylor & Francis)

Johnson, J. A. (1996) Social auditors: the new breed of expert. *Business Ethics,* March/April

Matarasso, F. (1997) *Use or ornament: the social impact of participation in the arts.* (Stroud: Comedia)

Morzota, B. de (1998) Challenge of design relationships. In: M. Bruce and B. Jevnaker (eds) *Management of design alliances.* (London: John Wiley & Sons) Chapter 11, pp. 243–260

Nonaka, I. (1991) The knowledge-creating company. *Harvard Business Review,* November–December

Oakley, M. (ed.) (1990) *Design management: a handbook of issues and methods.* (Oxford: Blackwell)

Olins, W. (1990) *Corporate identity.* (London: Thames and Hudson) pp. 28–42

Olson, E., Slater, S. and Cooper, R. (2000) Managing design for competitive advantage: a process approach. *Design Management Journal,* 11(4): 10–17

Pearce, J., Raynard, P. and Zadek, S. (1996) *Social auditing for small organisations: the workbook for trainers and practitioners.* (London: New Economics Foundation)

Pugh, S. (1991) *Total design.* (Reading, MA: Addison-Wesley)

Roberts, P. (2001) Corporate competence in FM: current problems and issues. *Facilities,* 19(7/8): 269–275

Roy, R. and Potter, S. (1993) The commercial impacts of investment in design. In: M. Bruce and R. Cooper, *Marketing and design management.* (London: International Thomson Business Press)

Sentence, A. and Clark, J. (1997) *The contribution of design to the UK economy: a Design Council research paper.* (London: Design Council)

Sentence, A. and Walters, C. (1997) *Design, competitiveness and UK manufacturing performance.* Design Council Working Paper. (London: Design Council)

Siegel, R. (1982) Ritasue Resources, http://www.ritasue.com/resources

Thackera, J. (1997) *Winners! How today's successful companies innovate by design.* (Aldershot: Gower)

Topalian, A. (1980) Designers as directors. *Designer,* February: 6–8

Topalian, A. (1994) *The Alto Design Management workbook.* (London: Alto)

UK Government (1993) *Realising our potential: a strategy for science, engineering and technology.* (London: HMSO)

UK Government (1994) *Helping business to win.* Government 1st White Paper on Competitiveness. May. (London: HMSO)

Walsh, V., Roy, R., Bruce, M. and Potter, S. (1992) *Winning by design: technology, product design and international competitiveness.* (Oxford: Blackwell Business)

Walton, T. (2002) Design and knowledge management. *Design Management Journal* (special issue), 2(1)

Wilson, E. (1994) Improving market success rates through better product definition. *World Class Design to Manufacture,* 1(4): 13–15

FURTHER READING

Aaker, D. A. (1991) *Managing brand equity: capitalising on the value of a brand name.* (New York: Free Press)

Alexander, M. (1985) Creative marketing and innovative consumer product design: some case studies. *Design Studies,* 1: 41–50

Ashcraft, D. and Slattery, L. (1996) Experiential design, strategy and market share. *Design Management Journal,* Fall

Baxter, M. (1995) *Product design: practical methods for systematic development of new products.* (London: Chapman & Hall)

Beer, S. (1979) *The heart of the enterprise.* (Chichester: Wiley)

Bruce, M. and Jevnaker, B. (1998) *Management of design alliances: sustaining competitive advantage*. (Chichester: Wiley)

Cooper, R. G. (1993) *Winning at new products: accelerating the process from idea to launch*. (Reading, MA: Addison-Wesley)

Cooper, R. G., Edgett, S. J. and Kleinschmidt, E. J. (1998) *Portfolio management for new products: picking the winners*. WP11. (Ontario: Product Development Institute)

Frascara, J. (2002) *Design and the social sciences*. (London: Taylor & Francis)

Hamel, G. (2000) *Leading the revolution*. (Boston, MA: Harvard Business School Press)

Handy, C. B. (1993) *Understanding organisations*. (Harmondsworth: Pelican)

Hayes, R. H., Wheelwright, S. C. and Clark, K. B. (1988) *Dynamic manufacturing: creating the learning organisation*. (New York: Free Press)

Kotler, P. and Rath, G. A. (1990) Design: a powerful but neglected strategic tool. *Journal of Business Strategy*, 5: 16

Leonard-Barton, D. (1995) *Wellsprings of knowledge: building and sustaining the sources of innovation*. (Boston, MA: Harvard Business School Press)

Lidwell, W., Holden, K. and Butler, J. (2003) *Universal principles of design*. (Beverly, MA: Rockport)

McGoldrick, P. J. (1990) *Retail marketing*. (London: McGraw-Hill)

Rickards, T. and Moger, S. (1999) *Handbook for creative team leaders*. (Aldershot: Gower)

Tidd, J. and Bessant, J. (1997) *Managing innovation: integrating technological, organisational and market change*. (Chichester: Wiley)

Tidd, J., Bessant, J. and Pavitt, K. (1997) *Managing innovation: integrating technological, market and organizational change*. (Chichester: Wiley)

Ulrich, K. T. and Eppinger, S. D. (1995) *Product design and development*. (New York: McGraw-Hill)

Upshaw, L. (1997) Transferable truths of brand identity. *Design Management Journal*, Winter: 9.

Walton, T. (1997) Insights on the theory and practice of branding. *Design Management Journal*, Winter: 5

Chapter 2

Design management, urban regeneration and the organisation of culture

Jonathan Vickery

INTRODUCTION

Design management involves organising innovative activity or constructing frameworks within which design takes place. Design management can be defined in terms of the management process or the design process, in terms of an individual 'design manager' or a collaborative process. Here we will be considering an example of the latter – a collaborative and interactive design management process, involving inter-organisational management and a multidimensional product. The object of this study is an urban design and regeneration project, which involved an enormous array of professionals. The project was the Coventry city centre Phoenix Initiative (1997–2004), a redesign of a three-hectare site, with four interconnected public areas and an urban focal point of a new city plaza.

Design in this urban context has many applications: enabling effective functionality and user experience of the space; enhancing habitability and material sustainability; facilitating communication and social interactivity; and, most visibly, constructing and displaying products, buildings and spaces in an aesthetically engaging way which coherently expresses a particular location and the cultural aspirations of its population. Such a project involves multiple forms of design and design managers: product design (public art, a plaza arch and the 'street furniture'); urban design (open public areas); landscape design (gardens and thoroughfares); architectural design (residential buildings, a new museum frontage and a visitors' interpretation centre); interior design (inside the buildings); graphic design (both the project branding and the city branding), and so on.

The visual focal point is the popularly named 'Whittle Arch', a monumental archway linking the compressed exit from the residential and retail zone with the city plaza. As a collaboration between Sir Richard MacCormac as architect-designer and structural engineer Mark Whitby, it is equalled only by the innovative cantilevered spiral ramp and glass bridge, another collaboration, between architects (Robert Rummey), engineers and an artist. A regeneration project is highly complex, and here we can only consider some general issues relevant to design management. Through this we will attempt to extend (1) our conception of design management research (and its vocabulary) and (2) our understanding of the professional tasks of design management practice.

THE PROJECT

As Roberts and Sykes (2000) testify, urban regeneration has become a major socio-economic phenomenon. Scholars like Graeme Evans (2001) have contended, however, that the cultural content of large-scale urban development projects is often ignored and our 'cultural planning' is haphazard. Charles Landry (1999) provides a compelling cultural-intellectual framework within which a vision for 'creative cities' can emerge, rethinking urban, economic and cultural development as part of the same social problematic. Along with a renewed interest in the cultural and creative industries in general, urban regeneration has been registered at the highest governmental levels, with varying impacts (Evans and Shaw 2004; Imrie and Raco 2003).

Significantly, the members of the Phoenix Initiative design team are professional participants in this growing discourse on urban transformation. Intellectually active as advocates of a renewed conception of public space, they were not only concerned with basic regeneration requirements, but with the relation between civic identity, cultural development and design aesthetics. The Phoenix Initiative project can be summarised as follows:

- Vision: To mark the turn of the millennium, a metaphorical journey (as an actual pedestrian route) is created through Coventry's historic centre, animated by the theme of reconciliation between the past, its industry and its conflicts, and the present and its aspirations for renewed productivity and for peace. This would provide an emotive and culturally inspiring fulcrum to the further regeneration and rebranding of Coventry city centre.
- Mission: To excavate the historic cathedral and medieval priory site, design and construct a new boulevard for both residential and retail use, and construct a visitors' interpretation centre in its own cloister, a city plaza, a new frontage to the Coventry Transport Museum, and a raised glass bridge leading to a 'Garden of International Friendship'. Within this project seven major public art commissions would take place, along with various events and a major poetry enterprise.
- Objectives: With a final budget of £55 million, and over £1 million spent on public art, it stands as the largest regeneration initiative in Coventry since the Second World War. It aims to make the historic portion of the city centre (1)

architecturally coherent in its design, (2) a site for both social interaction and retail business development, (3) a symbol of cultural identity and (4) a stimulus for a synergy between community groups, city authorities and institutions.

- Constituencies: Coventry City Council (as client); other local social and cultural institutions and organisations; Coventry's urban multiethnic population; and the international and national tourist industry.

- Agencies: Coventry City Council's project management team were the Phoenix Initiative; the Coventry Millennium Forum monitored the millennial objectives of the scheme (a major initial funding source was the Millennium Commission). Sir Richard MacCormac of MacCormac Jamieson Prichard (MJP) was commissioned as Master Planner; Robert Rummey Design Associates (RDA) were architects of the public realm; the Public Art Commissions Agency (now Modus Operandi: MO) were art consultants; and Ashgate Management Development Services (AMDS) were project managers and overseers of a multitude of other professionals: architects, consulting engineers, developers, lighting architects, project managers, landscape designers and structural engineers.

- Context: Coventry is the oldest recorded town in England, though largely renowned for its declining automotive industry and the massive damage suffered in the first major enemy air bombardment of the Second World War. Its contemporary popular image is a composite of Jaguar motor cars and the spectacular Coventry Cathedral (wedded by design to the bombed-out shell of the old cathedral); to this add memories of the very first shopping precinct in England, with its post-war urban planning and modernist 'brutalist' concrete buildings. Then came urban decay and skinheads (and, latterly, the 'chavs').

- Structure: A three-phased development over five years: Phase 1 included both ends of the site, from the old priory area at the south end to the Garden of International Friendship at the north; Phase 2: development of the 'boulevard area' with its residences and commercial lets; Phase 3: Millennium Place (the plaza), with the enormous 15-foot-high paired-arch structure, a new frontage to the Transport Museum, and a cantilevered spiral ramp leading to a glass bridge, with its 800 decorated glass fins. Public art was integral to all three phases.

This summary offers an idea of the many levels of demands, interests and design factors involved in an urban project. The Phoenix Initiative project was essentially a city council-initiated urban design and regeneration project involving, both explicitly and implicitly, the generic objectives of such projects. *Explicit* objectives are usually the aims stated in initial council planning or development policy and its urban 'masterplan'; its objectives are usually the physical reconstruction of an urban area, with new buildings and open spaces, in the hope

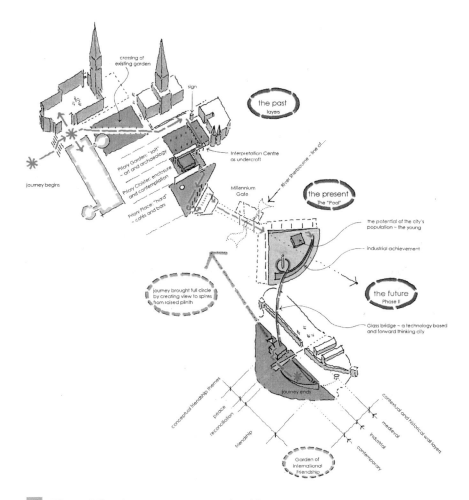

Figure 2.1 `'The Journey – concept sketch'`
By Rummey Design Associates, 1998. Supplied courtesy of Robert Rummey

of attracting tourism, investment and a renewed sense of civic pride. At the concept stage of a project of this kind a commissioning body may think they know what they need or want, but this often has to be challenged or extended. Effective design management articulates the *implicit* aims and aspirations the client or commissioning body cannot articulate; these emerge from an understanding of both site and the public or consumers. These implicit aims and aspirations have to be translated and then encoded in the initial design proposal, and carried through with flexibility within a financial and legal context that could constantly change.

Effective design management in a complex project of this kind must integrate the distinct demands of (1) the commissioning body (and the complex financial–legal–political networks within which it functions), (2) the physical and aesthetic dimensions of the urban site, and (3) the public and their social-cultural needs. In a project of this kind, however, no one individual is usually charged with the office of 'design manager'. Design management operates in several very different organisational contexts, and is only a coherent reality if some form of 'design leadership' emerges. Design leadership is more than just project management; it makes the aesthetic and social aspirations of regeneration internal to the practical process of physical urban reconstruction. The design leader (or team) synthesises the demands of client, site and public and 'translates' these demands within a specific unified vision, for which they then must act as advocate, rationalising and arguing this vision through multiple decision-making contexts with disparate stakeholders.

The formation and leadership of a design team was central to the Phoenix project. It functioned in managing the design and construction, but also in cultural leadership and diplomacy in ensuring that unfamiliar or creative design ideas maintained a safe passage through successive decision-making bodies. MJP subcontracted RDA and MO, and all three played a significant collaborative role in both developing the initial masterplan and then managing, in a coordinated way, the distinct tasks in the design and construction process. Their roles in the team were initially defined by their professional expertise, as architects (of buildings), landscape architects and art consultants respectively. However, the team dynamic worked effectively when the conceptual boundaries between buildings, space and art objects (the specialist terminologies embedded in institutionalised professional roles) became relative to the demands of the site, through office sharing, interaction and discussion. The work of MJP is not characterised by signature styles or preconceived architectural templates. Their designs emerge from an analysis of the site (its history, social specificity and use) and a dialogue with the various stakeholders. Sir Richard MacCormac is a major public intellectual involved in architectural research as much as public advocacy, and his ability to facilitate and maintain dialogue is one of his mechanisms of innovation. The necessity for design leadership is that, through possible conflicting demands from site and stakeholders, a coherent design concept survives intact. The design team's objectives were to:

- unite and reconnect the disconnected elements of the city centre
- re-establish the ancient topography of the city
- articulate both the past and a vision for the future
- facilitate the creativity of diverse contributors.

Through preliminary research, the design team understood the socio-cultural framework of their project. All public projects take place within a discursive context of already existing (and perhaps failing) urban, social and cultural planning strategies. These can include a city council 'urban development strategy', a 'local cultural strategy', a 'strategic arts policy', a 'heritage strategy' and a 'tourism strategy', along with many city planning conventions. Each strategy is the product of deliberation by the council and its professionals, and ignoring them could lead to political conflict or render further design proposals dysfunctional in the eyes of key stakeholders. As a city council invariably holds the power of veto at critical points of any public project, such strategy contexts must be acknowledged. The Phoenix project was fortunately undertaken at a time of political stability in the city council, and the council's forward thinking ensured that the two initial barriers of planning consent and public consultation were unproblematic. Moreover, this major project was sensibly used as a platform for policy renewal, clearing some cognitive space for innovation: civic projects of this kind can be crucial in 'importing' ideas and new concepts and setting up frameworks wherein different or more extensive renewal plans can germinate, be developed and become part of strategy. More often than not, however, public projects have to battle against basic and traditional political imperatives that have little to do with the feasibility or success of the design. The political framework of public decision making is usually animated by the following motivations:

1   Political prestige: how do we justify this? Public bodies strive to maintain credibility in the face of their various constituencies and in the context of other pressing financial priorities.
2   Social amenities: does this space meet our needs? Value judgments passed on the design can be purely instrumental and utilitarian.
3   Art for everyone: value judgments on the aesthetics of the design are often pitched low: how do ordinary people respond?

This last point is problematic: good design usually involves a certain aesthetic sophistication, and this is often inimical to popular taste. The Phoenix design team worked with an emphatic conception of cultural democracy – the reclaiming of 'lost' social space for public use was one of their prime objectives. This did not mean capitulating to an already existing consensus on design taste, but communicating in a public context remained a major challenge.

The criteria for successful design are never stable, but constantly negotiated through the process of design management. All practitioners work with a value system, and their values are derived both from the internal discourse of their profession and from other social and political frameworks. While the value systems of architects and artists are usually governed by visual values, the primacy of such visual values is notoriously problematic. 'Good design' can be rejected by both a commissioning body or client and the public for the following reasons:

■   Artistic complexity: The design (whether its unusual spatial functionality or its visual composition) might intimidate the general public or militate against other guiding objectives of the public project, such as brand objectives.

- Aesthetic values: The distinctive symbolic import of a design, or even materials, might be alien to its urban context or not develop a visual rapport with its urban context.

- Cultural signifiers: Style or artistic detail might emit meanings antagonistic to the socio-historical environment: for example, metropolitan architectural idioms or London art world trends can appear alien or even hostile in a regional cultural context.

- Contemporary design idiom: A visual language might 'date' swiftly or be too expressive of passing trends or fashion. Urban design needs to maintain a long lifespan, which is why 'classical' motifs are often favoured.

- High commercial risk: The design may not in itself cost beyond budget to construct, but its long-term maintenance costs may be prohibitive (for example, potential damage or material corrosion).

The Phoenix design team's 'holistic' concept of design went beyond the usual emphasis on buildings, symbols and public amenities. It entailed understanding the structure of spatial experience and the specific meanings embedded in the space. The historical character of Coventry as a city was written into the design at concept stage, and its historicity emerged through a series of visual hermeneutic strategies (ways in which the design directed the viewer's interpretation of its content). The design was not to be didactic, or work with literal symbols, pedantic literary references or local clichés. It involved interpretation of some-times subtle imagery within a loose chronological framework; the metaphoric journey demands some intellectual participation on the part of the public in order to make sense.

Modus Operandi's partnership with MJP ensured the public art strategy was to play a major role in the masterplanning process, whereby the artists have an input into how the large spatial zones, and parts of the historical narrative, will function. Artist–designer collaborations are not easy to manage. Artists make proposals based on a number of criteria, usually intrinsic to their own professional interests (continuing their own artistic project, style, subject matter, etc.). Collaboration mediated by an art consultant was crucial in initiating artists into this complex project, and integrating their proposals and personal creativity.

The central challenge for managing the art–design collaboration was that the public art proposals had to both be innovative and engage with popular sensibility. This seemingly impossible union was arguably achieved by using artists who were willing to respond to the particularity of the site and its public, using motifs or imagery historically familiar. Artist Chris Browne constructed *Cofa's Tree* ('Cofa Tree' being the historic centre point and linguistic root of 'Coventry') as a mosaic, using debris from the archaeological excavations, from medieval building remains to old mechanical car bits. David Ward's sound installation, *Here*, featured eight sound speakers in the priory cloister, each with concurrent voices recounting their

Figure 2.2 *The glass bridge by MacCormac Jamieson Prichard and Whitbybird with Alexander Beleschenko, the* Public Bench *by Jochen Gerz, and the* Time Zone Clock *by Françoise Schein, all 2003*

Photo: Jonathan Vickery

experiences of Coventry's past. Jochen Gerz's *Public Bench*, placed against the cyclorama wall forming the rim of the north of the plaza, featured over 2,000 plaques of names elected by Coventry people or friends, inserting private memories into public space. And on the plaza itself was a time zone map of the world, where artist Françoise Schein illustrated the concurrent time of the world's capitals and Coventry's 26 'twin cities'. Each art work was characterised by (1) conceptual clarity: its formal innovation did not preclude public intelligibility; (2) social objectivity: the art did not express an artist's ego or personal feelings but the topography of the public space; and (3) dialogic engagement: they each mediated a part of the narrative that was the metaphorical journey from past to future and thus give visual expression to civic identity.

The involvement of the art consultancy lasted as long as the commissioning and induction process; the artists were then 'project-managed' by the architects of the specific project phase or spatial zone. Practical collaboration between artist and architect, however, can generate intellectual property issues. For example, there is no simple demarcation between Susanna Heron's *Waterwindow* and the spatial structure within which it sits (designed by RDA); similarly, Kate Whiteford's land drawing, the *Priory Maze*, was also contextualised by RDA's spatial design. Every dimension of a work of public art, depending on its complexity, can demand collaboration: (1) the artistic idea, generated by the project context; (2) the

Figure 2.3 Waterwindow *by Susanna Heron; architectural surround by Rummey Design Associates, 2003*

Photo: Jonathan Vickery

concept – its meaning-function must cohere with the design scheme; (3) form – scale and impact *in situ* are negotiated; (4) its materials are coordinated with its physical-architectural context; (5) spatial function – it must facilitate a viewer or pedestrian movement in harmony with the spatial flow of the public area. A documented file of drawings and plans is usually the only way to demarcate the boundaries of intellectual property ownership.

PROJECT SUMMARY

The design innovation and artistic creativity altogether are embedded in non-negotiable project management contexts: we can summarise the project in terms of such contextual determinations:

- Proposal: The initial proposal for a public project takes pace within a matrix of urban development schemes and existing policies; the decision-making process can be mediated by many different 'authorities', and initial proposals are based on estimated receipts of funding, often not guaranteed. The proposal should not represent a fixed structure but a mutable template, having the facility to respond to shifting demands.
- Concept: A 'strong' proposal of assertive visual statements is always in

danger of repressing the historical specificity of the space and suppressing experience of the space as a site of social interactivity. For the 'public' to maintain a symbolic priority over buildings (almost always tacitly symbolic of 'authority' of one kind or another), the object–viewer relationship needs to be built into the production process at the level of the concept.

■ Research: Computer imagery or other visual simulations of the site are crucial public relations tools as well as a design necessity. The structure of the design itself also needs to maintain a flexibility, as public projects can suddenly expand or shrink. A central feature of the project – the proposed boulevard – was abandoned as a result of a late refusal by Sainsbury's Plc to vacate a part of the site; this resulted in a re-routeing of the pathway and a truncated entrance to the plaza. However, what transpired was a significant design solution in the form of an innovative arch, which provided a 'compression-release' mechanism for the now radical spatial transition between the zones.

■ Production assessment: Unforeseen pre-production problems can lead to a complete budget restructuring, or a delay in order to raise further funds. In the case of Phoenix, the composition of the ground (earth, rock and water) and positioning of the services (draining, water and gas mains, etc.) were more complex than anticipated, leading to more foundation work. The demolition of key buildings on the site required compulsory purchase agreements, and a public inquiry was required for this; further, there was large public resistance to the demolition of the Hippodrome theatre, whose location was to become the plaza.

■ Schedules and contracts: The design schedule is planned within the context of projected project income and expenditure. Contracts of various kinds need to be drawn up (ownership, maintenance, copyright, insurance, responsibilities, planning consents, liability, etc.). AMDS, the project managers, structured the scheduling, legal and financial activity on behalf of the city council. This usually includes a full business and implementation strategy for the longer term, involving the maximisation of land value, coordinating all contractors and subcontractors, budget scheduling and management, quality assurance, site acquisition and attracting private sector investment. Problems with initial prediction, risk analysis and programming on a regeneration project are substantial. Some spaces are contractually complex, riddled with concealed historical restrictions.

■ Production, construction and installation: The Phoenix project utilised the services of archaeologists (the medieval priory site), artists (the public art), lighting architects (the lighting scheme), street furniture designers (benches, paving and kerbing), other project managers (administration of financial, legal and logistical detail), developers (administration and finance of properties), engineers (civil works), structural engineers (bridge and the great arch), developers (the commercial lettings), quantity surveyors, and other legal,

43

administrative and financial services. Each of these services had to be scheduled and coordinated.

- Reception: Public and consumer response needs to be managed, and communication opportunities need to be seized. The archaeology of the site became more important than anticipated, and formed a focal point for the project, attracting the Channel 4 Time Team on discovering a twelfth-century medieval cathedral floor and the oldest medieval wall painting in Britain. Even the foundations of a medieval building can provide an opportunity for a small indoor archaeological park, as is now the Priory Undercroft. Publicity, public reaction, interpretation, and subsequent photographic reproduction of the public project play a significant role in design management. Both the Phoenix Initiative and the design team were independently engaged in countless public lectures and presentations.

Urban regeneration projects are a complex of interests and objectives, and these are never static but evolve, sometimes subject to convulsive changes in priorities. There are unique difficulties with public–private partnerships, and these difficulties can prevent private sector companies from being involved. These include working with low budgets, invoices often being paid late, political interference, a multitude of legal considerations, inconsistent decision-making processes, a willingness to settle for 'easy' options, and so on. The Phoenix Initiative was unusual in its efficiency, and this did not come at the cost of creative practice. A number of artists overspent, but were accommodated. However, MJP's design management role meant that they were undertaking coordination and creative responsibilities that were not costed under their professional services as planners and architects, and for this a severe financial price was paid.

DESIGN IN THE PUBLIC SPHERE

Public projects usually must conform to some basic social demands: they must (1) interest or stimulate the public or social community; (2) add to the environment in an affirmative way and not disturb or upset; (3) carry meanings both relevant and communicable to residents or visitors; and (4) meet with health and safety regulations (and all other manner of social regulations pertaining to the uses and abuses of public space). For this reason experimental or 'avant-garde' design or public art is not usually accepted; and, generally, the public art does not directly relate to art world discourse or radical social critique. Public aesthetic expression must usually be 'affirmative'. This means that innovation cannot simply be expressed through new artistic idiom, controversial representation, or technique; it must be constructed out of a broader dialogue with social context.

'Social context', however, is not one seamless environment, but a disjointed

a)

b)

Figure 2.4 *Two views: a) Priory Place looking towards Millennium Place; b) Millennium Place looking towards Priory Place, with transition articulated by the Whittle Arch, designed by MacCormac Jamieson Prichard and Whitbybird, 2003*

Photo: Jonathan Vickery

network of institutions, organisations and random representatives of the public; sites of contestation can emerge (and dissolve) quickly. One consistent source of instability in public projects is the perceived tension between 'public' and 'private' interests. Public sector objectives will usually concern (1) the representation of a complex of undefined stakeholders and state institutions, (2) economic development that expands the local tax base, (3) longer-term sustainable development that creates new employment opportunities, and (4) quality-of-environment factors involving integration of social communities and involvement and support of public sector services. Private sector interests are less expansive, and more easily and clearly quantified, usually involving fewer procedural constraints (like meetings or committees), structured by a cost-cutting profit-driven schedule and driven by clear profit, return on investment and further investment opportunities. For political or economic reasons, either set of interests could simply be ignored in a public project. The success of the Phoenix, however, was the way the design management process mediated the traditional public–private antagonisms. MJP, RDA, MO and ADMS do not simply work with a 'public sector ethos', however that is defined, but are developing a new conception of public value through creating a dialogue between public and private interests.

This 'dialogue' is not some convenient political fudge. The questions 'Who are the public?' and 'What is the public sphere?' articulate a chronic uncertainty in contemporary culture. That the 'general public' no longer exists as a simple generic entity is a sociological truism. Class, gender and ethnicity are complex, and how people are categorised and represented in the public sphere is problematic. The public sphere is now heavily integrated with private interests, and 'public' signifies dominant institutions and organisations, not 'people' as such. This issue is made more complex by the fact that urban regeneration is as much concerned about external investment and business immigration, and national and international tourism as about the indigenous population. The design team's approach to the sociological undefinability of public identity was to avoid creating a 'closed' visual statement, with stylistic and architecturally expressive buildings as a focal point; they opened up the space as a site for dialogue for the various 'forces' animating city life. The design team's solution was to redefine 'space' as 'place', in the sense that the area was not conceived as a site for interesting buildings but a sphere of the city where identity and history could be reconstructed, and public and private could reconceptualise their interests in terms of long-term cultural development.

In reconsidering the initial objectives which were the animating factors in the design conception of the Phoenix project, we can now articulate some basic implications for design management research:

- Unite and reconnect the disconnected elements of the city centre: Space was defined as 'place', with the continuity of a historical narrative providing

connections but the spaces differentiated by the diverse series of interconnected activity zones. The design concept emerged from an understanding
of social interactivity: how space was and is used and how the spaces are
interconnected.

- Re-establish the ancient topography of the city: Medieval and later archaeological remains were exposed and again became part of the fabric of the
  space; but the historical content of the design was not 'memorialised', alien-
  ating non-English residents. There is an open 'aesthetic' to the space, where the
  visual experiences of retail, art, media, design and heritage are co-extensive;
  the multiple functionality of the site can involve viewers on any level.

- Articulate both past and a vision for the future: A 'dialogic' approach to
  design involved responding to the site, not imposing a plan, and allowing its
  memories to speak and provide the terms by which to move forward. The
  ancient identity of the city is not 'fossilised', but is articulated in terms of a
  specific trajectory to the future; this was done through a historical narrative
  based not on beliefs or social rituals but on industry. The material conditions
  of existence were the context out of which a realistic move forward was
  imagined. Dialogue with the past grounded civic idealism.

- Facilitate the creativity of diverse contributors: A design-driven leadership
  did not attempt to micro-manage the creative output of contributing
  practitioners, but, through the mediation of the art consultancy, diverse
  creative aspirations were coordinated; the management model overall was a
  dynamic network model, not a fixed grid model. Moreover, the final outcome
  did not, as in so many urban projects, signify the authority of the State or
  top-down city authority cultural micro-management, but the mediation of
  stakeholder networks as well as political and civic networks generated an
  effective advocacy process.

CONCLUSION: DESIGN MANAGEMENT PRACTICE

The Phoenix project was highly complex and here our generalisation has simply
allowed us to make a few observations and hopefully extend our conception of
design management research and practice. In terms of research, our key concepts
have been social interactivity, aesthetics, dialogue and network: that is, we have
understood this project not primarily in terms of management structures and
plans, but in terms of communication. As for professional practice, the following
points have emerged:

- The visual presentation of the design plays a pre-eminent role at proposal
  stage in convincing the client and stakeholders, including the general public,
  that such a project is justified.

- The project concept was a creative and flexible conceptual framework (not a fixed-plan set of technical specifications); the framework maintained a flexibility in the advent of radical change.
- The collaborative design team was crucial in integrating the complexities of creativity and innovation into the project management process.
- The design team's collective experience and collaborative flexibility enabled it to engage in both advocacy of the project vision and management of the master plan through successive decision-making contexts, political, financial and social.
- Urban reconstruction is not a natural habitat for artists; artists usually need induction and mediation in the context of both contractual obligations and contractors' schedules.
- Miscommunication and indirect communication are the greatest problem concerning multi-organisational projects; specialist practitioner and contractor terminology, embedded in their own professional values, has to be 'translated'.

REVIEW QUESTIONS

1   Did the management complexities work well in Coventry, for example in utilising the services of archaeologists, artists and designers?
2   How were the public involved within the management process?
3   What were the unusual features of design management involved in the creativity of the diverse contributors?
4   How did a 'dialogue approach' contribute to achieving the final solution?
5   What were the main issues of mediation in both stakeholder and political and civic networks?

PROJECT QUESTIONS

1   Develop a 'snapshot' map of the project in terms of the multiple activities involved in the multiple forms of design and arts management at the mid-point of the project.
2   Compare traditional design management vocabulary with that used on the project. Highlight the differences in debate.
3   Utilise the project summary in considering the Coventry site with a similar site in another city; then compare, using additional secondary sources.
4   Devise a tabulated task and skills list for all potential project members that could have been valuable at the project's initial briefings.

REFERENCES AND BIBLIOGRAPHY

Campbell, L. and Cork, R. (2005) *Phoenix: architecture/art/regeneration*. (London: Black Dog Publishing)

Evans, G. (2001) *Cultural planning: an urban renaissance?* (London: Routledge)

Evans, G. and Shaw, P. (2004) *The contribution of culture to regeneration in the UK: a report to the DCMS*. (London: London Metropolitan University)

Imrie, R. and Raco, M. (2003) *Urban renaissance? New Labour, community and urban policy*. (Bristol: Policy Press)

Landry, C. (1999) *The creative city: a toolkit for urban innovators*. (London: Comedia and Earthscan)

Lovell, V. (1998) *Coventry Phoenix Initiative: public art strategy and programme*. (Birmingham: PACA)

Lovell, V. *et al.* (1998) *Public art: a decade of Public Art Commissions Agency, 1987–1997.* (London: Merrell Holberton)

MacCormac, R. (2004) Coventry Phoenix Initiative: achieving urban renaissance through public space and art. Available at http://www/mjparchitects.co.uk/essay/Cityscapepiece.pdf (accessed 3 April 2006)

MacCormac, R. (2004), Art and regeneration in the city of Coventry. Available at http://www/mjparchitects.co.uk/Art_Regeneration_Coventry.pdf (accessed 3 April 2006)

Mageean, A. and Wansborough, M. (2000) The role of urban design in cultural regeneration. *Journal of Urban Design*, 5(2): 181–197

Roberts, P. and Sykes, H. (2000) *Urban regeneration: a handbook*. (London: Urban Regeneration Association/Sage)

Verwijnen, J. and Lehtovouri, P. (eds) (1999) *Creative cities: cultural industries, urban development and the information society*. (Helsinki: UIAH)

Vickery, J. (2003) Interview with Chris Beck, Director, The Phoenix Initiative (unpublished), Coventry, 17 December

Vickery, J. (2004) Interview with Toby Johnson, Managing Director, MacCormac Jamieson Prichard Architects, London, 8 January

Vickery, J. (2004) Interview with Vivien Lovell, Managing Director, Modus Operandi Art Consultants, London, 15 January

FURTHER READING

Lynch, K. (1995) *City sense and city design*. (Cambridge, MA: MIT Press)

Moughtin, J. C., Cuesta, R., Sarris, C. and Signoretta, P. (2003) *Urban design*. (Oxford: Architectural Press)

49

Chapter 3

The Italian furniture industry and the Kartell case study

Gabriella Lojacono

INTRODUCTION

Establishing the borders of the furniture system is quite difficult, as is defining the homogeneous features the enterprises involved have in common.

This is partly because the furniture companies satisfy a very general need – that is to say, the need to 'furnish' to both aesthetic and functional requirements; also the products offered – namely, furniture, fitments, lighting units, household articles, accessories, curtains and flooring – are extremely varied. This is why it's appropriate to describe the structure and size of the most significant part of the system which has made the greatest contribution to creating the worldwide image of 'Italian design': furniture (e.g. chairs, tables, sofas, kitchen).

THE ITALIAN FURNITURE INDUSTRY

The Italian furniture industry is important in domestic terms because of its employment levels, turnover, contribution to gross domestic product and propensity for export, equal to 48 per cent of its total production value (Federlegno-Arredo 2004). The main market areas are the United Kingdom, France, Germany and the USA.

Exports as a proportion of turnover have increased considerably since 1991, a year in which they amounted to 28 per cent. Such an increase in exports may be explained by the crisis in domestic demand, which began in the early 1990s and which, together with increased competitive pressure in the Italian market, has forced many companies to strengthen their presence in foreign markets; Italian companies have had to look for new sales opportunities in non-European countries. In terms of product categories, above all Italy exports upholstered furniture (24 per cent in 2004 – Federlegno-Arredo 2004), furniture components

(15 per cent), lighting units (12 per cent) and dining- and living-room furniture (11 per cent). Imports at €1,685,715 million are up 13.2 per cent. A major factor in the recent growth in imports is delocalisation of production to low-labour-cost countries.

Growth of imports, instead, can be considered the effect of foreign retail network expansion in Italy (for instance, Ikea and Roche Bobois). A possible explanation is that these forms of distribution have managed to satisfy demand in the medium to low end of the market, one not covered by Italian producers.

The main areas of origin for furniture imported by Italy are China, Germany, Austria and Romania, amounting to 45 per cent of total value.

Apart from these characteristics, furniture is among the top manufacturing industries with a positive trade balance, evidence of a competitive advantage that has enabled Italy to achieve a position of leadership at the international level. However, there are signals of vulnerability: since 2003 Italy has not been the world's leading exporter of furniture – a primary position gained from 1979 onward.

The qualifying factors of the production industry, which at the same time make it inimitable, are specialised workforce skills, the creativity of both entrepreneurs and designers, the geographical concentration of the enterprises concerned, company flexibility, interaction with associated and support industries, growth of a specialised distribution structure, and sophisticated domestic demand.

In 2004 Italy's furniture production industry comprised 36,687 enterprises employing a total of 232,963 people. The average size is small (about six employees), reflecting a fragmented, craftsman-type production structure. Other data confirm this: 90 per cent of enterprises employ fewer than ten people, 1,657 have more than 20 employees, and around 140 enterprises have more than 100. Only one Italian company is listed on the New York Stock Exchange (NYSE) – Natuzzi.

In 2004, only 26 companies in the home and office furniture industry reported a turnover above 50 million euros (Bocconi University School of Management on Aida). These are mainly large companies in the upholstery and kitchen furniture field or diversified groups within the furniture system.

It should be emphasised that 'upmarket' enterprises such as Giorgetti, Tisettanta, Boffi and Poltrona Frau don't feature in the leading positions even though some of their products are considered excellent examples of Italian design. This can be explained by a combination of the 'niche' strategies pursued by these companies and the deep-rooted positions achieved in the Italian market, factors that limit possibilities for turnover growth. The majority of enterprises still continue to be family owned, even when they exceed a certain size, for example the Molteni, Natuzzi and Scavolini family companies.

Another important structural feature in this industry is the concentration of production units in only a few of Italy's regional industrial areas: Lombardy, Veneto, Tuscany, Friuli-Venezia Giulia and the Marches.

A few examples of production concentration are the Como–Milan Brianza area (diversified in terms of offer), Pesaro (production is mainly kitchens), Murgia Barese (upholstered furniture), Manzano (chairs) and Bassano (classic furniture). These areas differ considerably in terms of structural characteristics (history, production system network and international standing), strategic behavioural models seen within the territory, development trends and limitations for growth. Two examples might explain the diversity of furniture production areas: Brianza and Murgia Barese. Brianza is Italy's oldest furniture production area, accounts for 18.5 per cent of domestic and 5.2 per cent of European production and is marked by its varied product segments (mainly modern-styled, upholstered living-room, dining-room and bedroom furniture), focusing on the medium to high end. The area's production structure is highly fragmented: 75 per cent of Brianza's 6,000 enterprises are craftsman-type producers. Small size is characteristic of all production segments: for wooden furniture the average is 3.8 employees; 4 in upholstered furniture; and 5.4 in metal furniture. The top 100 enterprises in terms of turnover account for 35 per cent of the area's manufacturing production.

Murgia, however, is a relative newcomer. The Murgia area's first craftsman-type production of wooden furniture and accessories started back in the 1950s. Then in the 1970s a few of these craftsmen specialised in upholstery production and launched an international growth process that triggered off local economic development. It wasn't until the 1990s that Murgia began to adopt a production structure typical of an industrial area. This structural change was the result of increased specialisation by enterprises, in particular production phases and the founding and progressive growth of small enterprises operating autonomously in specific market niches.

THE STRATEGIC GROUPS OF PRODUCERS

Within the industry, those companies producing finished products can have a varying degree of production specialisation. The industry includes single-product companies, namely specialised in the production and sale of only one type of product, and companies diversified in numerous furnishing segments. Given the number of companies operating in the industry it would seem best initially to classify them based on two fundamental factors: degree of vertical integration and degree of production diversification. By combining these two factors the following groups appear to be the most widespread:

■ Integrated and specialised companies: This category includes enterprises where the majority of production takes place inside the company or group of companies controlled and managed by the one family. These enterprises normally engage in a high degree of innovation. In one of these, Natuzzi, company management covers a broad range of activities concerning the promotion, design and marketing of a specific product (armchairs and sofas). In this case the gradual integration of production, design and communication activities and a search for economies of scale were stimulated by the need for top-level service (volumes and delivery times) and low cost to large international customers.

- Integrated and diversified companies: In this category, direct control of production activities is combined with an offer covering various products, from kitchen units to fully equipped wall modules and bedroom furniture. Production is often diversified by means of external growth (acquisitions) and the formation of groups with different brands. Diversification has been dictated by a need for greater negotiating power with distribution and after having identified potential synergism with the companies acquired. For example, it often happens that wardrobe and 'equipped wall module' companies decide to apply their carpentry expertise in kitchen unit production. What appears to be fundamental here is that the acquisitions always concern homogeneous brands with a high intrinsic value. Some of the best-known cases of external growth strategy are the acquisitions of Varenna by Poliform, Salvarani by Feg, Ernesto Meda by Scavolini and Halifax by Tisettanta. Decisions to diversify are usually linked to basic technology. One particular example of this category is the Meritalia Group, which is specialised in large turnkey contract business for private and institutional customers, which led to the acquisition of specialised companies (in wood, metal and marble and stone-cutting) and the launch of lighting unit production. Companies that carry out all stages of woodworking also fall within this group – Molteni is a case in point – as do those that integrate activities that are normally decentralised by companies in the industry, for example B&B, the only company to internally produce cold-foamed polyurethane.

- Specialised 'assembler' companies in a given furniture segment: These companies outsource heavily and purchase all simple and complex components from sub-suppliers and third parties with which they have consolidated relationships, thanks to fiduciary relationships, their reputation in the local area, brand recognition in the market or agreeing special trade contracts. The offer mainly comprises mattresses, upholstery and kitchens. Accessories (for example, bedside tables and carpets) are purchased from external companies and marketed under their own brand. Certain examples of this are Flou (mattresses and beds), Chateau d'Ax (upholstered furniture and mattresses) and Calia (upholstered furniture).

- Diversified 'assembler' companies: This category includes both large companies focused on a volume strategy and small concerns of an artisan nature whose unique skills are gradually being lost (for instance, gilding and polishing). The latter work to order based on specific customer requirements and, therefore, have to be highly flexible in terms of production. For example, Kartell offers many items (from lighting to chairs to trolleys to bookcases) linked to the firm's original specialisation in plastics technology; the company coordinates the design and marketing process but all the components are manufactured by external suppliers.

Furniture producers can then market finished products either under their own brand – the most frequent case – or under commercial or other manufacturers' brands. Marketing activity can be focused on the domestic market and/or foreign markets, which leads to a different international approach of the companies concerned. This can be broken down into:

- companies with a stronger vocation for the domestic market – with exports amounting to less than 50 per cent – such as Flou, Berloni, Febal and Scavolini
- intermediate companies – with an export level of around 50 per cent – such as Poliform and Molteni
- companies with a strong international vocation – where only one-third of production is for the domestic market and that sell furniture to normal retail outlets, private customers, institutional buyers or large chains – such as Cassina, B&B Italia, Selva, Meritalia, Nicoletti and Natuzzi.

A consideration of design leads to the following typologies:

- Design-based companies, which apply design to the whole supply system – as their main differentiating criterion. For these companies, design is not just a stylistic study; it involves specific methodologies in relation to business management. It therefore becomes an element of the genetic inheritance that characterises the company's basic strategic approach (e.g. B&B Italia, Kartell and Zanotta). Often, these companies belong to the high end and outsource the creative activities of the design process to independent designers paid on royalties (a percentage of the turnover generated by the new product). The product results from a dialectic relationship between the external designer and research and development.
- Design-oriented companies, which don't focus exclusively upon product design, submitting it to production and marketing logic, such as Scavolini, Snaidero and Natuzzi.

THE DISTRIBUTION CHANNELS

Furniture distribution in Italy mainly relies on non-exclusive agents who sell to a large number of retail outlets. The length of the sales channel, marked by non-exclusive agents and traditional stores, can reduce production company profits.

About 86 per cent of production reaches the market through agents. This can be explained as follows:

- the need to keep in touch with a very high number of retail outlets widely distributed throughout the country
- the significant weight in Italy of traditional retail outlets as opposed to modern forms of distribution (large surface, low customer assistance, belonging to a chain with a central coordination, and wide assortment)
- the high value attributed to an 'information and consultancy service' by agents who benefit both the trade and producers.

Clearly, the fact there's an intermediary between production and distribution means producers only have limited direct relations with demand. This becomes critical when the agent concerned is less well qualified.

Direct contact between company and customer only occurs in contractor situations, when a company can either fulfil the role of prime contractor, co-ordinating a network of suppliers and representing the interface between the latter and the customer contracting party, or participate in production of part of the contract requirement without getting directly involved in bidding and negotiating activities.

A second characteristic feature of the Italian scene is the predominant form of retail. Italy has a highly fragmented distribution structure based heavily on traditional small independent retailers specialised in the sale of furniture. The average retail area is 350 square metres; 70 per cent of the stores have at most five employees; and about 80 per cent of the retailers are family businesses. The Italian average is one store per 2,300 inhabitants although, in areas with a high vocation for production, such as Lombardy, Veneto and the Marches, there's one retail outlet per 1,700 inhabitants. There are approximately 3,500 top-of-the-range specialists. The high number of retail outlets in Italy is confirmed by retail data for furniture and furnishing accessories, including carpets and household textiles (estimate by Bocconi University School of Management).

Recently, however, Italy has also witnessed an increase in modern forms of distribution and levels of concentration, above all thanks to the growth of certain specialised chains such as Ikea, Mercatone Uno, Divani & Divani, Chateau d'Ax and Ricci Casa.

THE KARTELL CASE

Kartell is the most important plastic furniture manufacturer in Italy. After establishing a leading position in the domestic furniture industry, the company gradually expanded its geographic scope. By 2004, Kartell had sales exceeding 60 million euros, 80 per cent outside Italy, and a return on investment (ROI) of 5.29 per cent (Table 3.1).

CEO Claudio Luti, who acquired the company in 1988, believed that the company reached a critical stage in 2003. Affected by Europe's recession, the company's sales had levelled in the previous three years. More fundamentally, Kartell faced a number of critical issues. Its domestic business had matured, while penetration into America challenged its management practices. In the meantime, other opportunities such as diversification appeared on the horizon. In order to continue its pattern of profitable growth, Mr Luti and top management had to plan a future growth path carefully.

The historical facts

Kartell was a company specialising in plastic furniture. The company was founded in 1949 by Giulio Castelli, a chemical engineer, to create a ski rack made of plastic. The friendship between Castelli and the director of the technical office at Pirelli, Piero Barassi, was a decisive factor because it allowed them to make maximum use of the technology used for the production of tyres and use of a well-known brand.

In 1951, Mr Castelli decided to experiment with the injection moulding of polythene in the home furnishing business (see Table 3.2 for the start-up and closing years of the Kartell divisions). Now lighting is included in the habitat catalogue, together with accessories and furniture.

The household goods division was born with an initial group of products (buckets, colanders and graters), the result of ergonomic research and the analysis of products acquired by Mr Castelli in the UK. At one time, the suppliers (Solvay and Bayer) financed the purchase of the moulds because they saw enormous potential in the household goods business. This company division was closed in 1979 because of a distribution problem: the channel was characterised by actors, like the wholesaler, unable to manage products with a design content.

Initially, Mr Castelli relied on a cooperation with Gino Colombini, a famous designer belonging to the rationalist design school, as director of the technical office. The importance of design had been clear ever since the company's foundation, as Mr Castelli recalled in 2003: 'I had to manage synthetic material without a structured aspect. For the chemical dusts to become objects the contribution of design was necessary.'

Table 3.1 *Kartell: economic profile*

	2000	2001	2002	2003	2004
Sales (euros)	46,948,909	50,924,183	52,742,296	55,087,186	60,884,784
Added value (euros)	12,528,795	10,589,736	10,265,168	13,224,220	16,726,764
Net income (euros)	2,713,385	1,422,127	967,586	2,667,646	1,935,993
Liquidity	0.92	1.02	1.18	1.59	0.37
Return on sales (ROS) (%)	10.5	3.96	3.25	7.84	8.03
Return on investment (ROI) (%)	9.34	3.9	3.48	8.52	5.29
Return on equity (ROE) (%)	8.87	4.8	3.27	8.45	6.2
Employees	82	118	122	no data available	79

Source: Aida

Table 3.2 *Kartell divisions*

Kartell divisions	Start-up year	Closing year
Car accessories	1950	1967
Household goods	1951	1979
Lighting	1958	1981
Labware	1958	Until now
Habitat	1963	Until now

Source: Kartell

In 1954, Kartell promoted a European network for the exchange of information about plastic materials. At this time, Kartell already provided a support activity to the company's image with various initiatives aimed at promoting the design culture. Among other things (catalogues and promotional and advertising material), the 'Qualità' house organ (1956) documented the problematics related to the use of synthetic material in production: 'It was a means to communicate that we were doing something different and that behind our products there were high research investments and a strong technological contribution', as Castelli recalls.

In 1958, Kartell created the labware division (objects for laboratory use like test tube boxes) and the lighting division for the production of the first injection-moulded lamp and the first lamp made of Raflon™.

The labware division is still considered to be the Kartell *palestra* ('gym') because it permits the acquisition of superior technological know-how and application of the plastic material in the field of scientific research. In 2004, the labware division represented more than 30 per cent of the overall production value.

The lighting fixtures were created with the English 'Rotaflex™' technology and were a result of cooperation with various designers. This division contributed to the company's growth (also to the high value per unit) and allowed it to have a presence in furniture stores, more able to make the most of the design content of the products. The division was closed in 1978 because it was no longer coherent with the strategic goals pursued by the company. The developing international strategy of the company was hampered by the existence of several laws on electrical mechanisms at a national level. The economic and human resources taken up by the household goods and lighting divisions were diverted towards new activities and products.

Following important international recognition (the Italian 'Compasso d'Oro' and the Design Award Interplast in London) in 1963, Kartell started up the habitat division for furniture production and participated in the Milan Furniture Exhibition. This period was characterised by fun, experimentation, communication initiatives and friendly relationships with the leading figures in the cultural and design world. In that period, Kartell designed important products such as the first chair produced by the injection moulding of polythene (1964), a best-seller still in production. The first, designed by Marco Zanuso and Richard Sapper, won the 'Compasso d'Oro', and it is exhibited in several museums, like the Museum of Modern Art (MOMA) in New York. The chair combined a strong communication ('a chair for children'), a technological challenge, cooperation with important designers and the relevance of investments (for the moulds, in particular). Unfortunately, this success in terms of image did not translate into good commercial results. In the meantime, the cooperation with architects and designers intensified.

In the 1960s and 1970s, furniture contributed more than the other divisions to turnover growth and to creating the image of the company, because it allowed its innovative orientation to become evident. The products that represented a kind of 'Kartell manifesto' were: the coloured fitted furniture, the flower boxes and the stools designed by Anna Castelli Ferrieri, Giulio's wife and Kartell's internal designer from 1968; the first chair created using a single mould; and the furniture system (armchairs, chairs and coffee tables) made of polyurethane, designed by Gae Aulenti, a famous Italian designer and architect. As Mr Castelli recalled in 2003:

> The Sixties and Seventies were years offering different kinds of challenges to the company. The idea of fitted furniture represented an important connection between the producer and the consumer. Kartell answered the need for more flexible and informal furniture pieces, coherent with the changes in the way of life of young people, consumers that would be protagonists of their own space. It was a system that could be used in different contexts. The injection-moulded chair, on the other hand, proved our ability to overcome technological constraints in order to follow the creativity of our designers. The same was true of the Gae Aulenti project: from the very beginning, I believed that I had to reject the idea because no plastic material could offer the necessary rigidity. The technical office suggested using polyurethane with the additional benefit of exploiting the internal line of production.

From 1972, the Kartell image was coordinated by CentroKappa, an internal team of design and communication experts who focused on the qualification of the international promotion of Kartell, by means of exhibitions, meetings and publications. In the same year, Kartell promoted 'Italy: The New Domestic Landscape' at MOMA in New York, where it presented three habitats designed by Gae Aulenti, Ettore Sottsass and Marco Zanuso. In 1978, Kartell began its editorial operation with *Kartell News* and *Modo*, the latter in association with other design-based companies such as Alessi.

The efforts of this period were rewarded in 1979 with two 'Gold Compasses', the former for the business policy based on design coherence and continuous research and the latter to the CentroKappa as a centre of research, design, promotion and image development.

The beginning of the 1980s confirmed the company's growth; turnover grew from 4 million euros (1978) to 9 million euros (1984), the geographical scope became larger (Japan for the habitat division; the USA and Japan for labware), the image was known to end customers and not only to industry operators, and new product lines were created. Anna Castelli Ferrieri was named as the art director, and had to mediate between the creativity of the designers – while continuing to design for the company – and the needs of the technical office, which decided on project feasibility.

Later in the 1980s, Kartell encountered cultural and ecological problems that represented the most difficult period of its life. Plastic was considered a poor, polluting material that could not be exhibited in a 'middle-class' house, while the cultural trend favoured unique, artisan furniture pieces. According to Mr Luti in 2003:

> Opinion leaders started to diffuse an image of Kartell as a company characterised by an outdated style. Kartell made the mistake of losing sight of the social evolution, continuing to design products with rounded shapes and basic colours (red, yellow, blue and black) rooted in the past.

The company's founder was ready to retire, leaving two consultants to identify some alternatives for his company's survival. As mentioned by the consultants, problems plaguing the company were related to the design philosophy and the product portfolio. Claudio Luti acquired Kartell in 1988, taking up the position of CEO.

Mr Luti began his career in Kartell after a long experience in the fashion industry as managing director of Versace. As he recalled in 2003:

> I needed continuous challenges and at a certain point in my career I had reached an excellent position but all aspects of it were static and routine. I was looking for something new and exciting; an ambitious project where I could concentrate my efforts. I considered different options in the fashion industry, but no alternative was a good enough substitute for Versace and in that company I had an important role. So I had to consider another industry where I could put my sensitivity for the symbolic product and my competencies in retail management to best use. I found that the furniture industry had some analogies with the fashion industry, but at the same time they had an urgent need for retailing innovation.

The opportunity came a few months after the decision to move into another business: Kartell, the design company owned by his father-in-law, was facing a bad period, confirmed by unsatisfactory economic results.

He knew that a great challenge lay ahead for him and that he had to rely on his own skills and efforts. He was having a hard time deciding what the priorities were, which people to remove and which people to involve in the strategy to revitalise the company: 'From the beginning, I believed that the key factor was to engage people in the mission of repositioning Kartell, leveraging on the excitement they could experience.'

While some operative changes had already been made, Mr Luti knew he faced several strategic challenges. The product portfolio and design management had to be rethought, facing new demand trends. Mr Luti wondered how he could develop a new design, internationalisation and retailing model, while also reinforcing the product orientation based on strong technological capabilities which had made Kartell famous.

When he began investigating the company's situation it felt like a nightmare, as he explained in 2003:

> I began talking with the key people in the company and asking for some basic data. The resulting picture was dramatic: an inefficient organisational structure; a self-referential design model based on centralisation; an ineffective commercial and marketing department. My impression was of being in a company which pivoted on technology but without a managerial guide. The marketing director explained to me the approach to the international market and I felt that it was absolutely wrong. Kartell lost the opportunity to diffuse the brand image abroad and to increase the export rate in a high potential market where you can see the return on investments after a long time. While Kartell exported directly in many European countries, in the USA, Mexico, Brazil, Argentina, Australia and Japan a financial holding gave licences for moulds to ten commercial subsidiaries that paid 6 per cent on sales to the holding. Such a policy was justified by high transportation costs and low labour costs. On the flip side, the licensing system prevented the company from increasing the export value and from controlling the quality of supply on single markets. An additional problem was that in the Eighties all the products sold by the commercial subsidiaries, often with private labels [the brand of large department stores such as Bloomingdales], dated back to the Seventies. Fundamentally, it was the negation of every theory on brand image and internationalisation. Further, this strategy caused significant economic problems and, for instance, the losses of the American subsidiary absorbed much of the Kartell profit. The old owners travelled around the world looking for people willing to produce the Kartell products, without evaluating their profile and real intentions.

Was it too late? How could wasted time be recovered? Mr Luti tried to figure out what the priorities were and how strategic challenges could be met by organisational changes.

The turnaround implemented by the new CEO

The situation Mr Luti inherited was challenging from every viewpoint. Using the intuition and inputs of talented employees, Mr Luti primarily focused on the idea that involved closing the financial holding and writing off the asset value and the non-collectable receivables. Then he revised the production planning by a modification in the minimum purchasing quantities and a reduction of the stocks. According to Mr Luti in 2003:

> I wanted to see us double the size of our business in a few years, restoring the image of Kartell. Within a week I terminated all the contracts with the subsidiaries and destroyed the moulds to start an export strategy. On the production side, Kartell produced minimum lots of 2,000 pieces of certain articles but the quantity sold was around 500. I tried to eliminate all the sources of loss in order to free up energy for new product development and the creation of a distribution channel. Unfortunately, at a time when I needed organisational support, my presence provoked a negative reaction in employees. I was supported by the prototyper, the vice-director of the technical office who taught me about materials and technologies and the vice-director of the administrative department. I promoted the last two people to the position of directors. I totally rebuilt the marketing department, removing the previous staff.

During the first year, he tried to reduce the fixed costs, above all related to personnel, and to centralise all the organisation's functions. Over time, a gradual delegation process was created, except for the design process.

After implementing these basic actions he felt were necessary to achieving his goals, he started making changes in the product portfolio, eliminating old furniture pieces from the catalogue and creating new products.

The product portfolio

The immediate intuition of Mr Luti was to valorise plastic material, by using pastel and fluorescent colours and new characteristics (glazing or opaque effect, transparency, and resistance to atmospheric agents). A further innovation was to combine plastics with various materials (aluminium, steel and wood).

The experience and aesthetic taste acquired in the fashion context prompted

Luti to contact external designers (Philippe Starck, Vico Magistretti, Ron Arad and Antonio Citterio) who would be able to interpret the Kartell identity. While Kartell complied with the designers' creativity, the projects had to be coherent with the company's image and technological skills.

The first new product was the Dr Glob chair by Starck. As Mr Luti explained in 2003:

> Creating the Dr Glob chair was an experiment. The technical office together with our specialised suppliers tried to achieve a soft touch, by mixing propylene and talc, and opacity, thanks to the special surface of the mould. Further, Dr Glob was the first chair made of two materials, plastic and metal. This chair led to the concept of 'product family': the chair was followed by tables, stools and stacking chairs.

Much to Mr Luti's surprise, the retailers of the low-end products didn't accept the new chair because it wasn't coherent with Kartell's traditional range, while high-end retailers liked the products but were suspicious, waiting for a totally new collection to be created. As Mr Luti explained in 2003: 'At that time in Italy we faced a big dilemma: retailers didn't understand the Starck design and didn't realise that the existing products were obsolete. They survived by selling shoe racks and chests of drawers.'

Mr Luti introduced a new catalogue in 1988 with three products by Starck and an office collection designed by Michele De Lucchi, another Italian designer, who had worked for Olivetti. To complete the offer, Mr Luti also decided to retain some products from the 1970s and 1980s, even if they were no longer appealing. As he said in 2003:

> It was a hard transition for our business. To develop new products was really difficult. I started with three pieces in order to keep the risk low. The creation of a mould costs 100 million euros. Kartell fought to sell the old products and to create an image with only three new products. Maybe it was an error to do three chairs belonging to the same family. If I had to make a decision now I would prefer to develop three different product families. In spite of this, we ended 1988 and 1989 with profits.

The second catalogue, dated 1992, reduced the number of old products and showed the public the new design direction. The catalogue had strong communication power, illustrating plastic furniture in a middle-class house. Along with this new image, Kartell set up its stand at the Milan Furniture Exhibition. In the 1992 catalogue, Kartell presented the first collection of trolleys made of plastics, metal and rubber by Antonio Citterio; it was considered the most important product of the period. As Mr Luti explained in 2003:

The idea was to fill a market gap, making the most of the existing technologies, and to introduce an industrial product into a private home. I contacted Citterio because he worked for other furniture companies at the high end of the market and he created excellent objects like sofas and chairs. Before our collection, the best seller was a white trolley produced by a German company. Our goal was to create something better. The problem was that the old sales representatives accustomed to selling objects at 25 euros believed the price of the trolleys (around 200 euros) too high and not appropriate for the plastic furniture market. Kartell sells around 10,000 trolleys per year, half the volume produced in the first years.

In 1996, the third catalogue presented a complete collection, with 80 per cent of the products being new, including the Mobil chest of drawers by Citterio (awarded the 'Compasso d'Oro'), the Bookworm bookcase by Starck, and various chairs and tables by Magistretti. Meanwhile, the company's overall business strategy remained the same: to provide the world market with excellent pieces of furniture thanks to the creativity of bright designers and the technological skills of Kartell. Thanks to the design contribution, plastics had to become a rich material that could be used in all homes.

In the following years the most relevant products in terms of process, material and aesthetic innovation were the Marie chair and the Bubble sofa, both designed by Philippe Starck.

The Marie chair was the first one made of transparent polycarbonate, a result of the technical and engineering skills of Kartell and the creative genius of Philippe Starck. It is curious that research commissioned with Bayer didn't assure the project success because of the material's low resistance and the production process based on a unique mould. Since 1999, 100,000 Marie chairs have been sold, many of them for use in high-profile locations (Fiat Lingotto, Turin; Cartier, Paris; Vitra Museum, Berlin; Saint Martin's Lane, London) and parties (The Glittering World of Vogue Italy, Monte Carlo). The Bubble is the first sofa produced by the rotation-moulding process that can be used inside and outside the home. In 2001, the jury of the Italian Designers Association awarded Kartell nine 'Compasso d'Oro' for this industrial sofa. Finally, the Boheme stool is an excellent example of technology transfer. Starck proposed a sketch of an amphora-shaped stool without knowing what technology to use. The technical office was in turmoil: someone in the technical office suggested moulding it in two parts and then combining them, while others proposed using the rotation mould. The chief of the technical office, Guido Borona, believed that they could use the process from the transparent lighting fixture. So Kartell applied the techniques of glass blowing to plastic. The effect was surprising.

Launching new products

Every year, Kartell launches around eight new products. New products typically represent 3–4 per cent of the total turnover.

Kartell considers design as an informal mix of intention by different actors: the CEO, the technical office and the external designers.

Traditionally, design for a product starts with an analysis of the current product portfolio. This analysis classifies the pieces of furniture according to the following criteria: price level, function (chair, table, sofa, etc.), sales value and contribution to image creation. The evaluation could reveal some gaps in the offer or inadequate commercial or image results.

Further analyses concern the strategies pursued by the main competitors, consumer taste and the evolution of technology. The stimuli for innovation are presentations at fairs, exploiting technological competencies, dissatisfaction with current results, and planned penetration into new markets.

This preliminary phase seeks ideas from many people inside (CEO, marketing, finance, etc.) and outside the company (key retailers, opinion leaders, etc.) and results in the definition of a 'design concept'. This is knowledge the company will achieve at the end of the process.

This data collection also serves to create information sharing among the personnel involved with product development and to write the design brief for external designers. It also includes the following:

- the goals of the project (to fill gaps in the product portfolio, to increase turnover, to achieve a new market segment, to react to competitors' actions, etc.)
- the characteristics of the competitive environment
- the company profile
- the available technology
- the supply needs
- the final price

Once the brief is defined, the CEO contacts one or two designers able to develop the project properly.

Working in compliance with the requirements included in the brief, the designers present sketches to the CEO and the technical office, who then select the proposal most able to meet the brief and some specific criteria (e.g. reproducibility on an industrial scale, investments for the moulds, difficulties in engineering, and desired aesthetic effects).

Not surprisingly, a Kartell product could originate from the spontaneous idea of a designer. This was the case for the Bookworm bookcase. Ron Arad had presented a sort of sculpture made of steel that was shaped on the wall, which represented an innovative bookcase. Arad and Luti decided to produce it industrially. The product research lasted one year because Kartell faced the problem of finding a plastic mixture that could resemble steel in terms of resistance and flexibility. A further difficulty was linked to the search for a technology that could allow efficient industrial production and a high price/quality ratio.

As Mr Luti noted in 2003:

> Thanks to the technology of extrusion, it was possible to create a sinuous bookcase that assumed the desired shape without compromising resistance and functionality. A peculiarity of Kartell is to put design first. The need to develop new shapes has always stimulated the invention or adoption of new technologies; technology has never been perceived as a constraint.

At Kartell, a new product could originate from the discovery of new materials or technologies. Mr Picazio, the prototyper at the technical office, underscores this side of the design process by presenting the Bubble sofa example:

> We realised that we could use the rotation moulding, not often used in the furniture industry due to the shortage of proper materials and technologies to create the moulds. This technology consists in introducing a powder of plastic in a mould; the mould rotates in two–three directions to distribute the material uniformly. Afterwards, the mould is put in an oven and the material, by warming, sticks to its sides. Finally, the mould is opened and the product is extracted. Because we could produce large-sized moulds, Starck proposed doing a sofa that has been awarded with nine Gold Compasses.

So a unique procedure doesn't exist: sometimes the company gives input to its external designers; sometimes the designer himself/herself suggests an idea that could be realised by plastics technology. The company has never carried out consumer research, considering the designers are the best antennae to capture the alternatives that could satisfy future needs.

Next the firm works toward the 'refinement' of the design idea by means of a dialectic between the designer and the technical office. Mr Luti follows the entire process and takes the final decision, because each product carries a significant mould investment. The first phases of the process rely on continuous teamwork between the CEO, the designer and the technical office. Once the idea has been approved – up to now the process has taken over one year – Kartell creates a three-dimensional model made of wood or polystyrene; this phase can generally be completed in seven to ten days.

In the words of Mr Luti in 2003:

It is important that the prototype is as close to reality as possible. For instance, for the Louis Ghost chair, presented at the 2002 Furniture Fair, we did a wooden model that didn't capture the final result. So we decided to do a handmade model made of plexiglas to better evaluate the visual effect. I believed that one of Kartell's strengths is technological know-how, flexibility and the innovative capacity of the technical office in prototyping.

Most of the product details originated from engineering and prototyping from internal competencies. This activity is essential for large objects where moulding machines don't yet exist.

Once the prototype model is produced, the challenge is to find the appropriate mix of plastic material. Suppliers help the technical office identify the adequate raw materials and develop the moulds for industrial production.

The production structure

Mr Luti knew he couldn't simply develop an efficient, innovative company without intervening in the production and logistic model: he had to start to outsource all production activities. However, since 1951, the company had focused on design, prototyping, engineering and a few production activities (polyurethane injection and the varnishing process) and outsourced mould production and the moulding process. This solution was also considered by the previous owners as being consistent with the need for flexibility; it contributed to the philosophy of a company founded on design.

Polyurethane injection and varnishing processes were also externalised so that the headquarters in Noviglio, Milan, became offices and a warehouse. As Mr Luti explained in 2003:

Polyurethane injection was used for the old products only, so there was no reason to keep it inside. Regarding the varnishing, I believed that internalisation would impede continuous upgrading and the search for more sophisticated techniques. For instance, in the case of the chest of drawers by Citterio I found a supplier who could give the plastic a satin finish without covering the material. Obviously, the purchasing department started identifying and selecting new suppliers, as well as components which were not necessary before. Over the years, the suppliers supported Kartell quality and innovation. Some of them worked closely with our technical office. Let's consider the example of Bookworm. For two years, Kartell worked together with the best company in the drawing process to obtain an irregular surface that looked like it was handmade.

67

In 2002, Kartell had around 100 suppliers.

Similarly, Kartell revised its approach to logistics. Before 1988, raw materials and simple components passed from the company's warehouse to other suppliers, which returned the semi-assembled products to Kartell. Such a mechanism increased costs, which had an effect on the final price. Luti decided to use the company's warehouse only for the assembly of the old products (1970s and 1980s) and for small deliveries of new products. It was the supplier's responsibility to package and deliver the products. Further, he intervened on design in order to reduce product size and packaging costs. (The estimated saving is around 10 per cent.) The most recent project involved introducing the bar code to coordinate the external warehouses.

The retailing strategy

At the beginning of the 1990s Italy was the key market for Kartell. Luti believed that to be a global player and to face the furniture demand crisis in Italy the company must have a market position in the United States, Japan and Europe, where other Italian design-based companies had been investing for many years. The 1992 catalogue offered the opportunity to launch the company in foreign markets. The export policy by direct agents seemed the most promising way to add incremental sales to the brand. Only Belgium, Holland and Japan had intermediate distributors. Until 1996, the company compensated for the low growth rate on the Italian market with good results in the other countries. As Mr Luti explained in 2003:

> In Italy, the new products didn't replace the old ones. In foreign countries, there weren't any old products so Kartell started from zero. The international retailers were happy because sales grew rapidly and they saw good opportunities for business in Kartell.

In 1996, with the production of the new catalogue, Kartell revised the Italian distribution channel following significant improvements to the product line. Initially, Kartell maintained its lead in the domestic market by reducing the number of stores and obtaining more space in shop windows. As Mr Luti confirmed in 2003:

> Kartell didn't have the bargaining power to impose the contractual conditions on our retailers but we tried to gradually recover the relationship with the distribution channel and the public by effective communication, and by appearing in the stores and at the most important exhibitions, in Italy and abroad.

Luti believed he had a complete collection; consequently, in 1997, he decided to open the first showroom in Milan. The Kartell international distribution project was born in 1999. In the same year, Kartell created a museum that presented the company history through products and documents.

While seeking to create modern structures to control distribution, Kartell also attempted to strengthen the company's image in the traditional independent and multi-brand stores by suggesting how to exhibit the products, through product families, a neutral context, a lot of light and many products in the windows to stimulate impulse buying.

After the success of the Milan showroom, Kartell opened other flagship stores of different sizes (100–400 square metres) in various cities. These shops had a different ownership structure: some of them were franchised, some were owned by Kartell and some were managed by autonomous entrepreneurs. At the same time, Kartell defined a strategy for the other stores in the world, trying to have as much space as possible and to define the product range in terms of type and quantity. Today, the distribution networks include 4,000 points of sale and 70 flagship stores in 85 countries.

Mr Luti argues that the actual distribution networks, with exclusive stores and agreements with the independent ones, function as an effective means to develop and maintain a brand identity throughout the world. As he explained in 2003:

> I did at Kartell what I had tried at Versace in the Eighties: mono-brand shops all over the world in order to create a concept of 'ad hoc' selling that can be recognised on the market and linked to Kartell's image.

CONCLUSIONS

This chapter has focused on the features of a specific industry: furniture in Italy. Italy is well known throughout the world for the aesthetic appeal and excellent quality of its furniture production. Amongst the characteristics of the furniture system, let us mention the high number and small size of manufacturing companies and retailers, the outsourcing of creativity to external designers, and the intermediation by multi-brand representatives.

The manufacturing companies are facing many challenges (both in the domestic market and abroad), resulting in declining competitive and economic performance, and Italy is no longer the leading exporter.

Some of the companies are reacting by developing a new managerial approach to distribution and internationalisation. Kartell represents a case of successful turnaround, as confirmed by its international positioning and the economic data. Starting from the core competencies in technology, the new owner, Mr Luti, was able to revise the business model, reaching a better control of the vertical channel, a focus on a few 'soft' activities and the creation of a brand image in target geographical areas.

REVIEW QUESTIONS

1   What are the key problems currently facing the Italian furniture industry?
2   Does the Italian furniture industry possess unique design qualities and strategies? If so, what are they?
3   What are the main differences between design-based and design-oriented companies?
4   What are the critical design management changes applied in Kartell since 1949?
5   Which technical processes contributed the most to the unique design qualities of Kartell's products?

PROJECT QUESTIONS

1   Consider the process by which Kartell currently develops new products and devise an appropriate briefing format for chairs.
2   Debate the relationship between design and retailing at Kartell and map the relationship.
3   Plan an adventurous design strategy for a new domestic product in furniture that would potentially increase Kartell's return on equity over the next three years. List the key tasks against the key objectives.
4   Devise a short questionnaire to analyse the key issues of new product development at Kartell.
5   Produce a 12-month plan for Kartell to enter the Japanese furniture market with existing products, listing the main tasks.

REFERENCE

Federlegno-Arredo (2004) *La tutela della progettualitià e del design nella filiera Legni-Arredo*. Italian Federation of Wood, Cork, Furniture and Furnishing Manufacturers. (Milano: Federlegno-Arredo)

FURTHER READING

Leslie, D. and Reimer, S. (2003) Fashioning furniture: restructuring the furniture commodity chain. *Area,* 35(4), December: 427–437

Verganti, R. (2003) Design as brokering of languages: innovation strategies in Italian firms. *Design Management Journal,* Summer

Kristensen, T. and Lojacono, G. (2002) Commissioning design: evidence from the furniture industry. *Technology Analysis and Strategic Management,* 14(1), 1 March: 107–121

Chapter 4

The long-term impacts of investment in design

The non-economic effects of subsidised design programmes in the UK

Mark Smith

INTRODUCTION

This is an account of a project designed to identify the long-term, non-economic impacts on business strategy of subsidised design-focused projects. Universities have an important role to play in knowledge and technology transfer, critical for the new knowledge-driven economy. In support of this objective, a range of UK government-funded schemes exist to promote innovation and competitiveness in business, for example through knowledge transfer partnerships (KTPs). Design-specific projects contribute towards both direct economic benefits and indirect, qualitative changes in business strategy and culture. The research presented draws on a series of case studies of companies that have participated in KTPs. The aim is to examine the impacts of design intervention, the resultant changes in the use and employment of designers, resources dedicated to design, attitudes towards design and the management of designers.

CONTEXT AND BACKGROUND

KTPs are a UK government strategy for encouraging greater interaction between universities (termed knowledge providers) and industry to provide innovative solutions to strategic business problems. The context of knowledge transfer is framed by political and economic objectives. In political terms, this engages with the restructuring of Europe away from manufacturing towards more service-oriented economies in response to increasing industrial globalisation. This has major implications for innovation and competitiveness, particularly for the small business community.

Innovation is also bound up with ideas of competitiveness, at international, national and individual business levels. The UK government position on competitiveness is guided by a review conducted by the Department of Trade and Industry (DTI 2003), which supports the argument that the UK needs to shift to a knowledge-based economy. It also suggests that stimulating innovation, particularly in small and medium-sized enterprises (SMEs), will be a crucial objective for future economic well-being. This view of innovation assumes that smaller firms have the capacity to deliver the post-industrial transformation through the process of knowledge transfer from the public to the private sector, although evidence suggests small enterprises lag behind other organisations when adopting new, innovative technologies (OECD 2003). A further assumption is that existing small businesses will gain and utilise knowledge, or new enterprises will be created using new, potentially disruptive technologies (EC 2001).

Innovation is the successful commercial exploitation of new ideas, products and processes and intimately connected to long-term economic growth. It is not limited to the narrow development of new technologies, but embraces organisational change and the exchange of ideas between different sectors and markets (DTI 2003). The key factor is the development, retention and diffusion of new ideas which will deliver the competitiveness of the new economic landscape through a process of technology transfer from the public into the private sector. For the purposes of this chapter, technology transfer and knowledge transfer are effectively synonymous.

Universities and other educational institutions have a central role to play in the policy objective of a knowledge-based economy through developing ideas and innovations through direct or indirect commercial exploitation, thus contributing to the competitiveness of the economy. Universities are encouraged to disseminate knowledge into the EU industrial fabric, including SMEs in traditional sectors, through the promotion of effective university–industry relationships, and exploit the results of their knowledge in relationships with industry. Knowledge is now a tradable commodity.

The process of knowledge transfer from the public to the private sector depends on universities to underpin the knowledge society, thus enabling 'the most competitive and dynamic knowledge-based economy in the world, capable of sustainable economic growth with more and better jobs and greater social cohesion' (CEC 2003).

This process is encouraged through the establishment of closer cooperation between universities and business to ensure better dissemination and exploitation of knowledge in the economy and society at large.

Research suggests there is little data that assesses the degree by which universities across the EU commercialise their research, so it is difficult to state how much is exploited by the private sector. However, some estimates suggest that less than 5 per cent of innovative companies regard data from government, private research institutes, or universities as important. It is therefore essential to shift the perception that universities are unable or unwilling to engage with commercial exploitation of new ideas. There are various routes for universities to diffuse expertise generated and develop commercial exploitation, such as through spin-out companies or incubator projects (EC 2001). In the UK, the theme of university–industry collaboration and innovation was promoted by the Lambert Review (HM Treasury 2003). The review noted:

> There has been a marked culture change in the UK's universities over the past decade. Most of them are actively seeking to play a broader role in the regional and national economy. The quality of their research in science and technology continues to compare well against most inter-national benchmarks . . . Business is changing too. Growing numbers of science-based companies are developing across the country, often clustered around a university base. New networks are being created to bring business people and academics together, often for the first time. The UK has real strengths in the creative industries, which are also learning to cooperate with university departments of all kinds.
>
> (HM Treasury 2003)

It is of particular significance that 'creative industries' (of which design is a major activity) appear increasingly to be regarded as critical to the national future economic well-being of the UK. In the mix of processes for delivering knowledge transfer, which include research networks, sponsored students, contract research, collaborative research and consultancy, the review highlighted the value of KTPs. KTPs are a useful mechanism for generating fruitful collaborations between innovative businesses and universities. The report also noted that the best form of knowledge transfer arises when a talented researcher moves out of the university and into business, or vice versa. Often, the most exciting collaborations emerge when like-minded people jointly address and resolve a problem. The process of knowledge transfer is tightly bound up with innovation, about which the review comments:

> Innovation processes are complex and non-linear. It is not simply a question of researchers coming up with clever ideas which are passed down a production line to commercial engineers and marketing experts who turn them into winning products. Great ideas emerge out of all kinds of feedback loops, development activities and sheer chance. This is another reason why it is so critical to build dynamic networks between academic researchers and their business counterparts.
>
> (HM Treasury 2003)

The observation that innovation is a non-linear process, affected by technology transfer mechanisms and the absorptive capacity among participating firms, is important in the context of this study. It also suggests that the benefits derived are not exclusively located in the private sector, and that knowledge transfer is therefore bidirectional. Innovation theory is generally discussed in connection with manufacturing industries, or those concerning new high-technology-based companies (e.g. Tidd *et al.* 2001). To date, little attention has been paid to the contribution made by the creative industries, which include design and designers, to the UK economy. The sector employs almost 2 million people, contributes £11.4 billion to the UK balance of trade, and produces almost 8 per cent of the gross domestic product. The sector is therefore larger than the construction industry, insurance and pensions, and twice the size of the pharmaceutical sector (HM Treasury 2005). The great majority of businesses in the design sector are micro or small-scale (Creative Enterprise 2006).

SUPPORT FOR KNOWLEDGE TRANSFER: KTPs IN THEORY AND PRACTICE

The UK industrial policy from the early 1980s onwards has promoted increased industry and university links, with selective support for generic technologies and an emphasis on new technology-based firms. Concern over growing regional economic disparities resulted in the establishment of regional technology support infrastructures, including science parks and innovation centres (Rothwell and Dodgson 1993). At the individual business level, the KTP programme was originally introduced in the UK in 1975 as a means of transferring engineering capabilities and expertise generated in universities to mainly small firms (SQW 2002). The programme aims to strengthen the competitiveness, wealth creation and economic performance of the UK by the enhancement of knowledge and skills and the stimulation of innovation through collaborative projects between business and educational institutions resulting in business development and growth. Increased competitiveness is realised through developing innovative products; improving quality, productivity and customer responsiveness; and increasing profitability and opportunities in new markets (Edge and Hands 2004).

These programmes increase the extent of interactions by businesses and academia in line with the recommendations of the Lambert Review. Projects might involve the development of new design or manufacturing methods, innovative marketing or the adoption of new technologies within the company's existing structure. Generally, the process is facilitated through an associate who is employed by the educational establishment and located within a commercial partner. KTPs are unique, as the benefits derived are not restricted to the commercial partner. Both the associate employed and the educational institution also derive benefits, for example through industrial experience and research (DTI 2004a). The objective of KTPs is to facilitate the transfer of knowledge and the spread of technical and business skills, through innovation projects undertaken by high-calibre, recently qualified people under the joint supervision of personnel from both business and educational institutions. This style of company-based training enables graduates to enhance their business and specialist skills, while the education partner gains relevant education and research. KTP projects are typically between one to three years in duration. The company and university are jointly responsible for the initial development of the project in partnership, project management methodology and monitoring. The company receives a government subsidy depending on its size for the duration of the project to cover specific costs such as training, travel and computing equipment. It provides the opportunity for a postgraduate student to gain pragmatic experience of the commercial marketplace whilst developing research and other skills that might be difficult to achieve within a purely academic environment (DTI 2004b).

The model for this collaborative relationship has remained essentially unchanged since its inception, and is recognised as one of the most successful forms of intervention for promoting innovation (SQW 2002). In summary, KTPs are a particularly effective form of intervention to resolve the following problems:

- firms, especially SMEs, having difficulty exploiting technological developments that are outside their established capabilities
- insufficient use being made by industry of the wealth of expertise and technology available from the UK knowledge base
- too few graduates with industrially relevant training and experience, combined with businesses' (particularly SMEs') reluctance to employ industrially inexperienced graduates
- the perceived disconnection between the knowledge base and business: both having difficulty accessing and communicating with the other.

(Adapted from SQW 2002)

The overall strategy seeks to address these problems through a portfolio of projects that are in tune with the social, technological and economic priorities of the UK. They aim to serve a broad cross-section of firms, regardless of size, and support projects that promote the greatest added value.

These points highlight key problems associated with technology or knowledge transfer. There is the assumption: firstly that SMEs are inherently capable of absorbing new ideas; secondly, that the expertise already exists and is capable of being transferred from universities, as suggested by the Lambert Review; and, thirdly, that graduates lack specific skills and commercial awareness.

A number of government departments and research councils sponsor KTPs. In practice most are technology- or management-oriented; the great majority (84 per cent) are sponsored by the DTI and the Engineering and Physical Sciences Research Council (EPSRC) (SQW 2002). The programme complements current design-oriented collaborative schemes. These include the joint Design Council and DTI campaign to promote innovation in emerging technologies, for example biotechnology, manufacturing and services, often with a focus on engineering and management. Other related support schemes involving higher education include:

- knowledge transfer networks, for example the Faraday Partnerships
- collaborative research and development (R&D)
- grants for R&D and investigations of innovative ideas.

(DTI 2003)

In contrast with most technology-oriented programmes, the cases featured in this study embarked on heavily design-oriented projects. To date, KTP research has tended to focus on case studies (e.g. Andrews *et al.* 2001; Edge and Hands 2004) often based on manufacturing innovation (e.g. Lipscomb and McEwan 2001) or draw on survey-based, econometric impact studies (e.g. SQW 2002, 2005). Although many schemes have focused on supporting manufacturing-based enterprises through technical assistance, little attention has been given to the capacity to develop and transfer *design* knowledge, and the implications for the long-term, strategic consequences of such intervention to the businesses involved. This study is novel, as it addresses an array of changes that occur in businesses, particularly design activities, and is not restricted to an assessment of technology transfer or narrow economic impacts.

METHODOLOGY

The aims of this study are to capture key aspects of design knowledge transfer from an academic context into industry, and the long-term impacts of this intervention on design practices and strategy in business. The analysis of financial benefits is not central to this study. Instead, the focus is on the more complex non-economic aspects, as these are traditionally more difficult to describe, determine and analyse. The research seeks to identify the reasons why companies embarked on the programme, and to determine the role of design and designers before and after the project, the changes introduced into firms, and the consequent effects on both design capacity and design management. It describes how design practice and attitudes towards design within businesses have changed following the conclusion of the programme. The indirect, non-economic impacts on a business may be highly significant, such as the way design management affects marketing, investment in new technology and so on.

There are two contrasting methodological approaches to conducting research. Quantitative studies use numbers for deductive reasoning and theory testing. The characteristics of the deductive, scientific form of inquiry are that quantitative data are a priority for testing theoretical models, usually based on limited numbers of variables in controlled, artificial conditions. Theory and research stimulate each other through a cyclical process of induction and deduction.

Qualitative research utilises non-numerical data for inductive interpretation. In this study, there is no specific theory or hypothesis testing. A strictly quantitative survey has been rejected in favour of a combination of both numerical and textual information. This ensures a richness of data that embraces a qualitative and inductive approach (Hammersley 1992). Qualitative information can also be quantified, because data can be enumerated, transformed and coded to recognise and describe differences. Conversely, quantitative data can also be descriptive, and both forms are not mutually exclusive. This study of the effects of KTPs on design and small businesses introduces questions about both quantifiable and qualitative issues. Narrow financial performance can be determined from quantitative information, while attitudes to aspects of commerce can be elucidated from loosely bounded or undelineated questions. This style of investigation is therefore iterative, and allows the inquiry to evolve as the study progresses.

The research method encompasses a range of techniques for collecting information. The most commonly used forms are surveys that can be conducted directly by the researcher. These may generate data that can be manipulated statistically and produce generalisations.

The principal alternative option is a case study approach. Case studies are useful for research that is informed by contextualised information using how, when and why questions to illuminate a set of decisions in a contemporary, real-life context (Yin 1994). Their defining feature is that they are able to encompass quantitative and qualitative data, and can be used singly or com-plementarily. Yin (1994) defined case study as: 'An empirical inquiry that investigates a contemporary phenomenon within its real-life context when the boundaries between phenomenon and context are not clearly evident and in which multiple sources of evidence are used.'

Case studies can celebrate the differences between apparently similar entities and therefore provide interesting insights (Stake 1994). Stake (1995) proceeded to argue that case studies represented three types of inquiry:

■ intrinsic, where the case itself is of interest
■ instrumental, where the aim is to accomplish or understand some particular factors
■ collective, involving coordination between a group of individual studies.

This study is a mixture of intrinsic and instrumental factors. The firms selected for this research shared a common experience of having participated in one or more KTP. An individual case may be a critical example; it can be used to test a significant theory, or it represents an extreme or unique situation. It may also be a revelatory case, useful for identifying critical issues and where the investigator has the opportunity to observe and analyse a phenomenon previously inaccessible to investigation or to reveal unforeseen phenomena.

Multiple case studies offer the advantage of being more robust than single cases, and can ascertain and track changes. Replication of circumstances is possible, enabling cross-case comparisons, and the results may indicate underlying patterns or provide contrasting opinions, as in this study.

The analysis of multiple studies follows a cross-experiment rather than an intra-experiment procedure. Each study should be selected to predict similar results, or provide contrary results, but for predictable reasons. This study draws on interviews conducted with one representative from each participating firm.

Glaser and Strauss (1967) argued that case studies demand analysis and reflection, with subsequent investigations modified by research findings. This is a highly iterative process, capable of producing extremely dense information, and enables the identification of themes. In ideal conditions, multiple case studies would be carried out to avoid the problems associated with limited access to company personnel, or information that is in a process of change.

The key criticism of qualitative data is the capacity to generalise from the findings (Brannen 1992; Schofield 1993). The qualitative method cannot be subjected to the same tests for reliability and validity as a quantitative experiment, but internal and external validity is still central. For qualitative data, a more appropriate term than 'generalisability' is 'fittingness', or the degree to which a situation studied matched others. A technique for increasing the validity of qualitative data is through a process of triangulation. This entails using multiple data sources to verify information or test opinions. In practice, this is rarely achieved. For example, under ideal conditions, this study would obtain data from a 'matched pair' research project. Similar firms in similar sectors could be compared and contrasted, and those that participated in the KTP programme compared with firms that had not. It could be further strengthened by interviews with other participants in the organisation, not just the businesses affected by the projects.

CASE SELECTION

The projects reported on in this study focus on the role of design in the context of the strategic development of businesses. Birmingham Institute of Art and Design has a long tradition of managing design-orientated KTP projects, in a range of industries, including architecture (e.g. Edge and Hands 2004; Edge *et al.* 2004), product design (Andrews *et al.* 2001) and jewellery. The associates appointed on each project had formal design qualifications at degree level and were registered for a relevant postgraduate course. The academic part of the course was conducted in a work-based learning environment. The projects and contact details were identified with the assistance of the KTP Office at BIAD (Walker 2005), which also provided the DTI project final reports. Four of the businesses contacted chose to participate in this study.

The information sources for this study are a mix of primary data, from questionnaires, and secondary data, from post-project assessment reports compiled for the DTI, the lead sponsor. The aim was to identify post-intervention impacts, so the firms were selected on the basis that the project had been completed at least one year before the interview. There was one exception to this, a jewellery manufacturer, where the project was current at the time of the interview. This served as a pilot study to test the validity of the research approach and to generate information which was useful in its own right. The study focuses on the effects on business and design practice of the programme. It does not address the impacts on BIAD, for example the expertise or research generated. With one exception the study does not consider the value of the experience gained by the associate, such as the commercial exposure, technical competences gained, qualifications and the role of work-based learning, employability or future career development. The information was collected from interviews conducted with the managing director, who in this study was also the founder of the business, responsible for the project implementation and the recruitment and direct management of the associate. The questionnaire was supplemented with field notes as additional, background information.

QUESTIONNAIRE DESIGN

The questionnaire, as Yin (1994) observed, was designed to uncover and celebrate differences between the projects. The questionnaire was partly derived from the methodology developed by Walsh *et al.* (1992) for the well-documented longitudinal study of design intervention and the subsequent study reported by Roy *et al.* (1999) that mapped the long-term benefits of subsidised design projects. The sections addressed general company information, such as size, market sectors and products; the role of the associate and design and innovation practice; the costs and non-financial benefits of the programme; changes in design resources; and the strategic role of design. The nine-part semi-structured questionnaire consisted of a mixture of closed, quantitative and open, qualitative questions, and was therefore a combination of hypothesis testing with grounded theory (Glaser and Strauss 1967). The closed style of questions included multiple-choice-style responses followed by more open questions to expand on specific topics. The closed questions often aimed to determine attitudes and opinions using a Likert Scale (Mogey 2006). It is therefore possible to use descriptive statistical techniques to analyse and present the information. The mode is probably the most suitable for easy interpretation. The small-scale, non-random sample in this survey precludes meaningful statistical analysis.

Examples of open-style questions include those relating to the nature of the client base. The interviewee was asked to name the clients that sold their products. Guidance notes and prompts were used to direct the interviewee. In this example, they included specific distributors, retail outlets or customers and end users. The themes of the questionnaire ranged across general company issues, markets, design and innovation of specific product ranges, the benefits and costs of investing in design, and the role of design at a strategic level.

Additional, unbounded discourse was also recorded in the questionnaire or supplemented the field notes. Thus the numerical information combined with the qualitative data provides a narrative thread; patterns and emphasis or reactions provide rapid visual checks. Research ethics demand that the businesses visited are referred to anonymously to maintain confidentiality. Pseudonyms have been used to protect their identities.

The responses were recorded directly on the questionnaire and compiled with other background information, such as marketing brochures that helped develop a more complete picture of the company. The exception was the initial interview with the associate located at the jewellery manufacturer's, which served as a pilot study to validate the questionnaire. In this instance, the project was still live and is unique in this study for gaining insights into the role of the associate. Permission was sought from the associate to record this interview, which was subsequently transcribed. This approach allowed for additional questions and further clarification.

OBSERVATIONS

This part of the chapter deals in turn with some observations about the general nature of the businesses that participated, the role of the associate, and discussion of the costs and benefits of investing in design, followed by an assessment of the non-financial consequences of the projects and finally the effects on design resources at a strategic business level.

General characteristics of the businesses, products and KTPs

The names and sectors of each company are summarised in Table 4.1.

All of the firms were founded within the last 20 years by the interviewees, the managing directors. All but one, Nicknax, is a UK-owned, independent firm. Nicknax is now part of a larger UK-based group of companies, and the founder now operates as a consultant to the larger company. All are small or medium-sized, with annual turnover ranging from around £1.2 million to some

Table 4.1 *Company markets and KTP project aims*

Business	Products/markets	Project aims
Nicknax	Giftware and memorabilia	Establish a design studio Establish computer technologies for developing in-house silk screen printing Establish a product development programme Establish a marketing philosophy for domestic and export markets
Kidstuff	Baby and children's clothing	Develop an in-house CAD facility Integrate CAD technologies and management information systems Develop industry intelligence and a marketing strategy
Taj	Design and manufacture of equestrian clothing	Develop fashion/textile CAD infrastructure to improve existing lines and develop new markets in outdoor pursuits
Falco	Jewellery	Create NPD systems Coordinate products and marketing Introduce managed new product ranges

£22 million. The smallest firm is Kidstuff, with seven employees, and the largest is Nicknax, with around 100 staff located at the interview site. The KTP projects in all but one case, Falco, were completed between five and eight years ago, so the strategic impacts should have percolated through each organisation. Each KTP lasted two years.

The use of additional field notes can be illustrated with reference to Nicknax. This business was originally set up by the interviewee in 1985. The firm specialises in designing and producing printed giftware and memorabilia, such as mugs, glasses and T-shirts associated with various tourist locations around the UK and abroad. There have been significant changes in the company structure and ownership. In 2004, the founder sold the business to a specialist company manufacturing greeting cards, and the firm operates as an autonomous group within the larger company. Nicknax retains control of the product design, while distribution and general administration are handled by the parent company. Design is considered to be a major contribution to its distinctive range of products.

The main change that has shaped business strategy in each case has been the shift to overseas manufacturing afforded by the opportunity of low-cost production. Low-cost overseas imports were a direct spur for Falco to investigate alternatives to jewellery that threatened its market niche. Access to low-cost manufacturing abroad has had an impact on both resource management and design management. Export markets are also significant. In the case of Taj, up to 70 per cent of its total output is geared to overseas markets. In the fashion-conscious children's clothing market, Kidstuff adapts its UK product ranges for European markets through subtle styling and colour changes.

Two of the interviewees cited the importance of the need to be perceived as a 'one-stop shop', that is, they provide a complete business service package, from design through production to distribution. In this way a small firm can become a hub and thus emulate a much larger corporation. This clearly demands considerable managerial and design management expertise to control supply chains or networks, and will be discussed in more depth.

The role of the KTP associate

The programme requires the prior negotiation of specific project responsibilities for the associate appointed. The appointment of a dedicated designer represented a major strategic development in business, and has implications for understanding design management. Prior to the programme, none of the firms surveyed had employed in-house designers, generally relying on freelance workers.

At Taj, the firm engaged an associate as a risk reduction strategy because the owner was cautious about investing in a full-time designer. The subsidy enabled the enterprise to develop more rapidly at reduced cost, one of the benefits of the programme. The appointment coincided with a move to new premises to accommodate rapid expansion that occurred at the time. The prime motive behind the appointment was to increase existing market share and expand the product ranges. Prior to the project, as in the other firms, design was sub-contracted, and this company had no recognised in-house design capability. The brief evolved as both the firm and the associate learned about the potential new products while gaining an understanding of the demands of the proposed new market, for which the associate also conducted some of the market research. The designs were continuously modified to reflect customer feedback. The arrival of the associate represented a culture shock in the business; the staff had no design history, having concentrated on manufacturing.

The most complex and demanding role of the associate was at Falco. Again, there was no history of formal design procedures at the business prior to the appointment of the associate, although she had previously worked for the firm as a freelance designer. This role changed with the requirements of the scheme. The two-year programme reflected the wider ambitions of the management team, who wanted to enter more profitable markets using platinum instead of gold. They recognised that good design could be pivotal in differentiating their products from those of their competitors. The extensive project brief included: systematic industry trend analysis; a new product development and cyclical review system; increased and efficient use of computer-aided design (CAD) to translate designs into reproducible commodities; and coordinating the range of directly employed staff and subcontracted elements of production. The research informs understanding of design management, and resources for design will be discussed further, and it is worth noting that in this study just one of the associates (Falco) completed the programme, although all made positive contributions.

This serves to illustrate that, even with the financial assistance and support of the university partner, investing in design is inherently risky. A key problem was identified as the selection of the associates. It is notable that in each case the associates had unrealistic expectations of working in a small firm environment. For example, at Kidstuff the interviewee acknowledged partial responsibility for selecting the wrong designer, which contributed to project failure.

In detail, the interviewee suggested that the project foundered for the following reasons:

- There was a lack of adequate market research of the proposed new markets.
- The designer was unsuited to the pressure of designing in a small business environment.
- There were personality clashes with staff and clients.
- The associate was too impatient, and tried to make a contribution before understanding the nature of the business.
- The designs produced were not commercial, being too complex and difficult to manufacture.
- The designs that did emerge did not reach production.

Nicknax eventually recruited three associates to develop design and marketing capabilities, but none completed the projects. The marketing associate left to join a new design company. Of the two designers recruited, the first was offered a partnership in a new design consultancy, and the next associate left to join a rival firm. The design brief for the project demanded an understanding of CAD systems, combined with an appreciation of the objectives of the business. A requirement of the project was to create designs using different decorating techniques on various media, such as textiles and ceramics. This technical problem was resolved independently of the associates through the introduction of a CAD system using proprietary software designed for the textile industry. This enabled Nicknax to make better-informed technical decisions, and so the firm recruited an experienced CAD technician with suitable expertise, who was subsequently trained in design. However, before leaving the associate enabled the firm to react more rapidly to customer needs by developing its existing CAD systems, something its competitors were unable to achieve.

Nicknax were not the only company to experience difficulties with locating the right person for the job; the same problem occurred at Kidstuff. Here, the designer selected was not suited to the pressures of working in a small firm environment, and left to join a major UK sports footwear manufacturer. This experience did not prejudice the manager, who continued to promote design within the firm. Kidstuff expected the designer to move the firm into new, upmarket clothing sectors and reorganise the operation using critical path analysis. In the event, as at Nicknax, the designer left before completing the project, largely owing to a personality clash with the staff. In this case, there was expected to be strong synergy between the quality of designs and the accompanying marketing material. To achieve this, the associate needed to display empathy for children's wear, which in turn demanded a thorough understanding of those markets. This exposed a problem with the aspirations and expectations of the associates of working in a small firm, often as the sole designer. Both Nicknax and Kidstuff understood that the associates were keen to establish themselves as early as possible in the business, but they needed to use the first year to understand the business environment, markets and objectives. The interviewees regarded the first year as an investment in the designer. The associate is expected to learn from the commercial exposure thus gained, implement ideas and contribute directly to the business during the second year. Despite these problems, the manager of Kidstuff has persisted with employing designers, and has increased design resources.

This insight suggests that the financial and non-financial contributions made by the projects require further developments in methodologies designed to capture the 'lag' or delay in measuring the impacts of investment in design and innovation. It is entirely feasible that further design-related changes will occur in the businesses in this study, and the full impacts of the KTP projects have yet to be realised.

The costs and benefits of investing in design

Although the questionnaire was intended to capture financial data concerning the costs and benefits of the innovations arising from the projects, in practice this information was unavailable or too complex to allow the determination of the contribution made by individual projects. The information collected from the questionnaire proved inadequate for the determination of causal relationships between specific project performance and investment.

In at least one case, the associate was expected to increase design capacity through greater use of design technologies such as CAD systems. Conventional metrics developed to quantify costs and benefits assume that financial benefits arising from specific projects can be adequately determined over a finite period. Any non-financial benefits or consequences cannot be conveniently categorised and quantified, a limitation of the assessment methodology used by the DTI (SQW 2002). Innovation is a notoriously unpredictable process, and the consequences may take some time to permeate through a firm. A narrow technological view of innovation may ignore the 'softer' or strategic effects of the projects undertaken. This study offers some possibilities for gaining insights into establishing not just practical outputs but also changes in attitudes towards design.

Some of the projects were primarily concerned with developing technical expertise. For example, Nicknax aimed to increase design capability through advanced design technology (CAD systems and software) to address the laborious task of manual design.

At Falco the project was still in progress, so the direct commercial benefits and the indirect consequences had not had time to become apparent. However, it was noted that the company had realised immediate financial gains of around £25,000 per annum plus significant efficiency savings through the introduction of a planned and documented new product development (NPD) process introduced by the associate. The post-project NPD system introduced is illustrated in Figure 4.1.

Where financial information was obtained, it was through a set of questions intended to determine the range of factors used to establish commercial performance. These ranged from sales, turnover, exports, profits and profit margins through to market share and return on investment. The interviewees generally used multiple financial criteria when assessing the financial performance of

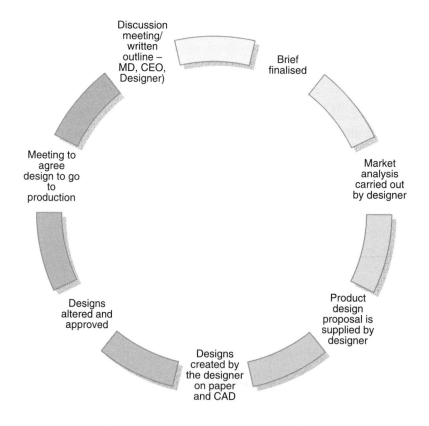

Figure 4.1 The NPD methodology post-project at Falco

products or projects; indeed Taj proposed that most of the factors combined to indicate success. For Nicknax, these criteria also translated into business growth, so aiding the company to develop organically to maximise profits and create good business relationships with its clients.

Non-financial benefits of design investment

The projects tended to generate a range of non-financial benefits for the businesses. For both the clothing manufacturers, Taj and Kidstuff, the design assistance contributed directly to technical textile expertise, functional garment design improvements and styling. Secondary benefits included significant impacts on marketing strategies, such as coordinated branding and packaging, which in turn influenced subsequent product lines. This is similar to the non-linear effects of design on business strategy reported by Smith et al. (1996), who focused on the impacts of environmentally conscious design strategies. However, in the textile industry as in other rapidly changing sectors including jewellery, while design can be a critical factor for product differentiation it is notoriously difficult to protect designs where plagiarism is a common practice.

The most striking effects of the scheme occurred in Falco. The associate showed considerable determination and initiative in entering the design competitions. As a result, the company gained considerable publicity arising from the nationally and internationally recognised jewellery industry design awards. The associate had designed a pendant that combined platinum with diamonds using the newly acquired CAD and rapid prototyping (RP) skills. The pendant was not originally conceived as a commercial project, but won the award for the high quality of the design. The resultant publicity arising from exposure in the industry trade press raised the profile of the company. The award prompted further explorations into designing with platinum and effectively signalled the company's intention to move upmarket. The associate proceeded to design a bangle, also using RP and CAD techniques, and won a further prestigious industry award, attracting further press coverage at trade shows in London and Basle.

Additional non-financial benefits to the companies involved include recognition of the value of branding and styling as intrinsic factors for conveying an image of quality. For Taj, the project provided a spur to the development of a family of related designs and contributed to the image that the business operated as a 'one-stop shop' for clients. This has been echoed by other interviewees. More interesting are attitudes to design, both inside and outside the businesses. Design has been articulated as contributing to product 'uniqueness', and the effects on Falco have already been outlined. In this case, the direct commercial consequences have been significantly enhanced by the design awards and resultant publicity. Other consequences of the KTP project affected the role of design, the designers and the resources allocated to design.

Figure 4.2 *The Falco award-winning bangle*
Permission obtained

Resources and the role of design and innovation at a strategic level: changes arising from the KTP

In each of these cases, resources and investment in design have increased following the KTPs. In Nicknax the language used by the interviewee suggests the business is heavily customer led and market oriented, but the rhetoric demonstrates an increased commitment to design. In absolute terms, the number of designers has decreased, from three to two full-time staff, but the efficiency and productivity gains made by in-house training more than compensate. In contrast, Kidstuff now employs three freelance designers and aims to recruit a full-time designer. At Falco, the designer has been retained by the company, in recognition of the direct commercial contribution and value as a prize-winning designer. At Taj the firm demonstrated its continued support for design by recruiting a full-time designer to replace the associate.

The strategic role of design and attitudes towards design that have occurred because of these projects are striking. The reaction to questions that probed attitudes towards design as a strategic function indicated considerable support for the hypothesis that investment in design delivers significant immediate and long-term benefits to both commercial and strategic goals in every company. For example, at Taj and Nicknax the associates helped the businesses gain an understanding of the design process, leading to more efficient use of design resources. The most striking impacts were at Falco, where the associate took control of the entire design process. This entailed managing the marketing strategy, conducting a major review of design strategy, and introducing NPD and design reviews. These activities increased the range of products and helped to develop a coherent company-wide visual style. The resultant industry awards generated unprecedented international trade exposure and established the business at the forefront of platinum jewellery design.

DISCUSSION

This study is an investigation of some of the design-related, non-financial impacts of design-led KTPs on small firms. The main focus of the research has been on the impacts of design and NPD strategies through increased design technology capacity and consequent organisational changes. The research has investigated the experience of associates in a small business environment and the non-financial impacts of design and innovation on business strategy, which complement the existing range of economic performance indicators.

KTPs represent an important mechanism for engendering knowledge, not just technology, transfer from HE to industry, and thus inform design management in practice. The strategy reinforces the theory that successful enterprises are those that utilise professional and social networks. Successful implementation of projects also depends on the assumption that participating firms are receptive to new ideas and capable of absorbing new techniques. This may be the case, since the scheme is voluntary, suggesting that the participants are favourably predisposed to investing in design and prepared to take risks associated with innovation. A business engaging in a KTP accepts a level of risk, mitigated by the subsidy and the access to academic expertise. The outcome is not guaranteed and can be mapped from, for example, a technological uncertainty perspective.

Networks

These businesses are clearly embedded in social and professional networks. They have demonstrated a capacity to establish and develop professional relationships between academics and government agencies that complement pre-existing informal networks. The KTP projects presuppose the firms have conducted a strategic review and, in these cases, identified the need to increase design capacity. The successful management of complex supply networks implies a reliance on multiple sources of tacit knowledge in the learning process. Manley (2003) claimed that interactive learning is essential for the long-term survival of an enterprise. A KTP is such a venture. A business must also demonstrate

89

adaptability to changing circumstances and technologies. Firms that do so through a broad array of innovation interests and external linkages, such as through KTP projects, are therefore more likely to survive. Manley (2003) also observes some key measures of innovation systems:

- Knowledge-intensive, long-term, multi-stranded linkages with external organisations are best, based on both market and non-market relationships.
- There is a diverse range of organisations of different types and varying levels of economic competence.
- Individual participants perceive benefits (analogous to opportunity costs) beyond what could be achieved in isolation, increasing the likelihood of a stable and productive system.

The idea of networks as being of importance to businesses has traditionally been deployed by engineers for understanding transport and communication systems. More recently, networks have become popular with economists and sociologists seeking to explain human systems, such as organisations in industry and particularly in relation to innovation. They can also be used to describe how strategic alliances evolve (e.g. Koza and Lewin 1999) or influence creativity in organisations (e.g. Stacey 1996). Despite the outcome of most of these cases, where the associates rarely completed the programmes, KTPs fulfil all the conditions for success outlined above. They are certainly knowledge-intensive and in business support terms relatively long-term, typically lasting two years, and the participants all mutually benefit. The opportunity cost is an issue that will be discussed in relation to the calculation of costs and benefits of investing in design.

A further factor in determining the effectiveness of knowledge transfer relates to the ability of enterprises to absorb the knowledge gained from the KTP experience and reflect that expertise in new products, processes or systems.

Innovation capacity

Firms differ widely in their technological strategies and 'absorptive capacity', or ability to encompass new ideas. Walsh et al. (1992) argued that firms tend to compete within well-defined technological corridors and build up specific competences, organise a knowledge base and develop a family of designs based on the technological corridor. It is further argued that successful companies are those which improve their products in response to user needs. These firms are also able to continuously modify and adapt their designs in response to new technologies and competing products. Innovations can be described using a market-based framework (for example, Ansoff and Stewart 1967) or a technological hierarchy (for example, Freeman 1982). The firms participating in these KTPs feature 'incremental' innovations, that is, the ideas and technologies applied are logical extensions of existing product lines, or design variants for new markets to generate competitive advantage. Possibly the most radical departure is in Falco, where the firm made a calculated gamble on shifting to an entirely new (for them) metal as the basis of their jewellery ranges. The successful implementation depended entirely on the skills of an experienced designer capable of developing a range of products using a novel metal and new design procedures. A useful technological capability typology has been developed by Arnold and Thuriaux (1993) (Table 4.2).

The innovative capacity of each company prior to the intervention of the KTP can also be mapped. Of the businesses interviewed for this study, only Falco had experience of using professional designers, and none had in-house expertise. All of the projects involved the acquisition and utilisation of CAD systems. This was viewed as central to supporting the NPD process. This meant a combination of technological understanding with appropriate personal skills. The manager of Taj is typical of the small business owner, being averse to taking financial risks. There is no guarantee of success to justify the initial investment in design. The KTP subsidy triggered the project, and the company, like the other companies visited, possessed no recognised previous design experience. Similarly, prior to the KTP, Kidstuff and Falco had no previous in-house design expertise, relying exclusively on freelance designers. With Falco, the associate had previously worked as a freelance designer for the company. At the time of the project, the management at Falco had made a strategic decision to engage with entirely new markets. Traditionally produced, low-design-content, low-value-added 9- and 18-carat gold jewellery was under threat from cheap imports, primarily from the Far East. The firm decided to counter this pressure by shifting away from gold-based products into platinum-based designs. This represented a high-risk, radical shift, as the management had no previous experience of working with the metal. They

Table 4.2 *Typology of absorptive capacity of firms*

Company type	Technological capacity
Research performers	Research department (or equivalent) Able to take long-run view of technological capabilities
Technological competence	Multiple engineers Some budgetary discipline Able to participate in technology networks
Minimum-capability companies	One engineer Able to adopt/adapt packaged solutions May need implementation help
Low-technology SMEs	No meaningful technological capacity No perceived need Possibly no actual need for technology

Adapted from Arnold and Thuriaux (1993)

had to employ the associate to implement this move into an upmarket, high-profit niche.

Using the Arnold and Thuriaux (1993) model to describe technological absorption capacity, the evidence suggests the participants in this study fall into the category of 'minimum capability'. All the companies recognised their inability to deliver new designs without external support. They were receptive to the strategic assistance offered by these KTP projects, which leads to the development of in-house design capability and, more importantly, creates systems to retain and capitalise on the new technological competences gained. Successful technological absorption depends on a number of factors, not least of which is the ability of businesses to adopt the appropriate set of techniques. This process is inevitably linked to the problems surrounding the uncertainty of innovation.

Mapping technological uncertainty

Innovation is by nature an uncertain and complex venture, epitomised by techno-logical uncertainty. This means that firms may be faced with a wide range of technological avenues, but in practice limited attention and resources. This is particularly relevant to smaller firms, where the wrong technological selection could be potentially catastrophic. KTPs provide a mechanism for allowing businesses to explore different options for identifying and obtaining new tech-niques through a process of technology transfer, thus reducing the risk of failure. In these cases, they tend to be design-oriented techniques and technologies. Technology transfer itself is uncertain, and there are many cautionary tales of technology transfer that has failed with disastrous consequences, particularly for smaller firms that are unable to absorb the costs of selecting the wrong technological options. The reasons for failure are numerous, and include over-dependency on experimental techniques, a poor history of technological adoption, and lack of selection capabilities. In an environment of rapid techno-logical change, businesses have to combine the search for external acquisition with the internal capacity to integrate new knowledge. A useful approach to classifying and analysing the uncertainties of technological selection faced by businesses is Pearson's uncertainty map (Figure 4.3).

Figure 4.3 can be interpreted as follows:

1 Output is unclear. The method of delivering results is unclear; work is *exploratory*, dependent on technologists. Feedback on performance is slow, and invisible externally.

2 Goals and outputs are more clearly defined; the means to achieve them are not. The research and development effort is described as *development engineer-ing* (e.g. Pilkington float glass). Considerable time, effort and the overcoming of technical problems are required, with a high probability of failure. Success

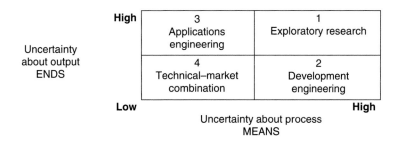

	Low	High
High	3 Applications engineering	1 Exploratory research
	4 Technical–market combination	2 Development engineering

Uncertainty about output ENDS — Uncertainty about process MEANS

Figure 4.3 *Uncertainties of technological selection faced by businesses*
Based on Pearson's uncertainty map, from Pearson and Brockhoff (1994)

is determined by the probability of alternative technologies. The long time scale means changing the external environment for innovation to realise the benefits.

3   The technology is relatively well known. The issue is exploitation through *applications engineering*. It demands close cooperation with customers and developing a range of applications simultaneously. Prioritisation is important.

4   Goals and outputs are clearly specified. The problem is the speed of producing the right *technical–market* combination; competition is potentially high. Appropriate and complementary assets are needed; competition is driven by forcing down price and introducing technical improvements to maintain leadership.

(Adapted from Pearson and Brockhoff 1994)

The nature of these projects is a mixture of both 3 and 4. The enterprises tend to explore relatively well-known design technology, such as CAD, and have close contacts with their client base. The solutions are based on design management techniques that are closely allied to market analysis; hence the technological risks are comparatively modest. The projects have enabled businesses to incorporate new techniques such as CAD through careful problem formulation. This has ensured that the appropriate techniques are more rapidly employed than if the projects had not been implemented. These strategies improve the likelihood of commercial success and, while evaluating the precise financial impact of these programmes remains a difficult issue, well-documented financial control techniques exist (see, for example, SQW 2002). The crux of this research concerns the less well-determined non-economic impacts of the KTP projects.

The costs and benefits of investing in design

There is a considerable literature on evaluating the financial consequences of investing in design and innovation (see, for example, Roy *et al.* 1999; Walsh *et al.* 1992), which have an impact on resource allocation for innovation. While innovation is an inherently risky activity, there are three main characteristics that influence corporate investment:

- Innovation is uncertain; success is not guaranteed.
- The process involves different stages that have different outputs that demand different techniques for evaluation.
- Many of the variables in evaluation cannot be reduced to a reliable set of figures to be used in a formula, but depend on expert judgement. It is critical that firms have effective communication between R&D and related innovative activities and the allocation of financial resources.

(Tidd *et al.* 2001)

These observations generally apply to large organisations, where the distinction between different (and often competing) departments can be critical for the political survival of a project. In this study of small firms, these divisions do not appear. The owner and managers are directly involved in the NPD process, although less so now at Falco owing to the design management strengths of the associate.

Research suggests it is difficult to determine the effectiveness of investment in innovation. For example, Mansfield *et al.* (1972) found that managers and R&D workers cannot accurately predict the development cost and time, markets and profits. On average, costs were greatly underestimated, while time periods were overestimated by between 140 and 280 per cent in products that required incremental modifications and by even greater margins (350–600 per cent) in major new products. Other research (Freeman and Soete 1997) also concludes that considerable effort is expended on failed projects. Unsuccessful projects are weeded out before major capital is invested. However, scientists and engineers are often deliberately over-optimistic in order to give the illusion of a high rate of return on investment to accountants and managers. Again, these observations are pertinent in large organisations with recognisable differentiated structures and functional departments.

Conventional financial evaluation methods rely on a mix of evaluation techniques, notably net present value (NPV) and discounted cash flow (DCF) (Cottrell 1986). A firm might invest in a negative NPV project to gain a market foothold, using a second-stage investment to justify the original investment. Thus, the second phase depends on the first, since if the firm could invest in the second alone the future opportunity would have no bearing on the immediate decision. This raises the problem of evaluation. Discounted cash flow estimates could be used to determine the NPV for both phases together. However, this would be misleading, since the second stage is an option, and discounted cash flows do not value options properly. The second stage remains an option since the firm has not made a commitment to proceed, and may only do so if the first stage is successful and the market still appears attractive. The firm can cut its losses if the first stage fails or market conditions change. Thus, investing in the first stage produces an intangible asset, an option on stage two. DCF is of no benefit for assessing pure R&D, which is almost all 'option value', analogous to exploratory research using the uncertainty map (Pearson and Brockhoff 1994).

DCF can also be used to examine the prospects for an enterprise if the management decides *not* to innovate. Eventually all its products and processes would become obsolete and its profits diminish over time. Predicting the future decline in profits is difficult, but using the accepted formula for calculating DCF means that long-range forecasts of future profits do not have to be precise (Georghiou 1986).

In the case of determining the economic effectiveness or the costs and benefits of KTP, the technique of 'additionality' is employed (SQW 2002). This approach is a computation based on estimates of the impacts attributed by the firms based on employment and turnover. This additional contribution to businesses is tempered with the estimates of businesses that would have proceeded regardless of the subsidy. This means there is a notional opportunity cost associated with the projects. In some cases the KTP enabled a business to undertake projects earlier than originally planned. The projects may have also resulted in some market displacement, gained at the expense of other UK competitors. The end result is an estimate of the net economic impact, and is valuable to guide policy makers based on the cost to the government of each additional job created by the programme.

In common with other research into the impacts of KTP, this study concurs with the findings of Edge and Hands (2004), Andrews *et al.* (2001) and Lipscomb and McEwan (2001). KTP can add considerable benefits to businesses through the application and management of design techniques. Technologically, the innovations introduced in these projects can be described as incremental rather than disruptive or radical (Tidd *et al.* 2001). This study suggests there are two types of outcomes of this form of design intervention. First, there are the short-term, direct financial benefits derived from the activities of the designers and the absorption of new design techniques. The second is the long-term, less easily quantified impacts arising from the less immediately apparent effects of investing in design on business strategy.

Although Edge and Hands (2004) comment on the changes in the case study of Haley Sharpe, which developed internationally distributed design teams, the firms in this study tended to retain the design expertise gained in the UK. Such expertise still demands close communication and effective control of the overseas production facilities. As Andrews *et al.* (2001) also reported, the enthusiasm for the project of senior management is fundamental. These cases suggest that the managers of these businesses were favourably predisposed to design, since few associates completed the programme. A critical shift in culture has been the formalisation of the design process, a prerequisite of the programme. This helps ensure that the new design techniques imported into the businesses are retained and utilised. This process increases innovation capacity and reduces technological uncertainty, and depends on the ability of managers to communicate the advantages that design can bring. Networking is an important factor for small firms, and KTPs represent an example of how businesses can access and use academic expertise. According to Manley (2003), knowledge is accessed by all partners through shared resources: a major constraint faced by SMEs. The links developed with HE institutions can therefore overcome some of these resource limitations. Another set of measures regarding the benefits that KTPs bring to the other partners, namely the academic partner and the associate, have not been addressed in this study but noted in other research (e.g. Lipscomb and McEwan 2001). For example the associate gains a design qualification obtained through work-based learning and commercial experience, and the HE gains from research and teaching materials.

CONCLUSIONS

The KTP projects reviewed in this study are atypical examples of the programme, as they focus on the integration of design and design-related technologies. In this sample it is the first time formal design strategies have been introduced at a strategic level in businesses through a collaborative partnership with an academic institution. The enterprises are favourably predisposed to design, and recognise the need to employ designers. The evidence suggests that these projects may have been initiated regardless of the existence of the programme. While KTPs are carefully planned and managed, with clear objectives to ensure reasonable success, they may also present management problems. The associates employed have to adjust to working in a small business environment, and not all can cope with the pressures or understand the business imperative. Indeed, some associates found employment better suited to their temperaments in larger organisations with recognised design departments. The projects undertaken enabled the firms to reduce the objective risk of investing in design through the ability of the designers to implement appropriate design technologies and skills. The projects thus enabled the firms to respond to client needs and create competitive advantage in the short term. The projects have in general helped to transform businesses by complementing existing core competences. Through this form of network, the enterprises have been able to utilise new techniques to increase their innovative capacity and reduce the uncertainty of investing in inappropriate technologies. In the short term, this generated economic benefits and, in the long term, less easily determined impacts. This can be illustrated most clearly with reference to Falco. The management took the strategic gamble to shift to an entirely new market niche, using the design skills of the associate. Indeed, it is noteworthy that commercial success was not purely based on narrow criteria, such as return on investment, but described with a wide range of attributes.

The non-financial impacts on business are highly significant. A common theme expressed by the participants in this study is the way formal design is integrated into the business process, often for the first time. Organisations have to adapt to accommodate the new skills; the presence of a designer can be a 'culture shock'. This was most apparent at Falco. Here, the associate introduced design processes that affected every aspect of the business, from corporate branding through to NPD strategies and marketing, and the publicity gained from the design awards is virtually incalculable.

These projects have been analysed through the lens of technology innovation and strategic management. The role of networks, or external linkages to other organisations including academia, is important to the development of small firms. The capacity for firms to innovate is not purely assessed on a technological selection perspective, but involves a wider assessment of organisational impacts. The process of innovation is itself a risky activity, but crucial for business evolution. In this study, it has been mapped using an uncertainty matrix. KTPs are carefully constructed to avoid the riskier elements of innovation, but may produce unforeseen benefits for the organisation beyond the purely financial. Indeed, the additionality model used to estimate the cost and benefits of the scheme fails to recognise the long-term benefits of design. Some of the changes to the participants have been quite profound and, while this study is indicative, these effects demand further research. This study has deliberately focused on the benefits to the enterprises reviewed. Further research should identify how the associates and participating HE institution profited. KTPs are an example of how technology transfer can be effected from HE to business, and could be evaluated alongside other knowledge transfer mechanisms, such as business spin-offs, consultancy and studentships. The overall picture from this study is that design-oriented projects have a positive impact on participating businesses. This suggests that the enterprises recognise the ways in which design contributes to their competitiveness.

ACKNOWLEDGEMENTS

The author would like to thank the participants who helped with the research for this study, and in particular permission for the use of the illustrations.

REVIEW QUESTIONS

1   Is there a proven relationship between (design) knowledge transfer from universities and innovation in design?

2   What is the nature of design resources held by small companies?
3   What makes knowledge transfer successful in design?
4   What are non-financial evaluation metrics?
5   Within the case studies, are the benefits from knowledge transfer similar?

PROJECT QUESTIONS

1   Small firms: develop criteria to evaluate non-financial benefits from design investment.
2   Consider and then map the various networks surrounding one of the case study companies. Identify at least three knowledge areas.
3   Devise a questionnaire to obtain measures of absorptive capacity around design in a small firm.
4   Debate and map the issues of communication involved in design-based knowledge transfer within the case studies. Illustrate a typical period of collaborative work between a university and a small firm.
5   Discuss issues of uncertainty and risk surrounding design costs within a case study. List the contributions that knowledge transfer might make to reducing that risk.

REFERENCES

Andrews, S., Ingram, J. and Muston, D. (2001) Product values and brand values. Paper presented at the 4th European Academy of Design conference, 'd3 desire designum design', Aveiro, Portugal, March

Ansoff, I. H. and Stewart, J. M. (1967) Strategies for a technology based business. *Harvard Business Review,* November–December: 71–83

Arnold, E. and Thuriaux, B. (1993) *Developing firms' technological capabilities.* Working paper. (Brighton: Technolopolis)

Brannen, J. (1992) Combining qualitative and quantitative approaches: an overview. In: J. Brannen (ed.) *Mixing methods: qualitative and quantitative research.* (Aldershot: Avebury)

CEC (2003) *The role of the universities in the Europe of knowledge.* Com (2003) 58 final. (Brussels: CEC)

Cottrell, A. H. (1986) Technological thresholds. In: R. Roy and D. Wield (eds) *Product design and technological innovation.* (Milton Keynes: Open University Press) pp. 112–118

Creative Enterprise (2006) From creative students to creative entrepreneurs. Conference held at the Custard Factory, Birmingham, 25 January

DTI (2003) *Innovation report: competing in the global economy – the innovation challenge*. December. (London: DTI)

DTI (2004a) *KTP strategic plan 2004–2007*. 29 November. Available at http://www.ktponline.org.uk/admin/documents/ktp_strategy_revised.doc (accessed 22 September 2005)

DTI (2004b) KTP strategic plan: Key Business Technologies Directorate presentation to UCE, Birmingham, 1 October

EC (European Commission) (2001) *Innovation policy in Europe 2001*. Innovation Papers No. 17, Fifth Research Framework Programme. (Brussels: European Commission)

Edge, S., Jerrard, R. and Hands, D. (2004) Design as an integrated process: Haley Sharpe Associates – ten years on. *Design Journal*, 7(1): 3–14

Freeman, C. (1982) *The economics of industrial innovation*. (London: Francis Pinter)

Freeman, C. and Soete, L. (1997) *The economics of industrial innovation*, 3rd edn. (London: Pinter)

Georghiou, L. (1986) *Post-innovation performance*. (Basingstoke: Macmillan)

Glaser, B. and Strauss, A. (1967) *The discovery of grounded theory: strategies for qualitative research*. (Chicago, IL: Aldine)

Hammersley, M. (1992) Deconstructing the qualitative–quantitative divide. In: J. Brannen (ed.) *Mixing methods: qualitative and quantitative research*. (Aldershot: Avebury)

HM Treasury (2003) *Lambert Review of business–university collaboration*. Final Report. December. (London: HM Treasury)

HM Treasury (2005) *The Cox Review of creativity in business: building on the UK's strengths*. December. (London: HM Treasury)

Koza, M. P. and Lewin, A. (1999) The coevolution of network alliances: a longitudinal analysis of an international professional service network. *Organization Science*, 10(5): 638–653

Lipscomb, M. and McEwan, A. M. (2001) Technology transfer in SMEs: the TCS model at Kingston University. Paper presented at the fourth SMESME international conference, 'Manufacturing Information Systems', Aalborg, Denmark, 14–16 May

Manley, K. (2003) Frameworks for understanding interactive innovation processes. *Entrepreneurship and Innovation*, 4(1), February: 25–36

Mansfield, E., Rappaport, J., Schnee, J., Wagner, S. and Hamburger, M. (1972) *Research and innovation in the modern corporation*. (London: Macmillan)

Mogey, N. (2006) So you want to use a Likert Scale? Available at http://www.icbl.hw.ac.uk/ltdi/cookbook/info_likert_scale/index.html (accessed 11 April 2006)

OECD (2003) *Seizing the benefits of ICT in a digital economy*. Meeting of the OECD Council at ministerial level, Montreal. (Paris: OECD)

Pearson, A. and Brockhoff, K. (1994) The uncertainty map and project management. *Project Appraisal*, 9(3): 211–215

Rothwell, R. and Dodgson, M. (1993) Technology-based SMEs: their role in industrial and economic change. *International Journal of Technology Management*, special edition on 'Small firms and innovation: the external influences', ed. M. Dodgson and R. Rothwell, 8(5/6): 8–22

Roy, R., Potter, S. and Riedel, J. C. K. H. (1999) The long-term benefits of investment in product design and innovation. In: R. Jerrard, R. Newport and M. Trueman (eds) *Managing new product innovation*. (London: Taylor & Francis) pp. 142–154

Schofield, J. W. (1993) Increasing the generalizability of qualitative research. In: M. Hammersley (ed.) *Educational research: current issues*, 1. (London: Chapman) pp. 91–113

Smith, M. T., Roy, R. and Potter, S. (1996) *The commercial impacts of green product development*. DIG-05, July. (Milton Keynes: Design Innovation Group, Open University)

SQW (Segal Quince Wicksteed) (2002) *Evaluation of TCS: final report to the Small Business Service*. DTI Evaluation Report Series No. 7, September. (London: DTI)

SQW (2005) *Interim evaluation of knowledge transfer programmes funded by the Office of Science and Technology through the Science Budget: final report*. February. (Cambridge: SQW)

Stacey, R. D. (1996) *Complexity and creativity in organisations*. (San Francisco, CA: Berrett-Koehler)

Stake, R. E. (1994) Case studies. In: N. K. Denzin and Y. S. Lincoln (eds) *Handbook of qualitative research*. (Thousand Oaks, CA: Sage Publications)

Stake, R. E. (1995) *The art of case study research*. (London: Sage Publications)

Tidd, J., Bessant, J. and Pavitt, K. (2001) *Managing innovation*, 2nd edn. (Chichester: Wiley)

Walker, S. (2005) Personal communication

Walsh, V., Roy, R., Bruce, M. and Potter, S. (1992) *Winning by design: technology, product design and international competitiveness*. (Oxford: Blackwell)

Yin, R. K. (1994) *Case study research: design and methods*, 2nd edn. (Thousand Oaks, CA: Sage Publications)

FURTHER READING

Easterby-Smith, M. and Lyles, M. A. (2003) *The Blackwell handbook of organizational learning and knowledge management.* (Oxford: Blackwell)

Salvador, T., Bell, G. and Anderson, K. (1999) Design ethnography. *Design Management Journal*, 10(4): 35–41

Tidd, J., Bessant, J. and Pavitt, K. (2001) *Managing innovation*, 2nd edn. (Chichester: Wiley)

Chapter 5

Researching risk in design

Robert Jerrard, Nicholas Barnes and Adele Reid

INTRODUCTION

The process of design is complex and implicit. Consequently the underlying components of the process can be difficult to separate without losing some information, the 'whole' being greater then the 'sum' of the parts. Risk perception and risk sharing are a positive part of the design process. The essence of innovation in product design should welcome risk to facilitate and encourage a creative design environment. Risk perception and risk sharing are inherently a fundamental part of this process. They will be reflected upon from current viewpoints and also from the perspective of case studies from five design-led companies.

The environment surrounding the design and development of new products is particularly complex, encompassing a range of risks at a number of levels in a broad range of situations. The literature about risk is equally diverse, ranging from that which is calculable to consideration of the perceptions of adventure and creativity in design (Jerrard 2000). As a consequence of the interdisciplinary nature of design-based new product development (NPD), the study of the associated risks is especially important (Jerrard *et al.* 1999). As the role and importance of creative industries in the UK economy become more widely recognised (e.g. Department of Trade and Industry 2005), understanding the nature of risk in NPD has significance both for successful business management and for the development of sound economic policy (Cox 2005).

Risk is often difficult to define and deal with and, while frequently linked to design and creativity management, it may be addressed in different ways. In essence, researching risk requires decision making during the design process to be considered from a number of different perspectives (Jerrard *et al.* 2002a). Other work (Horne Martin and Jerrard 2002) identified *critical decision points* through case studies which looked retrospectively at the evolution of NPD. Research focusing on the human or non-measurable characteristics of risk in design is rare

(Jerrard and Barnes 2006), yet hazards that are not normally 'calculated' by standard risk assessment tools are an essential feature of the work domain of designers. These are particularly important in small and medium-sized companies that do not have the structure or resources that larger companies have to perform such assessments. In small companies, many of these judgements are viewed simply as 'what feels right', and decisions are often made using 'gut feelings' or intuitive thinking. Typically, the new product development process occupies multiple work domains that may be represented by a critical path flow. The path, however, needs to pragmatically embody the unexpected and opportunistic themes associated with the design process. As a general rule, financial risks tend to be a predominant concern, closely followed by personal risks (Jerrard *et al.* 2002b).

RISK PERCEPTION

Despite numerous government invitations, companies frequently fail to invest in design, owing to their perceptions of the downside of risk. Indeed, even when companies decide to invest in design they often tend to be risk-averse and much opportunity and market potential may therefore be lost. For UK manufacturing the situation is made more difficult with the continual development of new products designed and developed specifically for European consumption, resulting in a rising import tide.

The large literature base on risk management is not normally applied to the management of design or indeed to a typical environment for NPD, the small company. Day-to-day risk is traditionally linked to design investment but has never really been quantified in a detailed way (Jerrard and Barnes 2006). This may be due to a variety of factors, including the relatively imprecise nature of both consumer response and the creative nature of designers in relation to NPD. Accordingly, such issues in management are viewed as being more socially or culturally based than business based. The issues surrounding the potential of design are well known, particularly where a company may calculate reinvestment from an in-house benchmark or from an established simulation. The 'sub-culture' of design within general management is viewed sometimes as an identifiable element but more often as an associated or even marginal issue. Investment in design within small companies involves comparisons with other areas of financial investment, potentially providing potent intelligence. Likewise, product innovation appears to be measured against other work cultures that are in the immediate vicinity. Literature to support investment in design risk may appear in government documents, or via consultancy, though little academic research is published demonstrating the rationale for initial design investment.

Studying the perception of risks is based on a developed assumption that people

103

do not behave in an expected manner (Renn 1998). The use of risk in everyday life is complex and context related, and these variable contexts include all social and cultural conditions. A psychological concept of risk perception is however less complex (Renn 1998), and risk may be considered as inherently social because of the natural process of sharing. Therefore a 'socially realistic' concept of risk is one that places an individual with independent perspectives into a society concerned with the minimisation of risk. This naturally segregates the 'newness' values traditionally associated with the design process.

The covert nature of individually based risk perception makes its observation difficult, and the preference of certainty over the love of taking risks will, like all perceptions, vary within individuals. The attitude or mood of an individual will determine the weight applied to risk judgements and produce a precise perception. Risk sharing may be important here, where others influence perceptions and a group consciousness is developed between certainty and uncertainty. The preference people and groups have for taking a risk is, however, different to the concept of uncertainty. Risk perception considers possible outcomes, whilst to be uncertain is to sense a risk without consequence. Therefore uncertainty perception may be only negative (i.e. the risk of making a loss) whilst risk perception may represent a challenge, a gamble and an opportunity. In this way risk management often proposes formalised risk-sharing strategies. Perceiving risk accurately is a measure of managerial competency, as is the distribution of risks, for example by using risk analysis to develop success factors for new products (Montoya-Weiss and Calantone 1994). 'Success' may, however, be as slippery a perception as the associated risks. Cooper and Kleinschmidt (2000) explicitly recognise this:

> New products can be successful in a variety of ways; they can have a major impact on the firm; they can be seen as great 'technical' successes; they can have a significant impact in the market by achieving a high market share.

Such success, if considered holistically, equates to the complexity of the design task. Interesting questions surround the relationship risk perception may have with product success where design is a strong feature. If we are able to determine design as a clear feature of success then investing in it becomes less risky; we might say that low-risk-product companies are likely to invest the least in adding value through design. Perceiving risk in product development requires an approach to the complexities of the product and the emergent associated events. In this context, too much perceived risk has been identified as detrimental (Cooper and Kleinschmidt 2000). Most designers would agree that high-risk product development represents a key opportunity to provide a difference; such perception however may not be shared throughout the company.

Risk perception is value laden and subjective. Sharing such subjectivity ought to represent a learning process for designers, and this learning may only result from recognising the expert authority within the NPD arena. In this way, sharing risk perception ought to be synonymous with project options and choice. This may only occur when the important meaning and associated essential issues are communicated. Good communication therefore has a direct effect on how risk perceptions are treated and shared. An agreed ambient quality of communication, without irresponsible speculation potentially replacing shared risk perception, is likely to be important. Communication of risk is, of course, a significant and widespread preoccupation. Situation safety is communicated through warning signs; their effectiveness has been recently reviewed (Wogalter *et al.* 2002), as have product safety (Sui and Wong 2002) and safety perception (O'Toole 2002). Such research is representative of major commitments to risk perception between employers, employees, product developers and consumers.

RISK SHARING

Risk sharing may also be viewed as being related to common commitments. For example, Cox and Jimernez (1998) describe risk sharing in private households. In these studies the transfer of resources over long distances, from financially buoyant households to poor ones within the same family, is recognised (family networks may well be a model for better risk sharing). The common recognition of problems and their communication within structures of loyalty and cultural perspective appear to be a natural human consequence of facing risk and uncertainty. One of the interesting conclusions in the area of household risk sharing is that (according to Cox and Jimernez 1998) major changes to social situations have little effect on the behaviours found in the network. Social networks associated with values in design may be seen in all design offices and one might conclude that groups of designers share both values and perceptions of risk.

Mutual insurance through risk sharing as a product of need and security has size limitations (Genicot and Ray 2003). A concentrated group of like-minded, need-driven individuals will share a more accurate and truthful perception than those in diverse areas. At the level of the firm this is likely to be an area of intellectual management rather than 'gut feeling'. Determination of risk importance is difficult, and the magnitude of a risk may be inaccurately inflated or underestimated by the broadcast of individual perceptions. Inherent risk perception does, however, always appear to be influenced by an ambient recognition of an issue. This may not represent knowledge at a high level but is important because ultimately the public arena is linked to the risk (see Frewer *et al.* 1998).

Shared risk perception appears to be a non-linear process. Once a risk is acknowledged, its acceptance level is individually negotiated and not easily shared, even with such common beliefs associated with design excellence being present. This broadcasting of negative or positive perceptions may, however, produce irreversible damage. Knowing other perceptions may only be useful if a positive intention is present to independently develop.

DIAGNOSING RISK

The word 'risk' itself represents an intangible focus within professional environments. Nevertheless, such environments increasingly require accurate support through their complexity, and risk calculation is viewed as a way of correctly assisting choice. Diagnosing risk and its calculation develop a fixed commitment to a future events forecast. Such a commitment, however, is actually an acknowledgement of the unpredictable nature of projects. The dilemma for designers lies in the conflict between common mathematical absolutes and professional experiential judgement. Management's role in design is clear: the identification of and preparation for risks, together with their reduction.

Risk calculation in business environments is typically applied to a logistical aspect where competing operations need to be evaluated, whilst risk calculation in the design process elevates management involvement in product development to be paramount. What is 'calculable' in product design development? Ahmadi and Wang (1999) state that product development risk is determined by characteristics such as product complexity, technological requirements or difficulty, and a firm's product and process development capability. Risk calculation as a control tool for management offers choice in the variation of time and cost aspects of projects. These 'critical points' may divide a design process into chronological parts with timed reviews linked to forward risk calculation. Thus risk calculation represents a significant move away from intuitive problem-solving.

The calculation of risk varies from industry to industry; each prefers its own methodology. In engineering, for example, risk calculation is derived from mathematical combinations of probability and consequences. The quantification of 'undesirable outcome possibility' appears central by factoring probability with effect. How a social conception is placed on such calculation appears to be important especially where absolute issues of safety apply. This risk reduction by degrees, down to an acceptable level, may easily justify the reduction of calculation. However, numeric values as a characterisation of risk magnitude and the equivalent in probabilities may assume 'equal' weight (Renn 1998).

The communities as described by Pratt (2000) chart the frontiers of acceptance within self-referencing groups. This kind of mathematical modelling considers the boundaries within which risk takers operate and the potential to model boundary crossing. Ward and Chapman (1995) specify risk levels 'primary' or 'secondary' within a staged assessment of risk in architectural projects. Thus impact assessment is made up of the relationship between probability and consequences in the complex process of constructing a building. Unsurprisingly, risk identification within such professionally complex projects received priority from project managers. Intermittent 'design' risks according to Ward and Chapman are both integrated and separate within the calculation. This approach presupposes that all involved are able to use a common risk identification and calculation 'language'.

The risk calculation involved in 'shared platform' design development, where a product may be developed in a modular style, is described by Gonzalez-Zugasti *et al.* (2001). The manufacturing and cost flexible benefits of shared platforms are set against the set of choices that are made by consumers around novelty and security. This approach formulates the confidence factors of design choice and relates these to other specific design factors. This highlights uncertainty within this type of product planning and allows for (1) the selection of alternative platforms and (2) the selection of variants. The models allowed a company to create future options but also to defer investment decision until risks have been isolated.

Within the process of economic planning, Eckwert and Zilcha (2003) isolate two types of risk: 'the insurable' (hedged from future markets) and the 'uninsurable'. This assumes that the value of public information useful to economic allocation is measurable. These divisions may not exist at the level of the firm, although market development investment is always macro-dependent. Other work, by Hall (2004), describes software to support uncertainty, where a clearer level of understanding complexity is reached through improved communication within management decisions.

The process of risk auditing (Shailer *et al.* 1998) and linked research highlight structural issues in developing an understanding of risk calculation. Shailer uses 'inherent control' and detection as distinct concepts in studies of auditors. This showed that the risk concept (calculation) was featured less in audits than within discrete problem calculation. Here a professional auditing standard appears to be inflectional where complex models involving risk calculation need to be usefully applied to increasingly diverse applications.

Companies must invariably take risks when launching new products. The ability to diagnose and manage those risks is increasingly considered essential within high-risk innovation. Project risk is determined by not only its likelihood and effects but also the ability of a company to influence the risk factors.

There is a tendency for research to develop tools and methodologies to calculate the risk in new product development. Scientists often appear compelled by nature to calculate and measure almost everything. The literature tends to describe the need for caution when handling risk, rather then recognising and promoting the value of adventure in design. However, excessive caution may prove counter-productive.

Emerging literature indicates there is a need for a more humanistic approach towards risk in the area of new product development encompassing a positive attitude towards risk. Changing companies' attitudes towards risk is a complex task. It requires a deeper understanding of their culture and the ability to challenge individuals' embedded perceptions of risk. Interestingly, in design the perception of risk is difficult at the heart of its diagnosis.

NEW PRODUCT DEVELOPMENT

New product development is, of course, inherently risky, and new consumer products have always failed at high rates (see Hopkins and Bailey 1971), although 'failure' is often difficult to define until some point in the future. At the heart of risk perception associated with consumer products is the unpredictable nature of consumers at the point of sale. Consequently, the risks associated with new products are perceived as very high, and market share strategies are important in reducing risk but may also stifle the creativity and design associated with such products. The classification of consumers into risk takers and non-risk takers reminds us that risk perceptions are often stakeholder derived. By taking this view we assume that when consumers purchase a product they take a similar risk to the designer – it's a new experience. This assumes we are able to precisely understand specific individual motivations. Mitchell and Boustani (1992) describe a process by which the act of purchase reduces the perception of risk. In other words engagements involve product commitment and risk tolerance. Such involvement in risk frameworks represents the central aspect of risk sharing. Perceiving risks is at the heart of the design process and for designers to avoid playing it safe, and thereby to take risks, is to extend design boundaries. Similarly risk perception by designers may include initial views of the way others deal with risk.

The ability to recognise and take prompt action when a product launch has failed is essential. Consequently it is interesting that senior managers in a new product launch setting are inclined to remain committed to new products that are failing. The issue of how best to deal with new product failures was raised by Boulding et al. (1997). They identified that the most effective methods of reducing commitment to a losing course of action appear to be either pre-commitment to a predetermined discussion rule or the introduction to a new decision maker at the time of judgement to either 'stop' or 'continue'. The latter method appeared to produce slightly less commitment to a losing course of action. Ultimately they found that none of the decision procedures were completely reduced to the commitment of a losing course of action.

As a whole, the design process with its intention to delight a customer often defies objective description. Interestingly, the separation of 'objective' risk and 'subjective' (or perceived) risk has become increasingly difficult (Royal Society

1992), thus creating new value systems where aspects of NPD are managed more by recognition of tacit knowledge domains than risk calculation.

THE CASE STUDIES

The main aim of this study was to gain specific insight into risk perception and sharing and design decision making by small companies. The authors utilised a number of methods to research risk in design, including the development of case studies from companies which are developing new design-based products.

Fieldwork was based on an investigation of 'live projects' in small companies. *Critical decision points* were tracked while decisions were being made. Current practices in risk assessment were observed and the techniques used to minimise risks were also examined. The design process was mapped and areas of risk such as financial, personal, design and sales were also considered. The main area of focus was on the human/non-measurable aspects of risk, which are generally not 'calculated' by standard tools and formulas.

Methodology

A novel and staged methodology was developed to identify risk areas and track decision making during NPD in design-led SMEs. The primary aim of the process was to establish trust between key company personnel and the fieldworker/ researcher in order that rich and insightful (essentially) qualitative data might be collected. This 'evolving methods' process needed to be flexible enough to suit a wide range of company cultures and yet robust enough to ensure relevance over the extended period of the product pipeline. Ultimately, the goal was for the fieldworker to become an embedded participant (though still essentially an 'out-sider') in the company culture. The process aimed to track decision making live (as it happened) in light of changing risk perception over the sampling period. We believe this research process has not been attempted in this way before. The methodology adopted was participant based, which means the participant, not the researcher, defined the risk factors.

Establishing trust requires time and work, but the rewards for researchers are potentially significant. As with all relationships, the success of interaction between fieldworker and company is directly proportional to the capacity of those con-cerned to give and receive freely (information, time, support, etc.).

First stage – identifying participating companies

Initially, 40 suitable companies were identified. The companies were identified from an established database of approximately 350 design-led companies from across the UK. An introductory letter outlining the aims of the project was then sent to the sample set of companies together with a short questionnaire to establish suitability and willingness to participate. The first criterion for suitability was for the companies to be located in the UK and to be small or medium-sized in terms of the number of employees. It was also important that the participating companies were in the process of starting a new product lifecycle and that the product was considered innovative by those producing it. Additional criteria included the product being of a household type and small in size in order to limit interference of variables. Lastly, it was essential that the companies utilised either in-house design or design via a consultancy during the NPD.

Ten companies were initially short-listed that expressed a positive initial attitude to participation and fulfilled the core project criteria.

Second stage – the selection of companies for study

Companies were contacted by telephone, and meetings were arranged with the relevant personnel (managers, designers, etc.). The meetings provided the opportunity for the researchers to fully explain the aims of the project and to explore the possible approaches to collaboration. At this point confidentiality issues were assured. It is essential from the outset that company personnel feel both secure and comfortable when discussing sensitive information. This can be dealt with, to some extent, by appropriate use of formal confidentiality agreements. Whilst useful to both 'sides' these may, however, shape and limit the way in which information is later disseminated.

Semi-structured interviews were used to help identify risk areas. Following the meetings, the five companies were selected for detailed study. The products under development by the selected companies included protective safety clothing, catering equipment, aids for the visually impaired, and home entertainment equipment. During this period a wide range of other material was collected to help characterise the company culture and the products and their development process. These included photographs, company literature and websites, notes from telephone conversations, emails, informal interactions, etc.

The semi-structured interviews were initially undertaken with selected key personnel, the aim being that the perceived risk areas would be identified at the onset of the NPD. This material was also used to draw up individual 'risk forms' for each participant (Figure 5.1).

Third stage – the risk forms and ongoing interviews

A risk form (reflective diary) was tailor-made for each person/company and was used as a prompt for the participants. It had the scope for grading the relative importance of each risk area over time. The interviewees were able to reflect on

Risk in design project – reflective table for development of new printer/heater product						
Date completed:				Completed by:		

High risk   Low risk

5   4   3   2   1

Identified risk areas	Critical	Significant	Important	Marginal	Negligible	Comments
Protecting intellectual property – patents, etc.						
Coordinating product development with funding deadlines (Smart, etc.)						
Acquiring small numbers of specialist components at affordable prices (minimum orders required, etc.), e.g. lamps						
Suppliers changing component specifications (e.g. motor circuit board)						
Cash flow (e.g. stocking right number of components)						
Change in premises – finding replacement leaseholder, affording new premises, etc.						
Change of location – impact on staff						
Expense of outer mouldings (box)						
High initial costs on relatively low sales – time lapse before costs recouped						
Loss of components (e.g. breakages) during design phase						
Retaining/ replacing key personnel, e.g. engineering role						
Original printer from Minolta now discontinued – finding adequate replacement						
Potential competition, e.g. American company						
Financial risks – expenditure on tooling costs, CAD and other investment						
Wastage losses, e.g. faulty guillotine						
Property issues, e.g. leaking roof						

Figure 5.1 *Sample of risk form*

their original selection of risk areas and also to (re)consider in light of the current situation. Each risk area was graded according to a five-point scale of relative importance, and 'new' risk areas were added as required.

Further semi-structured interviews were undertaken on a regular basis to provide detailed 'commentary' on risk issues as the NPD continued. The risk forms were again used in conjunction with the interviews as prompts and to record the perceived relative importance of risk areas. However, given the need to fit into the 'real world' of product cycles, sampling periods were inevitably 'ragged'. Coordinating the start/finish of data capture with the start/finish of the product development timeline is unlikely to produce a perfect fit in any design/ new product development process research project.

Fourth stage – the final interviews and provision of feedback to the companies

On completion of the fieldwork process, the final interviews were conducted and 'feedback' sessions were offered to the companies, thus providing an opportunity to reflect overall on the material gathered. It also enabled personnel to access a structured record of their judgements and responses to risk areas and issues.

Potential methodological difficulties

Participant methodologies can mean that judgements or impressions by field-workers may be 'clouded', i.e. their observation will inevitably be subjective to some extent.

The act of observation changes what is observed. This well-known principle is true for all research, though participatory work may be particularly prone to this effect.

Sampling bias can also occur during the selection of a company; for example, those companies willing to invest significant resources such as time, information and costs, etc. in the research process might be considered more 'public-spirited' than those that do not. Alternatively, they might simply be more 'savvy', that is more open to the potential benefits of their participation in the research. Either way, it raises the question 'Are the participating companies representative? And if so, of what?'

There is also a danger of the fieldworker becoming a burden, as he or she will probably have to walk a fine line between persistence and annoyance. Inevitably, participation in research being conducted by 'distant' academics will be seen, at times, as low-priority by busy managers and designers operating in the commercial arena. The fieldworker therefore has to be persistent in order to ensure continuity of data collection but also needs to take a careful judgement on how far to 'push' for contributions.

Thus, maintaining the flow of information when conducting fieldwork is not always easy for the researcher. One-way flows of energy and information may become unsustainable, and for the data capture process to work successfully over extended periods the fieldworker(s) must give something 'back' to the firms. This might include ideas, good will, time, information, and practical or emotional support.

Results

During the study the interviewees were asked to identify the future risks which they perceived to be significant during a forthcoming NPD process. Despite the relatively small sample size, a very wide range of risks (total = 70) was identified (Table 5.1). Notably, only two of these specific risks were common to three or more companies, and only six were common to two companies. This highlights the very individual nature of risk perception in companies, even where firms share a number of core characteristics (small, focused on product design, etc.). Regardless of the common features of the companies, there is no management process which follows a generic risk process pattern. The only recognisably common risk issues are: competition, correct pricing, developing and protecting IPR, technical risks (around components) and the retention of key personnel. This might suggest that there is a preoccupation with developing a management consistency within a complex process.

The research generated a wide variety of interrelated material – part physical (questionnaire, transcript, risk form, photograph), part human (memory, impression, judgement, feeling). Valid interpretation and robust analysis of this rich and potentially insightful material requires careful consideration. It is likely that, ultimately, in all situations the companies, personnel, products, risks and researchers are essentially unique in time and space, and attempts to reduce or generalise are consequently both difficult and of limited value. It is clear though that a number of highly informative and even delightful 'stories' may be derived – a narrative on risk and creativity in the adventure that is design and NPD.

Also, as a consequence of the lengthy fieldwork process, the fieldworker will build an extensive set of experiences concerning the sampled companies and the individual personnel involved. At the end of the process this could provide a valuable and unique perspective which could be translated into further 'secondary' material. Judgements, feelings, recollections, memories, impressions, etc. can all provide potentially powerful additional insights which can be usefully considered in tandem with the 'primary' data.

CONCLUSIONS

Previous work by the authors (Jerrard *et al.* 2002b) suggested that risk around NPD for design-based entrepreneurs was dominated by financial risk and risk of 'reputation'. These results suggest that this may not always be the case (financial risk is limited to the promotion and selling process and how the product is viewed in competitive markets). Developing IPR is not as strong as one might assume, and in terms of risk will probably relate to a planned lifespan for certain products together with the required development speed, i.e. some products have short lives

Table 5.1 *Specific risks perceived by five companies embarking on NPD*

Companies	1	2	3	4	5
Competition:					
Competition in niche market	X		X		
Growing international competition	X			X	X
Growing UK competition				X	
Financial:					
Relatively high costs for low-quantity components		X			X
Overrunning budgets		X			
Front-end loading, supplying all stockists gives high artificial demand		X			
Ability to produce cost-effective products			X		
Correct pricing		X	X		
Building adequate sales				X	
Continuity/predictability of supplier costs				X	
Controlling costs				X	
Cash flow – stocking issues					X
High initial costs on relatively low sales					X
Loans – high gearing	X				
Premises:					
Affording new premises					X
Finding new premises		X			
Finding replacement leaseholder					X
Property maintenance					X
Design-related:					
Waiting for industrial design to come through		X			
Many iterations – 'fuzzy front end'		X			
Incorporating enough USPs			X		
Public perceptions of product efficacy	X				
Suppliers:					
Key suppliers – will they deliver?	X	X		X	
Suppliers changing component specifications					X
Reliance on limited number of suppliers	X				
Components and parts:					
Packaging		X			
Development of crossovers and drive units		X			
Complexity and expense of cabinet		X			
Cabinet manufacturing/production capability		X			
Expense of outer mouldings					X
Unusual paint		X			
Damage to components during design phase					X
Components becoming discontinued					X
Specialist new dye needed	X				

Companies	1	2	3	4	5
Intellectual property rights (IPR):					
Developing and protecting IPR				X	X
Developing strong branding (trademark)	X				
Research needed to validate products	X				
Legislation and compliance:					
Test compliances, e.g. drop test, transit test – late in process		X			
Compliance with new standards	X				
Legal issues with competitors	X				
Technical:					
Technical risks – components		X		X	
Capacitors – variable impact on sound quality		X			
Technology development risks whilst on timeline		X			
Production of technical manuals – tends to be late		X			
Psycho-acoustic phenomena		X			
Markets:					
Reaction of customers			X		
Sales – direct vs shops			X		
New market (high end)		X			
Developing international markets				X	
Seasonality of products	X				
Human resources and organisation:					
Retention of key personnel		X			X
Internal competencies				X	
Internal organisation change				X	
Redundancies				X	
Impact on staff through change of location					X
Coordination strategic:					
Timescale for components, e.g. final crossover usually late in process		X			
Lead time for tooling, bedding in components, etc.		X			
Attempting to meet ideal launch periods (September and January) means compressed timescales for tooling, etc.		X			
Late decision changes		X			
Clarifying/agreeing objectives				X	
Decision changes by key partners				X	
Overstretched management				X	
Coordinating product development with external funding deadlines					X

Continued

115

Table 5.1 — *continued*

Companies	1	2	3	4	5
Business relationships:					
Delivery of services from external partners			X		
Building relationships with key customers	X				
Personal:					
Personal financial investment	X				
Other:					
Manufacturability within factory (new technologies, high weights, etc.)		X			
Manual handling – weighty products		X			
Damage in transit (high-quality product – internal and external damage)		X			
Other wastage					X

and their development may be 'held up' by considering protection. The retention of key personnel may be assumed to be a feature of technical competence – employing people with the necessary skills – although these do appear to link. One might assume therefore that risk responsibility will be within entrepreneurial individuals with reduced risk sharing. Other strongly recognisable features are growing international competition and the perceived capacity for key suppliers to deliver. This is, perhaps, unsurprising, as these risk areas may be seen as outside a control locus but central to the design-based NPD process. Design often represents a key set of features related to speculative markets as well as quality assurance from suppliers.

Risks in NPD are interlinked with design within a complex process where risks are temporary, and risk areas easily linked to design may be difficult to portray. Although specific risks may be (conveniently) grouped into a number of risk themes in largely predictable categories (e.g. finance, competition, etc.), such groupings mask the underlying diversity of risk faced (or at least perceived) by creative companies; personal commitment to design carries personal risks. For those concerned with trying to predict and address risk in small creative companies, this diversity of risk perception reveals some of the potential complexity faced by managers.

The development of a risk culture (and therefore an innovatory one) is partly based on the ability of individuals to collectively construct and then model 'unknown' space, beyond current experience. The potentially uncomfortable nature of such external space and scenarios means that companies are often 'shocked' into innovation (Schroeder *et al.* 2000). Such shocks may include impending business failure of any kind or entrepreneurial rivalry and ambition. The changing nature of business, however, often develops an existing space into something feeling more uncomfortable than the unknown, and what is experimental becomes a safer place, even a haven. Risk is often the first point of reflection within an emergent contractual business process. This is normally followed by complex judgements on returns, controls, duration and finally termination. Innovation risks therefore may be viewed in a variety of different ways depending on both individual perception and the ambient risk-sharing culture within the firm. Consequently, studying risk in innovation is difficult; 'the big picture' of a company's innovation process is populated by a large number of risky positions and strategies which are difficult to attribute or assemble in common space.

Day-to-day risk is traditionally linked to design investment but has never really been quantified in a detailed way, and the literature surrounding risk is surprisingly quiet about design. This may be due to a variety of factors, including the relatively imprecise nature of both consumer response and quality of designer performance in relation to NPD. The risky labelling of design decision making may be a reflection of our inability to describe complexity, and the calculation of risk is equally mysterious within a human resource context. It is not clear whether management decisions to, for example, employ new designers to reposition product ranges are perceived by most as anything but a 'gamble'. Similarly, potential design performance in a new marketplace defies accurate calculation although more predictable incremental output will have recent case detail.

The knowledge resulting from this type of research can contribute greatly to the companies being studied, providing a reflective tool for their creative practice. It is also informative to other small companies' NPD process when considering their decision making and risk assessments. The academic audience will also benefit from the outcomes of this research work as further development of knowledge in the fields of creativity and design management, with potentially important implications for the development of business support policy.

Overall, this study has provided unique insight into the way in which small companies perceive and assess design and risk during new product development. What makes this study distinctive is that the main area of focus is on the human/non-measurable aspects of risk and does not try to 'calculate' it by standard tools or formulas. In addition the knowledge gained has only inspired further research questions. The foremost of these questions are 'What are the benefits of risk management in design once the potential procedures are recognised?', 'Is it possible to map the considerable literature based on management of risk in general management to the design function in creative industries?', 'Is it more appropriate to establish design as an integrated feature where risk is shared between decision "locations" (that is, establish design investment initially to be openly financially *and* culturally based, thereby providing an expectation that two "types" of investment may be concurrently required)?', and lastly 'Should we acknowledge that creativity in the design of new products is *delightfully* risky and defies description?'

REVIEW QUESTIONS

1   What are the advantages and disadvantages of sharing risks across multi-skilled NPD teams?
2   In what practical ways can risks be effectively shared during the design and development of new products?
3   For a given new product type of your choice, consider and list the potential risk areas.
4   Is it possible to grade these risk areas, in advance, in terms of perceived relative importance?
5   How might the relative importance of these risks change during the cycle of development for this new product?
6   And how might these specific risk areas be perceived differently by different company personnel (e.g. product designer, project manager, technical specialist, finance officer, etc.)?
7   What are the advantages and disadvantages of attempting to 'formally' identify and manage risks through mechanistic/formulaic management tools?
8   Risk perception and approaches to risk sharing will vary according to many factors, including size of company involved. How might the approach of very small 'micro' companies (say, fewer than ten employees) differ from that of larger companies which may have more resources and more complex organisational structures?
9   How might we best recognise and embrace risk in a positive manner, as an essential part of creativity in general and NPD in particular?
10 Some parts of the NPD process may inevitably include an element of chance or luck, or at least involve factors beyond our control. Is it possible to perceive and manage these types of risk and, if so, how?

PROJECT QUESTIONS

1   The data presented in Table 5.1 highlight the extremely diverse nature of risk in NPD, with potentially little commonality even between similar product types. Discuss why this might be so.
2   For small companies developing new products, what are the potential benefits of participating in collaborative research projects with universities or other research institutions? What type of potential problem might you associate with such risks?
3   For a given new product type, and referring to the example in the text,

develop a simple tailor-made pro forma to track risks during the product's design and development.

4   Consider three specific ways in which a new product might be perceived to have failed following the completion of NPD (e.g. specific financial or technical aspects). Attempt to reframe each of these 'failures' in such a way as to generate a positive perspective in some manner (e.g. development of new skills or a valuable learning experience).

5   Establishing, developing and maintaining working links with partner companies can be a difficult process. With reference to the methodology described in the text, consider the ways in which you could maintain and strengthen positive working relationships with your partner organisations.

REFERENCES

Ahmadi, R. and Wang, R. H. (1999) Managing development risk in product design processes. *Operations Research*, 47(2): 235–246

Boulding, W., Ruskin, M. and Staelin, R. (1997) Pulling the plug to stop the new product drain. *Journal of Marketing Research*, 43: 164–176

Cooper, R. G. and Kleinschmidt, E. J. (2000) New product performance: what distinguishes the star products. *Australian Journal of Management*, 25(1): 17–45

Cox, D. and Jimernez, E. (1998) Risk sharing and private transfers: what about urban households? *Economic Development and Cultural Change*, 46(3): 621–637

Cox, G. (2005) *Cox review of creativity in business: building on the UK's strengths.* (London: HM Treasury)

Department of Trade and Industry (2005) *Creativity, design and business performance.* DTI Economics Paper No. 15. (London: DTI)

Eckwert, B. and Zilcha, I. (2003) Incomplete risk sharing arrangements and the value of information. *Economic Theory*, 21(1): 43–58

Frewer, L. J., Howard, C. and Shepherd, R. (1998) Understanding public attitudes to technology. *Journal of Risk Research*, 1(3): 221–235

Genicot, G. and Ray, D. (2003) Group formation in risk-sharing arrangements. *Review of Economic Studies*, 70: 87–113

Gonzalez-Zugasti, J. P., Otto, K. and Baker, J. (2001) Assessing value in platformed product family design. *Research in Engineering Design*, 13(1): 30–41

Hall, B. D. (2004) On the propagation of uncertainty in complex-valued quantities. *Metrologia*, 41: 173–177

Hopkins, D. S. and Bailey, E. L. (1971) New product resources, Conference Board Record, pp. 16–24. (Reviewed in: V. W. Mitchell and P. Boustani (1993) *European Journal of Marketing*, 27(2): 17–32)

119

Horne Martin, S. and Jerrard, B. (2002) *Risk in innovation.* University of Central England, Birmingham. (London: Design Council)

Jerrard, R. (2000) *Researching designing: cycles of design research, foundations for the future – doctoral education in design, La Clusaz, France.* (Stoke-on-Trent: Staffordshire University Press)

Jerrard, R. and Barnes, N. J. (2006) Risk in design: key issues from the literature. *Design Journal,* 9(2): 25–38

Jerrard, R., Horne Martin, S., Newport, R. and Burns, K. (2002a) Risk in new product development: six case studies. *New Product Development and Innovation Management,* September/October: 231–246

Jerrard, R., Ingram. J. and Hands, D. (2002b) *Design management case studies.* (London: Routledge)

Mitchell, V. W. and Boustani, P. (1992) Market development using new products and new customers: a role for perceived risk. *European Journal of Marketing,* 27(2): 17–32

Montoya-Weiss, M. M. and Calantone, R. (1994) Determinants of new product performance: a review and meta analysis. *Journal of Product Innovation Management,* 2(5): 397–417

O'Toole, M. (2002) The relationship between employees' perceptions of safety and organizational culture. *Journal of Safety Research,* 33: 231–243

Pratt, J. W. (2000) Efficient risk sharing: the last frontier. *Management Science,* 46(12): 1545–1553

Renn, O. (1998) Three decades of risk research: accomplishments and new challenges. *Journal of Risk Research,* 1(1): 49–71

Royal Society (1992) *Risk: analysis perception and management – a group study report.* (London: Royal Society)

Schroeder, R. G., Van de Ven, A. H., Scudder, G. D. and Polly, D. (2000) The development of innovative ideas. In: A. Van de Ven, H. L. Angle and M. Scott Poole (eds) *Research on the management of innovation: the Minnesota studies.* (Oxford: Oxford University Press) pp. 107–134.

Shailer, G., Wade, M., Willett, R. and Kim L. Y. (1998) Inherent risk and indicative factors: senior auditors' perceptions. *Managerial Auditing Journal,* 13(8): 455–464

Sui, N. Y.-M. and Wong, H.-Y. (2002) The impact of product-related factors on perceived product safety. *Market Intelligence and Planning,* 20(3): 185–194

Ward, S. C. and Chapman, C. B. (1995) Risk-management perspective on the project. *Lifecycle: International Journal of Project Management,* 13(3): 145–149

Wogalter, M. S., Conzola, V. C. and Smith Jackson, T. L. (2002) Research-based guidelines for warning design and evaluation. *Applied Economics,* 33: 219–230

FURTHER READING

Jerrard, R., Trueman, M. and Newport, R. (eds) (1999) *Managing new product innovation*. (London: Taylor & Francis)

Kleizer, J. A., Halman, J. I. M. and Song, M. (2002) From experience: applying the risk diagnosing methodology. *Journal of Product Innovation Management*, 19: 213–232

Oakley, K. and Leadbetter, K. (2001) *Surfing the long wave: knowledge entrepreneurship in Britain*. (London: Demos)

Von Hippel, E. (2005) *Democratizing innovation*. (Cambridge, MA: MIT Press)

Chapter 6

Design for the strategic repositioning of a sub-supplier

Lisbeth Svengren Holm and Ulla Johansson

INTRODUCTION

Within most industrial sectors, for instance transportation, furniture and tele-communication to name just a few, there are a vast number of sub-suppliers for every part of a company's operation. Many of the sub-suppliers are small and medium-sized enterprises (SMEs), rather anonymous outside their sector. A few of the large component suppliers are very well known. One example is Intel, manufacturer of computer chips, typical commodity products with few possibilities for differentiation. Chips are components consumers neither want to see nor know very much about. Intel, however, managed to create Intel as an ingredient brand name. The computers with an Intel chip have an Intel label, the Intel Inside sticker, on the computer case as a kind of quality guarantee. This kind of branding strategy is rare for most sub-suppliers of components that become parts of a product that might be very well known among customers and con-sumers. How many consumers know who is developing and manufacturing the parts that make up a car, the instrument panel, the chairs, the safety belt, etc.? With the strategy of outsourcing, most large manufacturers have built a network of sub-suppliers for a large part of the product. These sub-suppliers are maybe known within the car industry and among purchasers and those involved in product development but outside this circle very few know anything about them. Many of these sub-suppliers are small or medium-sized and they often work with a small number of customers, especially if they have a very specialised product.

The normal situation for all those SMEs that constitute a large part of a country's industrial sector is that they are not only anonymous but also quite dependent on small numbers of customers. Their role as sub-suppliers could be as strategic partners, developing the products together with their customers, or just as suppliers of a pre-specified product. A study we conducted of Swedish sub-suppliers in plastic and textiles showed that many of these companies have concerns about their dependency on their customers and the vulnerability of this position. The sub-suppliers within the plastic sector especially have very little influence on product development and, for instance, no design development of their own. The sub-suppliers in the textile sector have more design activities of their own and they viewed themselves as more active partners with their customers.

One sector that operates a huge number of sub-suppliers is the transportation sector. In Sweden it is estimated that around 70,000 people are working in small and medium-sized companies in related areas connected to the transportation industry. As Sweden has three major manufacturers within this sector, Volvo, Saab and Scania, their sub-suppliers have grown to a substantial number of companies (around 1,000). These companies are also operating internationally with customers outside Sweden but they are still in a position of dependency on their Swedish customers. If any of the Swedish manufacturers ceased to exist or moved abroad it would have a significant impact on several regions in Sweden.

As these often anonymous, often small companies are quite dependent on their customers they are vulnerable to the changes of their customers, changes over which they have no influence. To survive as suppliers these companies focus on cost and technical development for high quality at reasonable and competitive prices. Some suppliers also manage to become strategic partners to their customers and have joint development projects. Other companies have only a minor role in the customer's product development processes. The latter type of companies especially face a high risk of losing customers in times of outsourcing manufacturing to low-cost countries. In addition to the cost side, the low-cost manufacturers in South-East Asia have technological knowledge that is or is soon at the same level as in the West. This will further enhance the price competition. The general strategy has been to reduce the price competition by emphasising quality and knowledge, but the question is whether this is possible with the development of the Asian competitors. One way of remaining competitive is to outsource manufacturing to Asia, and this has been one way also for sub-suppliers. Another way is to become a larger actor through acquisition and merger. Regardless of this we can still identify that many of these sub-suppliers have a technology-dominant culture where marketing is often equal to sales and less strategic, for instance, in terms of creating a recognisable brand name.

Design is another field that is not well recognised among these technically focused companies, regardless of size. In a study of how design is related to and utilised as a strategic partner to the disciplines of marketing and engineering we selected one sub-supplier with an interesting story of repositioning itself as a strategic actor through design. The aim of the design project was to show the market how two companies merged, the Swedish company Berifors and the

Scottish company TVI, when they were both bought by the American Stoneridge Inc. The means for communicating this merger was to show the result of a joint project at the large industrial fair in Hannover. The result was much better and different from how they had thought it would be. The conceptual product attracted much attention and led to their customers discovering the synergy of their competence. This in turn led to another type of project where the new Stoneridge Electronics became involved earlier in the design process of their customers. Stoneridge could then work with the total solutions instead of just supplying panels according to specified orders.

The authors will present this case study of Stoneridge Electronics and at the end draw some conclusions on the use of design for strategic development. The case is based on interviews with the project manager and two project participants at Stoneridge Electronics in Stockholm, previously Berifors. We also interviewed the external industrial designer from the design company Propeller, also in Stockholm. Although the company case is Stoneridge Electronics, we refer to them as Berifors in the case study, as we have focused on the Swedish part of the company and will present their story only.

THE STONERIDGE ELECTRONICS CASE

Company background

In 1988 some managers working at Ericsson Radio System initiated a management buyout of the car electronics department and took over the operation. The company was called Berifors, and it had enjoyed a good growth rate for many years. The company had its head office with product development, marketing and finance in Stockholm, with about 300 people employed. In Örebro, a city 300 kilometres west of Stockholm, it had its manufacturing plant, with about 180 people employed. The turnover at the beginning of the 2000s was about SEK700 million. In 1998 Berifors was sold to the American Corporation Stoneridge Inc., a global leading manufacturer of advanced electronics within the transportation sector, focusing on heavy transportation vehicles.

Berifors is a typical component supplier of products and services to the automotive, truck, bus, agriculture and off-road industries and the after-market. Its products range from telematics and driver information systems through electronic control units and power distribution centres to multiplex systems and cockpit switch modules. In 1999 Berifors merged with the Scottish company TVI, also a part of Stoneridge Inc., and the merged company was named Stoneridge Electronics. The Scottish company's product is tachographs, and it has an assembly plant in Dundee.

The merger

When the two companies, Berifors and TVI, were about to merge, certain engineers at Berifors suggested that they should start a shared development project. The purpose of this was to get to understand each other and integrate their activities but also to show the market what they could achieve together. The internal integration was important, as it would motivate the personnel towards the merger and maybe encourage them to make further developments.

But external aspects were also important. Certain customers saw Berifors as an electrical component supplier – an identity it did not want to have, as the engineers thought they had a larger capacity than that. An important objective for the new project was to do something that would visually increase the value for both the customer, i.e. the truck manufacturer, and the end user, i.e. the truck driver.

One ambition was therefore to show the market that Berifors and TVI, now one company, could increase the value of their services and the products they sold. In a customer-focused project the car and truck manufacturers specified in detail what they wanted. Hence, both Berifors and TVI were limited and had little influence on the development outside the brief, not the least because of time and cost limitations. Therefore they rarely had an opportunity to communicate and show what they thought they could accomplish. As one of the engineers commented:

> Often when we work with design, future visions, we do it upon a request from the customer. It is often a tough deadline . . . And we have thought . . . we have not really any opportunity to show our customers what we are capable of. So then our discussion with the management aimed at getting a budget for a project where we had this opportunity.

When the merger with TVI was a fact, some of the engineers at Berifors started to discuss with their management how now was the right time to do a project that was outside the routine. Mikael became project manager. From Berifors there were another four engineers and from TVI four engineers assigned to the project.

These two aspects, the internal collaboration and the aim of developing something of greater value for both customers and end users, were part of the first ideas of the development project. They had, however, no idea of the size the project would become – or the strong strategic impact it would have.

The concept project

The idea of the project was well received by both companies. The Swedes and the Scottish partners therefore met in March 2000 in Scotland to discuss what kind of project they should and could carry out. One conclusion was that the Internationale Automobil Ausstellung (IAA) fair in Hannover would be a suitable forum to deliver the project. TVI had participated before, but not Berifors. It would be an ideal opportunity to display not only the standard products but also this new shared product.

Another conclusion was that it was going to be a conceptual project with no 'real customer' of the kind both companies were used to. The purpose was just to show the market what Berifors and TVI could accomplish together, the synergy effects without the normal restrictions. At the same time they would get the experience of working together and getting to understand each other. With September, i.e. seven months ahead, as delivery time there was no talk about *not* having a pressing time schedule. The freedom was the fact that there were no customer specifications that guided or limited the project.

There were no limits to the creativity and ideas, but they realised the need for some guidelines. The first discussions during the spring therefore centred on how to delineate the project. There were some ideas about having three different products for three different segments. One product would be a low-end panel with a simple instrument, a small display and a built-in tachograph. The second one would be a little more advanced, with a tachograph and instrument integrated into one product, including GPS and GSM, etc. The third one would be a colour screen and have a display with everything on the screen. Another idea was to develop three different products: one instrument that was like the ones that exist today, one that showed the next generation, i.e. three to five years ahead, and one that was more visionary, about 10 years ahead. This concept survived for some time, but no decision was taken about exactly what to do. The Scottish partners, however, broadened the discussion and argued that they needed to look at the total needs of a driver in a truck, including styling, functions, and requirements from authorities. During these discussions they considered the need to engage designers who could help them visualise the ideas.

An industrial design company is engaged

Prior to this project Berifors had never commissioned an industrial designer itself but met industrial designers at the customer's site. The proposal was accepted, and Berifors started to look for an industrial design partner. In this case they had no customer so they had to find an industrial designer themselves. In spring 2000, Mikael and one of the design engineers at Berifors, Liselott, spoke to various design companies, and after some searching they finally decided to engage the industrial design company Propeller. They had met Fredrik Magnusson, head of Propeller, before at the truck manufacturer Scania. Mikael knew a little about what Propeller had done for Scania and hence he knew that Propeller had experience in the transportation sector. This was an important factor in their decision. In May 2000 a contract was signed for collaboration in the concept project.

For Berifors this was an investment project, as there was no customer to pay for the costs. Mikael, the project manager, had received a budget of approximately SEK1.5 million (approximately £110,000). In negotiation with Propeller, Berifors agreed to see this as an investment project for themselves. Propeller had a policy of doing conceptual visionary projects with their customers so the project was in tune with this.

In the end the project turned out to cost around SEK4 million; Propeller also invested many more hours than they had calculated. But, according to Mikael, it was worth every penny. The company invested around 3,000 hours, and material and other expenditures were about 25 per cent of the costs. Propeller invested another 1,000 hours on the project, but it was also considered a good investment for Propeller. Mikael commented on the size of the project and the budget:

> Well, we had thought of an instrument with a tachograph and some predefined pictures. It was imagined as an instrument that was part of a panel. But Propeller opened it up into something more and the project became much larger and took on another character.

The meeting between the Swedes and the Scots had broadened the project's frame, but with the involvement of Propeller the scope of the project took another step. Both a broadening and a focusing took place – and many intensive brainstorming meetings around the objectives of the project – before the project team could decide at the end of May upon the final concept that 'everybody felt was right', as they expressed it. It was a new instrument panel with many new features and functions built in.

The idea generation phase took much longer than they had foreseen. Afterwards they realised that it was necessary. The commission to the design company was not very detailed, but it included four key areas:

- research, sketches and ideas
- design work
- refined design work
- final model.

In reality the tasks and work did not occur as they had planned. Some tasks that Berifors thought Propeller would work on were completed in-house and vice versa. When Berifors argued that a solution was not possible, Propeller worked day and night to prove them wrong, etc.

Propeller was quite aware of the character of the conceptual project without an end customer. But, still, Propeller argued that the project team had to clarify who the end customer might be, as otherwise it would be less efficient. There would be many customers at the fair and they had to focus on whom to address. Fredrik, the industrial design team leader, commented:

> Who is visiting the fair, who is going to look at this and what is it they are going to look at? What will they see? You have to start with what message they are going to find. Our whole idea was to visualise the competence of Stoneridge, as they are now called. They had a lot of knowledge, a lot of ideas, but they were very much a component supplier . . . Could we package their technology in a visual way that people could understand?
>
> Their market, the people in this case, is the purchasing people. And then you have to understand what the purchasing people are looking for. Our strategy in this project was to profile Berifors and TVI not as a sub-supplier of components but as experts in their field. Instead of being the last in the supply chain, when all the designs are ready, when everything is developed and the customers call Berifors and ask for the cheapest price for these components . . . This was the scenario we wanted them to get rid of . . . They should be thought of much earlier and they should say 'We are experts on cab communications. Come to us when you need help to develop new systems.'

The ideas that Berifors and TVI had discussed so far, the context in which the products were thought of, were rejected by Propeller. The commission to Propeller was introduced as 'to look at the next generation of clusters'. At Berifors the team had different ideas of both the project content and how to present the ideas at the fair. One idea was a low-budget version of a PowerPoint presentation. Another idea was to make different display cases with different levels of solutions. Propeller discussed this and aimed to understand what this was really about. When Propeller came back to Berifors, Fredrik presented his critical view, arguing: 'We don't believe it will have any impact. If you want to be visible you have to do something bigger!'

Berifors and TVI accepted the critique and started with a new brainstorming phase that took several weeks. Many ideas went back and forth. Mikael remembered this:

> One thing is that there are so many ideas that pop up. The first idea that I really liked was the one where we wanted to do a movie where a person walks up to the truck, takes a seat in the truck cabin and where the person watching the movie stands just behind him or her and watches how the driver starts up and drives – starts first far up in the North with ice and snow and then drives through Stockholm and the big cities and

then finally ends up in Egypt and a completely different culture and climate and partly also a different design of the truck exterior . . . to show that cross system would work in all places . . . But it turned out to be impossible because of both time and costs.

The project soon started to focus on one single product for the truck driver cabin. The time pressure was significant and it increased as summer and the holidays arrived. The fair in September was an absolute deadline. Propeller did a background study of future instruments but realised the project could not be too large. After all the discussions the team had to go for one idea that could be realised, first as a prototype but also then as a real product within a five-year period. Björn, one of the Berifors engineers, recalled:

> When we ended up with this panel, that only was a panel, it felt right at once, even if . . . the day before everything had been so unstructured. So, it was a big step. Then, the whole development, the design. . . it was everything from very futuristic to very, very retro.

When the team decided that they should focus on an instrument panel there were still many discussions and decisions needed about what to include in the panel. Berifors had carried out thorough driver studies earlier and these studies could now be utilised. The knowledge from these studies about the desires and expectations of drivers became a starting point for new solutions. Transferring from earlier market research became a major part of the idea generation and conceptualisation process.

The cross system is born

After the first 'wild ideas' there was a focus on the information that the driver needed at different points on the route and during driving. Propeller undertook some functional and ergonomic studies to identify risks and possibilities. At the same time they brainstormed freely on how to communicate information. The designers showed the engineers possibilities that do not exist in today's trucks. Fredrik explained:

> We started by saying 'How do we tell the driver that he is driving too fast? One way could be that it starts to smell like something is burning and . . .' Berifors looked at us as if we were crazy. But sometimes you have to go very far to find solutions . . . The GPS you have today, with a small display, that is placed in the mid-bracket and there is an arrow that points in the direction you should go . . . It's really dangerous, because people stare at the arrow instead of the road . . . I think we could have

vibrations under the left leg in the chair, or knock at your left shoulder or something like that . . . To find new ways . . . But none of these ideas were realised. But we have to start far away to get this far, and then we started to visualise and sketch these ideas, present them to Berifors, get new comments, go back and continue to sketch. There were a lot. Meeting, presentations, discussing ideas, go back, sketch again, etc. Until we started to find something that they felt they could stand for but that was a step far enough into the future. That's what the project looked like at the beginning . . . A lot of sketches and discussions.

The discussion soon also started to include the single driver's need for other kinds of information, like planning the route, times, contacts with other truck drivers, etc. The idea of the project of integrating the instrumentation from Berifors and the tachograph from TVI was important. The designers contributed with sketches, but the engineers at Berifors also made sketches, which were discussed and commented on by the designers. The project team met at Berifors but also several times at Propeller's studios. The atmosphere was described as open and without prestige constraints, with a flow of ideas that were openly discussed.

The ideas around how to communicate information soon led to a new integrated instrument panel. Most importantly there were two functions that were radically new. One was a joystick as gearing tool and the other was a new concept for measuring functions. Fredrik talked about the ideas that led to the solution of a joystick:

> Having a vibrating chair was of course not a clever solution, as Berifors is not a chair manufacturer, so we had to focus. A lot of the interaction we develop is based upon a geometric interface. You get information on a display and you are supposed to react to that; you get a new message and you react to that. But it means you have to look at the display. Human beings are very good at remembering physical positions. Regardless of the mess on your desk, for instance, you remember quite well in which pile you will find the important paper. And physical positions are something that people are good at memorising . . . An interface in a truck: can we find an interface where you don't have to look? . . . There is one interface that is close by and that is the gear stick. The gear stick is physical, tactile. Very few drivers have to look down at the gear stick and wonder where the next one is positioned. So we wanted to have something similar. It was then we started to build the joystick . . . instead of having menus or chapters in the interface, like a mobile phone, we had physical positions. Up to the right we had everything that had to do with the office functions . . . down to the left everything that had to do with

the truck, down to the right everything to do with navigation, and then within these positions we could navigate sideways, upwards, etc. So, when I know that my mails are on Office, up to the right, two steps sideways, there are all my mails. When I want to know where a map is, I press down to the left, put pressure sideways . . . you create a mental picture of a tree.

The idea was well received at Berifors, and they started to put it into effect. But problems soon occurred. The joystick manufacturer was not as enthusiastic. It claimed it was not possible to make a joystick with 16 positions, i.e. four positions with four positions in each. Berifors suggested that Propeller should make buttons instead. But the designers did not give up their joystick idea:

We felt that, no, we could not . . . it would be too much of a compromise. But then we were forced to say . . . to become good enough you have to prove your case; sometimes you find yourself in that situation. And then the question is: is it a bad solution only because the joystick manufacturer cannot do it? Or is it such a good design solution that we have to manage to make it ourselves?

We locked a bunch of designers into a room overnight and said 'You are not allowed to come out before it works.' And we really built a mechanical joystick that worked. And this is the way it is. Sometimes you just have to take this and ignore the budget, because the idea is so good and you have to do it although people say no. Then we showed that a bunch of designers could manage to build it like this, suddenly.

It was probably not as simple as first thought. According to Fredrik it took three nights before the problems were solved and they could get a result that they could present to the project team:

And once you have done it . . . then people start to say 'Ah, it worked, oh, very good.' And this interface that we had done, it has become so intuitive that people come up to this, grab the joystick and understand immediately how it works. And it is not that you have to ask 15 other people 'How do you programme this?' People took it, grabbed it and . . . OK, I shall draw it like this, because it is visible if you draw it; you can see what happens on the screen.

Although the project had no defined customer, the concept should still appeal to different types of drivers and purchasers. Although the concept should stand out from the crowd, it should also be neutral so as to fit different customers' truck environments. Fredrik thought they had managed to achieve this:

This was one of the reasons for choosing this. We also need to be able to show business value in the solution. If it looks different enough it sticks out. It doesn't matter how good the solution is if people don't notice it.

Another important part of the concept was to find a good solution to how to explore the joystick and ingrate it with all the measuring functions that were needed for a truck. All truck manufacturers have a modular system for different meters. There are many different meters, with the result that every usage has special meters. The driver needs a lot of information about the truck's technical functions. The solution to this has been to have different measuring meters for each function. The result is a panel crowded with meters.

One idea that came up in this project was to have a neutral meter that was analogue in the middle, but with a digital information frame. Instead of showing all information at the same time, the driver could through the joystick choose a position in the cross selection and there get a graphic sheet with different parts of the information, for instance fuel, oil pressure, braking pressure, etc. In this position the driver can get more information through the joystick. It is then the software that is updated, but the hardware remains the same. You can therefore have a standard cluster, which is much cheaper for all truck manufacturers. Fredrik was well aware of this:

> Instead of the truck having nine different meters here and there . . . it is almost a handmade panel in every truck. It is very expensive. We said that instead we will do four neutral meters that have max/min and empty/full, or whatever.

Figure 6.1 *The instrument cluster features the traditional speedometer, revolution counter and four gauges, which are designed as multimeters. Each multimeter function is freely configurable by the driver and indicated by a symbol on the display. By adding gauges on the display more information, like the temperature of the power train or cargo conditions, can be monitored if needed. Standard warning lamps are placed in the driver's viewing area on the upper side of the instrument cluster. When illuminated, the lamps appear three-dimensional for excellent readability*

Figure 6.2 *The drivercard provides the storage capabilities required by law for saving driver information over a rolling 28-day period. To enhance convenience and efficiency, the personal driver ID taken from the drivercard can be used to activate personal driver settings of the cross system when put in place*

Figure 6.3 *The display is organised in a central and peripheral information area. The peripheral area displays more basic information and the selected function of the multimeters, which are located next to the display. The central information area organises detailed information in four groups about driver, vehicle, cargo and route. Each information group is accessed by the cross selector*

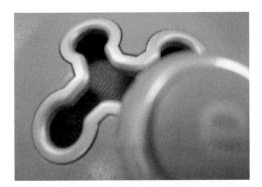

Figure 6.4 *The cross selector can be moved by gear shifting, as in one of the four possible positions corresponding to the different information groups. In each position the stick can be moved slightly up, down, left and right, and a click button placed on top of the cross selector allows further selection. Utilising built-in human muscle memory, the cross selector ensures minimised distraction from traffic when selecting desired information*

Many of the solutions were new and not always easy to realise. The electronics were also a challenge. They needed to fit into the physical models. Berifors's engineers allocated considerable time to fit the models that Propeller made for the electronics. Although everybody in the team was enthusiastic about the ideas, they certainly needed a prototype that worked at the fair. After the holidays, with a few weeks to go, the problem to get the joystick and the software to function together was not resolved. Everybody wanted to succeed and they worked continuously until the last minute. Even once they arrived at the fair they continued to work on some of the details. The last work on the prototype was done the night before the fair opened. But in the end they made it.

When asked about the stress and the chaos, Björn commented: 'No, it was not chaotic, but . . . one never felt stressed . . . a lot to do, but not . . . It was at the end very intensive. I never thought we would not make it in time. You always do.'

A successful product launch

The key stakeholders that we interviewed at Berifors seemed to collectively agree that the cross system was a huge success and that the goal they had with the project was accomplished. Berifors and TVI, now Stoneridge Electronics, got a lot of attention at the fair. The cross system concept has had an influence on their relationship with their customers and the projects they have received afterwards. Mikael described it as follows:

> What we know is that we have received certain important business since then. We cannot directly see, but we know that they have seen . . . and we have got a lot of response . . . The project cross system gave us a closer dialogue with the customers and we get involved earlier in the telematic part where we have not been before. We had not done that in customer projects before.

At Berifors they could see that the collaboration with the design company in this project discovered what they experienced as the right strategy for a dialogue with their customers. They were also capable of making the right judgement about what the customers wanted to have. The collaboration with the designers to find the right level for communication with the customers was, according to the project manager, Mikael, important: 'I believe that, physically, the project would have been much smaller. If we had stopped and not used their support as much as we did we would not have got this complete product.'

Björn reflected upon what the project meant and whether it has had any impact on later projects:

It was of course very difficult . . . partly during the development phase, partly the way we worked, the contacts it gave both externally, with Propeller, and internally, most of all with TVI, that has been very valuable. Then the reactions we got at the fair were also very valuable. They were all positive. I got no negative reactions. Then some can say 'I don't like the linear meters, or the colours' or something like that. But that we found the right level feels like the big win, that we got the right information in the display, the right information in the instrument as such, the right size . . . we have one of the largest competitors – or colleagues – in Germany, who also have big display cases . . . They also had similar systems. They had a very, very futuristic design, more of a space shuttle and functions . . . just as a comparison between the system, and a lot of entertainment, etc. It looked more like a space capsule . . . The reaction we got from customers was 'What a relief that you don't have those parts which do not belong.' Because there is nobody in this industry who is willing to pay for those production costs. Road carriers do not buy TV games for their drivers. They buy a truck that is cost-efficient, maybe also comfortable, but as cheap as possible and the most efficient. That's what's important . . . it is easier to communicate with our customers, partly to show that we have done a thing like this ourselves, and we have shown all our ideas to everybody and got this information in return. That's what I believe is important. That's what we really got out of it.

Besides the importance the project had for the relationship with their customers it was also important that Berifors and TVI, now one company, Stoneridge Electronics, got to understand each other internally.

REFLECTIONS ON THE STONERIDGE CASE STUDY

The collaboration between Stoneridge Electronics and Propeller has continued since the cross system project but now in customer projects. The competence that the industrial designers have is appreciated by the engineers at Berifors:

I personally found it very stimulating to work with them. Different perspectives met. I draw squares and straight lines. I cannot do anything different. If I discuss with a colleague I automatically think economically. Do we have time to do it? Do the customers want it? Do we need to invest in a new thing to make it? It becomes more basic and simple and cheap. It is as if the basic questions are on a different level . . . but it is not certain that the customers want it like that. The customer maybe wants something completely different if he can see it. They [Propeller] are very intrepid. They saw no limitations – only possibilities. It sounds like a cliché but it fits them well, I believe. It was something else as well. Their creativity and curiosity. They threw themselves headlong into the project . . . We see a lot of mass production – but they only see one piece of product and its possibilities . . . We are used to thinking in terms of 'Is there enough material, etc.?' That's our thing. But the mix between them and us . . . it was very stimulating.

One aspect of the collaboration was the difference of the environment and facilities between the engineering and the design company. Mikael commented on this as a positive part of the collaboration: 'I remember how it was to visit their office. With all the coloured pens and brushes and . . . yes, it was quite a different environment compared to ours.'

Björn noted the difference in the physical rooms for building models. Berifors has small rooms for doing details, whereas Propeller has a large room for painting and building models. A design company often has workshops and the possibility of making different types of models and prototypes. The larger design companies can make quite big models, which is not always the case for their customers, who often have no manufacturing of their own in-house. As CAD modelling dominates, most companies do not build their own physical models and there is also no need to have the equipment and facilities to do this. But for the design company the physical models are more part of their work and an important communication device. Therefore the big workshop is an important part of their operations.

The role of the project manager is to take responsibility for the accomplishment of the project, deadlines and budget. To keep the deadline was probably the most crucial issue in this project. The budget was, as mentioned before, overspent by quite a bit. To encourage people in the project to keep deadlines was not the difficult part in this project. Everybody knew about the deadline and worked day and night to get ready in time. The problem for the project manager was rather to force the people to go home to have some rest and see their families. 'It was a great fun. It was enormously stimulating. I think everybody felt like that', concluded Mikael.

Doing the impossible and having challenges that you meet are probably part of all successful projects. Even if you cannot do this kind of project all the time, it is probably quite a stimulating strategy every now and then to have this kind of visionary, challenging project and to create something.

For many sub-suppliers the transformation to a problem solver and being viewed as an expert and partner requires a new identity. This is often a transformation that needs external support and is what many consultants do, not least management consultants. But many sub-suppliers are technical experts and see themselves as such. They do not change the market, or the product, but they need to package their knowledge in a different way if they want to make the transformation, i.e. to become a problem solver or strategic partner in the customer's product development process. In this chapter the authors have argued that designers are excellent partners for these kinds of technical companies. Industrial designers have the technical and technological understanding without being the experts. They are visionary and strategic thinkers who can force and inspire the engineers to think in a more strategic and visionary way.

REVIEW QUESTIONS

1 How could design be effectively used within the extended supply chain network in the pursuit of creative product development?

2 How could the supply chain partners contribute their specialist knowledge to solve particular complex problems in the NPD process?

3 The process of innovation is often regarded as a complex activity; where do you see the role of design within this process?

4 Small and medium-sized enterprises encounter particular problems throughout the process of new product development; what problems do you think they could be?

5 How would you define an SME? What other definitions are used to define SMEs? Why is it so difficult to accurately establish a generic definition?

6 How would you promote the value and benefits of design to a small enterprise operating in difficult and dynamic marketplaces?

7 What phase of new product development do you consider the most crucial to the success of the final product?

8 The success of NPD relies on the involvement of key stakeholders; how would you identify and embrace stakeholders within the design process?

9 How important is user feedback on the performance and benefits of new product introductions?

10 How can this often complex and contradictory information be translated into subsequent design projects?

PROJECT QUESTIONS

1   What distinct problems did Berifors encounter in delineating project parameters at the initial stages of the NPD programme? Why is it important to clearly identify and articulate these to the design team?
2   Berifors had never commissioned an industrial design team before; what criteria would you suggest in selecting the most appropriate design partner?
3   In the development of the joystick concept, the designers encountered difficult technical problems; as a design manager what course of action would you have recommended to surmount these problems?
4   Berifors were successful in developing the unique 'cross system' concept through collaboration with their supply chain partners; how was design leveraged within this collaborative partnership?
5   The design team relied heavily upon the use of prototype models throughout product design and development; what are the drawbacks and benefits of this traditional approach?

FURTHER READING

Aaker, D. A. and Shansby, J. G. (1982) Positioning your product. *Business Horizons,* 25(3): 56–62

Abell, D. F. (1980) *Defining the business: the starting point of strategic planning.* (Englewood Cliffs, NJ, and London: Prentice Hall)

Calderon, H., Cervera, A. and Molla, A. (1997) Brand assessment: a key element of marketing strategy. *Journal of Product and Brand Management,* 6: 293

Collis, D. J. and Montgomery, C. A. (1995) Competing on resources: strategy in the 1990's. *Harvard Business Review,* 73: 118

Myers, J. H. (1976) Benefit structure analysis: a new tool for product planning. *Journal of Marketing,* 40

Park, C. W. and Moon, B. J. (2003) The relationship between product involvement and product knowledge: moderating roles of product type and product knowledge type. *Psychology and Marketing,* 20: 977

Zeithaml, V. A., Berry, L. L. and Parasuraman, A. (1990) *Delivering quality service: balancing customer perceptions and expectations.* (New York and London: Free Press/Collier Macmillan)

Chapter 7

Adopting a user-centred approach to designing against crime

David Hands and Robert Jerrard

INTRODUCTION

Designing out crime presents many complex challenges for the design development team. These may include: access to specialist crime prevention knowledge; and utilisation of appropriate tools and techniques to enable crime 'misuse' scenarios within the front-end stages (in particular during the design 'briefing' stages, which are the primary focus of this chapter) and the design concept development and production/construction phases.

Furthermore, the complexity of attendant design issues related to crime requires access to current research and data, which are often either unavailable or difficult to obtain. This account is an exploration as to how the design manager can facilitate and focus the design development team to develop a crime-'aware' consciousness at the initial stages of the design briefing process. It discusses how designing against crime is an emergent issue within design and how the designer can contribute valuable skills and approaches to reducing crime throughout the development programme. This account then provides two complementary case studies focusing upon Cityspace/Adshel and Parksafe, Derby, UK, discussing how the design manager was central to the successful development of a new product/service that embodied robust yet elegant design against crime thinking.

DESIGNING AGAINST CRIME: AN EMERGENT ISSUE

Designing against crime has featured highly in the disciplines of spatial design and urban planning. Architects and planners have become more understanding of the public's perceived fear of crime and started to develop new ways of addressing these issues in the design programme. Although the British Crime Survey (Home Office 2002) identifies a downward trend in crime activity, the public's perception of crime and fear of crime are high. A BBC News feature (BBC News 2004a) attempted to explain this phenomenon by suggesting that 'crimes are now being committed in more affluent areas . . . making the crimes more visible'. It further added that, 'if the media report even a small number of cases, readers may see themselves as being indirect victims'.

Public transport and travel is another area that has received considerable attention in reducing criminal activity through a more enlightened approach to designing out crime. Mature industries such as the automotive manufacturing sector have taken crime prevention into account, focusing heavily on securing their vehicles or making it harder to steal from the vehicles. Vehicle crime accounts for just less than one-fifth of all crime recorded by the police (Home Office 2002). Although the number of crimes has been falling steadily since 1992, around 340,000 vehicles are still stolen every year (HOCD 2001).

The role of design and designers can make an effective contribution to reducing the impact of crime. Designing against crime can be utilised throughout many different contexts, which include the built environment, product design, packaging design, new media and textiles.

Crime reduction thinking is already considered in certain disciplines of design, in particular the built environment – where crime reduction is an integral part of the design process. Environmental design, most notably architecture, can significantly contribute to situational crime prevention. Situational crime prevention (SCP) has developed considerably since the late 1970s, in a further attempt to minimise the occurrence of crime. SCP is based on the premise that crime is context-specific, predominantly opportunist in nature and influenced by the predisposition of the offender. To reduce opportunist crime, measures can be taken to reduce the likelihood of success for the criminal by implementing 'control' measures within a given situation.

Situational crime prevention measures are predominantly applied to the built environment, in particular to reduce the likelihood of burglary, vandalism and shoplifting. SCP can apply to every kind of crime, not just to 'opportunistic' or acquisitive property offences; there are examples of successful applications to more calculated or deeply motivated crimes, as well as ones committed by hardened offenders, e.g. hijacking, homicide and sexual harassment (Ekblom 1999).

Crime prevention features are most often considered retrospectively, applied to both products and built environments after the event of crime, rather than at the initial stages of their design development. Consequently, crime prevention attributes are often 'added on' or considered as an afterthought rather than 'embedded' within the product or system at the initial stages. To overcome this perception of thinking in relation to crime, designers need to view the way that they develop design proposals from an alternative perspective. This will involve looking at the final design as 'misuser-unfriendly' as opposed to 'user-friendly', thus requiring a paradigm shift in designers' understanding and involvement in the way that they identify and solve design problems.

Ekblom and Tilley (2000) argue that: 'We must start "thinking thief", anticipating criminals' actions, researching the tools, knowledge and skills available to them now and in the near future and incorporating attack-testing into the design process.' Changing the designers' approach to the way that they design, taking into account crime-resistant measures at the initial stages of the design programme, requires an understanding of how the final product or environment could be misused by the criminal (Design Policy Partnership 2002). Designers are required to take fully into account not only the user's experience of the product but also how the product could be misused or abused in support of criminal activity or be a target of crime itself. Neglecting to do this could result in the failure of designers to anticipate the vulnerability of their product to crime.

THE IMPACT OF CRIME: TRENDS AND PERCEPTIONS

The most recent and sophisticated analysis of crime in England and Wales puts the total annual cost at a staggering £60 billion, with, on average, burglaries costing £2,300 each, vehicle thefts £4,700, and robberies £5,000 (Brand and Price 2000). Although recorded crime has witnessed a slight decrease, more than half of the population in England and Wales considers crime as the number one problem facing the country (ICPC 1997). The British Crime Survey (Home Office 2000) shows a fall between 1997 and 1999 in nearly all the offences it measures. Burglary fell by 21 per cent and vehicle-related theft by 15 per cent. Robbery increased by 14 per cent and theft from the person by 4 per cent. If one measures the importance of property offences in terms of value, rather than the quantity of incidents, fraud is of far greater significance. By contrast, the combined costs of prolific offences of 'auto-crime' and burglary for 1990 were estimated by the Association of British Insurers to be just under £1.3 billion (Maguire 1997).

Although statistics from the 2000 British Crime Survey (Home Office 2000) report highlight a downturn in incidents of recorded crime, to fully understand its effects on society as a whole we would need to move beyond mere statistics. The perception of crime is heightened by high-profile court cases in the media having a profound effect on society at large.

The general public's concern about crime in the 2000 British Crime Survey (Home Office 2000) highlighted the following key issues:

- They are pessimistic about the problem of crime, with over one-third believing that national crime levels had risen considerably.
- A substantial minority (29 per cent) thought that it was likely that they would have their vehicle stolen in the next year; that they would have items (such as

141

a radio, camera, bags, etc.) stolen from a car (32 per cent); or that they would have their home burgled (20 per cent). One-tenth thought it was likely that they would be a victim of mugging or attacked by a stranger, although in reality the average risks of victimisation are far lower.

- Around one-fifth of people were 'very worried' about burglary, car crime, mugging, and physical attack by a stranger and rape.
- Concern about crime will be linked both to people's beliefs about their chances of being victimised and to what they feel about the consequences of victimisation. Levels of worry are higher among those living in high crime areas, recent victims of crime, those who consider it likely they will be victimised and those who are socially or economically vulnerable (e.g. the elderly or single mothers).

The level of anxiety of being a victim of crime can range from mild concern through to high anxiety. The survey also highlighted that:

- 8 per cent of adults in the UK say that they never walk in their local areas after dark, at least in part because of the fear of attack. Amongst the elderly and women this figure rises to 19 per cent.
- 13 per cent are 'very' or 'fairly' worried about their home being burgled all or most of the time.
- 6 per cent consider that the fear of crime greatly impacts on their quality of life, slightly more than those (4 per cent) who said the same about crime itself.

DESIGNING AGAINST CRIME IN THE BUILT ENVIRONMENT

Crime prevention through environmental design (CPTED) is a well-recognised and suitably mature approach to reducing the opportunity for crime under the broader framework of situational crime prevention (SCP). McKay (1996) argues that 'it is defined as a proactive crime prevention technique in which proper design and effective use of a building and its surroundings leads to a reduction in crime as well as an improvement in the quality of life'. Ekblom and Tilley (1998) add that 'offenders can only exploit potential crime opportunities if they have the resources to take advantage of them', then suggesting that 'situational crime prevention must also consider offender resources and their distribution and social-technical change'.

CPTED aims to reduce the opportunity for crime by focusing on the specific contextual situation as opposed to hardening the crime target or product; in essence it is a context-specific approach to crime reduction. Ekblom (1991) details how situational crime prevention rests on the observation that people's behaviour is not influenced simply by their fundamental personality, but by the physical and social situation they find themselves in at a given moment in time, for a crime to happen. By its very nature, environmental design is a broad, multi-disciplinary aspect of design practice, requiring the input of architects, planners, statutory and legal professionals, and key stakeholders in the use and functioning of the designed space. Hence, CPTED requires the close involvement and collaboration of all the various stakeholders for it to be effective in reducing the opportunities for crime (McKay 1996). Owing to the flexibility of CPTED principles, they may be embedded into the design early within the design pro-gramme or, alternatively, applied retrospectively after the design has been com-pleted. Crowe (1991) defines the distinction between CPTED principles and commonplace crime reduction techniques, suggesting that:

> where CPTED differs from traditional target hardening strategies is that the techniques employed seek to use environmental factors to affect the perceptions of all users of a given space – addressing not only the opportunity for the crime but also perceptions of fear on the part of those who may otherwise be victims.

CPTED draws heavily on behavioural psychology, with its key strategies and concepts taking advantage of the relationships between people and their immedi-ate environment. Crowe (1991) further explains this relationship by highlighting the 'softer' side of CPTED, arguing that:

> the way we react to an environment is more often than not determined by the cues we are picking up from that environment. Those things which make normal or legitimate users of a space feel safe (such as good lighting) make abnormal or illegitimate users of the same space feel unsafe in pursuing undesirable behaviours (such as stealing from motor vehicles).

CPTED: MECHANISMS AND APPLICATIONS

Secured by Design (SBD) is an accreditation scheme based upon CPTED principles intended to reduce criminal activity in the built environment. The key designed elements it advocates in the early planning stages are:

- Defensible space: positioning and detailing of boundary treatments, thus preventing unauthorised access. Boundaries will provide the first line of defence in securing the development from both the opportunist and the dedicated criminal.

- Improved surveillance: natural surveillance is enhanced, thus allowing a high degree of 'social control' to minimise criminal activity. The guidelines argue that 'optimum natural surveillance should be incorporated, whereby residents can see and be seen'.

- Promotion of territoriality: designing in a clear demarcation between public and private space. Rachel Armitage (2000) talks about territoriality in the context that, 'if space has a clearly defined ownership, purpose and role, it is evident to residents within the neighbourhood who should and more importantly who should not be in a given area'.

- Community interaction: by creating a sense of community through mixed-use developments encouraging social interaction and a human scale in the architecture, the community will exercise a high degree of control over their environment.

- Circulation management: reducing the number of 'unnecessary' footpaths and access points within the development. Armitage (2000) argues that 'through routes and footpaths provide the opportunity for offenders to attach to an area for criminal intent and purposes'.

The following are typical examples where CPTED principles are often applied:

- hospitals
- schools and colleges
- public transport networks
- vehicle parks
- residential, commercial and industrial developments
- hotels, bars and restaurants
- city centre developments.

DESIGN BRIEFING: AN OVERVIEW

The design brief acts as a central point of reference from which dialogue and the sharing of values can depart, and to provide a firm basis for all subsequent design decisions within and throughout the design programme (Philips 2004). The design brief is to get everyone started with a common understanding of what is to be accomplished. It gives direction and provides clarity to designers as well as to clients. According to the AIGA (2001), 'a brief can be as valuable internally as it is externally'.

Often briefing encapsulates the findings and conclusions of a whole process that precede the creation, review and approval of the document. When referring to the design management process, Olson *et al.* (2000) describe the three discrete steps within briefing:

- Step 1: Clearly articulate the firm's competitive strategy to designers and design managers.
- Step 2: Develop a detailed understanding of the design requirements inherent in the adopted competitive strategy.
- Step 3: Ensure open lines of communication among the design group and other functional units.

Furthermore, they highlight that the review of the design brief and the assessment of design performance will depend on whether the client is briefing in-house or outsourced designers. Contrasting with the cases in which the company is briefing in-house designers familiarised with the company's business and overall strategy, when companies contract out their design work and no single design group is typically retained the review of design briefs and the assessment of design performance will be, by necessity, an ongoing activity (Olson *et al.* 2000).

In an ideal situation, the client is aware of the value of discussing the brief with the designers or designers' representatives and so incorporates designers into the group at the initial stages of the design programme. However, on a day-to-day basis, this practice is often the exception rather than the norm among the briefing makers. In general, once briefing is considered finished, it is often given to the design team to act upon (Topalian 1994).

Depending on many factors, the designer's response can vary. For instance, it could be: 'Start right away generating the design solution.' This may be the case for a *small* project, or a typical design competition, which does not allow the design firm to thoroughly understand its client in order to give valid advice. It could be the case that, to protect their investment in the design competition, the competing design firms will play it safe, not questioning the brief and simply providing the client with what it is expecting. When discussing how to get creative results, the AIGA highlight (2001) that design competitions, in which the client receives artwork at a cost below market value, owns the intellectual or creative property and can exploit the work without the involvement of its creator, are a threat to the designer, the client and the profession. 'The designer gives up creative property without a fair level of control or compensation. The client fails to get the full benefit of the designer's talent and guidance. The profession is misrepresented, indeed compromised, by speculative commercial art.'

The Design Council (2002) suggests 'an outline brief can be developed [from the beginning or] further with the designer to help form a common understanding of objectives throughout the project'. Alternatively, the process of debriefing the client is extremely important for the designer, who can often complete or even discuss the information contained in the briefing.

As the Italian designer Michele DeLucchi learned, even the perfect translation of a client's brief cannot guarantee that designer and client mean the same things

145

when they talk about design and its subtle qualities. So he always produces a *contrabrief* in response to the owner's brief, to clarify his terms and his vision.

The Design Council suggests that the brief for a designer should be a comprehensive document. It should contain all of the information a designer needs to fulfil the design objectives of the project. The AIGA (2001) adds that 'the brief should not tell the designers how to do the work'. To decide what makes sense in terms of how to structure the brief is a process of thinking, not just completing a standardised form.

Cooper and Press (1995) describe a design brief as something 'that defines the nature of the problem to be solved', whilst Ken Allinson (1998) describes it as 'relating to problem framing and problem finding as opposed to problem solving'. Hymans (2001) succinctly argues that 'systematic briefing defines the problem to which design is the answer'. In a report prepared by Frank Duffy for the Construction Industry Board (1997), *Briefing the team*, briefing is defined as: 'the process by which a client informs others of his or her needs, aspirations and desires, either formally or informally and a brief is a formal document which sets out a client's requirements in detail'. Michael Slade (1990) talks about how quick decisions early on prior to briefing can actually jeopardise new projects, offering advice to overcome the common pitfalls in pre-project activity. He argues that:

> An attempt in instant solutions often places the projects team in a false position. Either the initial response is anodyne – key problems have not been exposed, but everyone is happy. Or the response does not meet with approval and inevitably more detailed requirements begin to emerge from the subsequent debate. Especially in this latter case, valuable credibility is lost and the project begins to fall in the classic pattern of continually moving goalposts.

CASE STUDY 1: CITYSPACE/ADSHEL

This section of the chapter focuses on the design of the Adshel I+ information terminal. It discusses how the design brief provided a focal point for discussion between Cityspace/Adshel and the design consultancy PSD. Through lengthy iteration and testing, the design brief developed from an initial statement of aims to a fully detailed document outlining a large variety of potential design interventions that would enable the final designed product to be able to withstand criminal misuse within a public environment. After the first-generation product entered the marketplace, Cityspace/Adshel developed a crime-focused strategy that embedded crime reduction thinking into all aspects of new product development.

> Our key driver is to have our kiosk usable the maximum period of time, so that it is always on and always working. Crime obviously prevents us doing that. It is one of the things that prevent us doing it, so it is a key driver for us. Business period considerations and potential rules for company focusing on DAC example – to gain competitive advantage but also to protect our brand is the biggest one here.
>
> (Peter Quinlan, Design Manager, Cityspace/Adshel)

The research was the result of three in-depth interviews in 2004 with Peter Quinlan, Design Manager at Cityspace/Adshel, and two interviews with Roger Crabtree at Wood and Wood in 2004. (*Note:* Roger Crabtree was the lead designer along with Barry Jenkins at PSD who worked on the first generation of the Adshel I+ information terminal; since restructuring at PSD, Roger Crabtree is now Design Director at Wood and Wood.) An interview was conducted in 2004 with Michael Thomas at Buxton Wall McPeak, who was one of the original investigators for the first pilot case study in 1999. Specialist literature was consulted which included: the Design against Crime report (2000) to the Home Office; a research paper (Press *et al.* 2001) discussing findings from the initial research investigation into the Adshel I+ information terminal; and an unpublished report (Learmount 1999) to the Home Office compiled by the Judge Institute of Management Studies, Cambridge University.

Company history

Cityspace/Adshel has been installing street furniture for many years, considering itself to be the leading world brand in the market, operating over 3,000 street furniture agreements with municipalities in 20 countries. This is an electronic service that provides free, up-to-date, interactive information on towns and cities in a visual and attractive format, with touch-screen technology and attractive graphics, combining editorial information with video, music, voice-over and maps. In operation since 1997, I+ has proved successful in cities across the UK and abroad. As each city has different needs and issues to address, each I+ network is implemented in close consultation with the municipal authority to provide a solution tailored to the local area (Adshel 2004).

Table 7.1 provides a brief summary of I+ applications within different areas of the UK.

Whereas traditional Adshel products were prone to vandalism, the I+ would also be vulnerable to theft owing to its housing a PC and other items of electronic equipment. PSD were appointed to redesign the first-generation Adshel I+ with these considerations in mind. Roger Crabtree explains:

> The brief that we worked up with Cityspace was formed with everything we'd known and learned from the first kiosk. We were looking to design

Table 7.1 *I+* applications in the UK

Area	Description
Bristol, UK	Bristol City Council wanted to improve the quality of visitors' experience in terms of both information and direction around the city centre. This was achieved through the Legible City Initiative, which links together the diverse parts of the city with a flow of consistently designed information. The initiative provides the city with a clear identity, reinforces the character of individual neighbourhoods and encourages more people to use public transport. As a key part of the scheme, the city-wide network of I+ points provides information at strategic locations around Bristol, putting the needs of the user first.
Knowsley, UK	The local authority is one of the UK's leaders in integrating technology and service provision. The I+ network provides an integrated solution, assisting the council with its social inclusion agenda, helping to bridge the digital divide and supporting local employment initiatives. Utilising Knowsley's existing high-speed telecommunications infrastructure, the I+ network delivers a number of innovative solutions developed in consultation with the municipal authority, including a dedicated housing repair system, allowing residents of local government housing to report any problem directly to the authority, making services more efficient and highly accessible.
Islington, UK	In Islington the municipality had a requirement to provide its citizens with greater exposure to digital technology and to make its services more accessible to residents and businesses in the area. In consultation with the municipality, the StreetScene application was developed, allowing residents to report problems directly to the relevant council department. With the ability to report problems with waste collection, faulty streetlights, broken pavements and other general environmental issues, Islington residents have been brought closer to the municipality, allowing services to be more efficient and relevant and the council to be more responsive to the needs of the residents. The I+ infrastructure is a public demonstration of the council's ongoing commitment to bringing e-government electronic services to all of its residents. With an I+ network deployed in areas of high pedestrian usage, the number of residents contacting the municipality leapt when the StreetScene application was installed, demonstrating how I+ empowers residents to interface simply and directly with their local authority.

Source: Adapted from Adshel (2004)

out all those problem areas and we're looking to design in all those desirables, such as ease of maintenance on the street, ease of repair on the street, ease of installation, all of which have come out of years of experience. So, we have now agreed these very challenging terms and conditions, and through and across the table discussion, in terms of confirming the brief, we were able to listen to clients who say 'I would like a high level of modularity', for example, or 'I would like, across the product, interface panels to be interchangeable so that I can come along and I can change a panel and put a replacement panel working interface, even replace it with a different interface and I can do that very quickly and very simply.'

Key briefing activities

In order to identify and solve the many complex safety and crime issues with the second-generation I+ information terminal, he developed a pro forma that assisted the design briefing phases. Table 7.2 is an extract from the V4 Scope, a software tool developed within Cityspace to enable and guide the process of briefing.

Peter Quinlan directed the design team, asking them to envision many different scenarios of potential misuse to the product, in terms of how the unit could be vandalised, tampered with and broken into, and how internal components could be removed. The design team were asked to consider improving significant aspects of the products, including strengthening the area around the monitor and removing spaces which could be used to conceal bombs or allow the accumulation of litter underneath. The door was positioned at the back of the unit, with the lock interface being located inside the shell to prevent it from being prised open. At the same time, feedback was gained from a variety of stakeholders for the units, which gave the design team unique insights into maintenance and security issues learned from the first-generation units deployed in the public sphere. Peter Quinlan adds:

> We go out to the kiosks twice a week to clean them, so we're getting feedback then. We'll get feedback from the local authority, because we deploy all our kiosks in conjunction with the local authority, so they have a vested interest, so their staff will call back. Within the Adshel Group, there's a hotline number, and any Adshel employee is responsible if they see any damage to any Adshel product, including the kiosks . . . But if they see any damage, they are obliged to phone in . . . Adshel are extremely good at this and very fast and they do our maintenance as well. They tend to respond; their first call is a sensitive issue – so is there broken glass, get it cleaned, get it safe, get the damaged product removed from site, that's their real urgency and they've got a guarantee that they'll do it within 24 hours . . . We get feedback from our engineers, the actual cleaners, the council, so we are pretty aware, but not always. People . . . we do get a fair amount of feedback from our users; people do develop a little bit of loyalty to our kiosks and tend to possess them. I've often spoken to users who refer to it as 'my kiosk'.

Table 7.2 The V4 Scope

Item	v. final (unviable)	v. final (difficulty – 1: low)
Feeling of enclosure/privacy	X	
Interchangeable modules (I+ RTI, ticketing, 2nd I+, 2nd screen, etc.) within single expandable modular frame	X	
Screen faces any direction	X	
No obvious front, back or sides	X	
No legs	X	
Increased stability	X	
Disabled access	X	
Screen cover (sunlight)	X	
Ticketing	X	
Simplified curve work (remove curved interfaces)		3
No sharp returns (hard to form)		3
No bespoke manufacturing tools required		3
17- or 19-inch screen		3
Provides three attractor zones		2
Vandal panels		3
Branding and LA panels (no vinyls)		3
No low-level paint – all SS or enamel or cheap-to-refurbish powder coat – to be costed		3
Ease of installation – sunken FP – pre-formed foundations – reinstatement plate – install casework – add I+ modules		2
No low-level glass		1
Enclosure for power meter		3
Scrolling attractor		2
2g/3g		1
Street Net/WiFi		1
Transactional (including Chip & Pin and coins)		3
Help point		1
Webcam		1
CE		2
Taller (for WiFi – roofline visibility)		3
Distinctive generic roof		2
Alarm		2
Vibration sensor		3
Motion sensor		3
Surround sound		3
Fortress version		3
Boundary markings		1
Exclude water (rather than manage)		3
Induction loop		3

Design 'brief' development

Once an outline or 'preliminary' brief was agreed upon, Adshel and Cityspace assembled a 'design briefing' team to develop and build upon the first brief proposal. At this stage of development the brief changed into more of a formal document and process, involving many different stakeholders, not only from within the two companies, but also external stakeholders that included British Telecom and the municipal authority. The V4 Scope provided a basis for focus and development, with both crime and safety issues being paramount. Peter Quinlan adds:

> I've been thinking about how we're going to do this and I think what we must do is design the brief; then at the end of it we must take a design against crime approach because it's got to be inherent in the overall design but it also has to be inherent in the detail. So I'm going to add that just as a general statement so that, all the way through our thinking of the design, we're thinking how is this preventing crime.

Figure 7.1 illustrates the relationship between Adshel and Cityspace, and the involvement of the diverse stakeholders in the briefing process for the I+ information terminal.

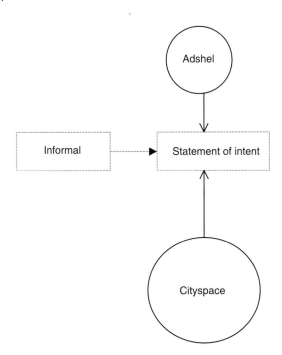

Figure 7.1 *Informal brief development between Adshel and Cityspace*

After an initial statement of intent between the two organisations, the design brief acted as a focal point between the two organisations, providing an opportunity (or statement of intent) for the development of second- and third-generation concepts for the I+ information kiosk. Roger Crabtree explains:

> So we found ourselves and Cityspace having to acknowledge that the market's changed, there are different clients out there, the needs of these clients are different and that their existing kiosks can't deliver it. So we now need to look at I say new kiosks but they're additional ones. The original ones will continue to have a place for a specific market and that, primarily, will be local authorities who want on-the-street digital information. The new kiosks are driven primarily by the need to integrate digital information into the transport industry and service transport users and transport providers. Now that requires a new level of thinking, because the information that you're carrying is usually of a different format, it's presented to a different audience and it's subsequently presented in a different configuration.

Once the approval for the redesign of the existing terminals was obtained by Adshel and Cityspace, the briefing process developed into a more formalised process (Figure 7.2), engaging the views, opinions and expertise of external stakeholders, ranging across the users, British Telecom (BT), installation engineers (I), service operatives (S) and cleaners of the units (C). Peter Quinlan comments:

> Obviously, we take a lot of feedback from our engineers. I am also going out and visiting the kiosks and making up my own mind. The previous question . . . that's where we get feedback from but we are also taking feedback from the local authorities and we listen very carefully – particularly in selecting locations; you know, if they say that's a known crime area and that's one to avoid, then we will listen to them. So yes, we are taking into account their feedback. Part of our product is aimed at social inclusion so we do also have to install in areas which we know are difficult, such as Knowsley.

Key issues arising from the briefing

On reflection, Peter Quinlan agrees that many issues arose that he did not anticipate at the beginning of the briefing process. By including and soliciting the views of a diverse range of stakeholders, the following aspects were raised and included within the design brief:

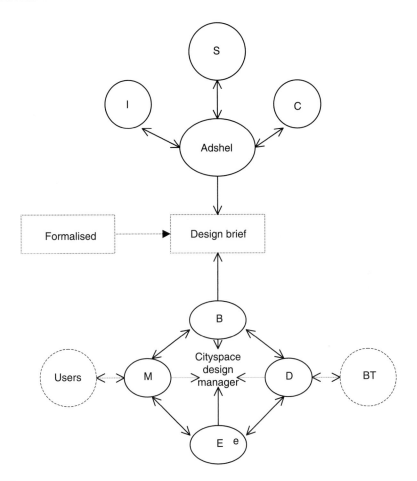

Figure 7.2 *Formal brief development between Adshel and Cityspace*

- Durability: The touch surface of the screen was prone to abuse by vandals, in particular by people who scratched their name on the surface or defaced it with 'tags' or graffiti. This information was imparted by the engineers within Adshel, who discovered that vandals were stealing safety hammers from buses and using them to vandalise the screens on the terminals. Consequently, the designers were able to design and specify replacements screens that could be easily and quickly refitted if required. Also, the screens were coated with vinyl, which is impossible to replace, thus reducing the incentive to steal the screens.

- Modularisation: Component parts were designed so they could be replaced quickly and effectively. Adshel has a rigorous policy of repairing any damaged or vandalised information units within 24 hours. By designing parts of the unit within a modular format, repairs can be undertaken relatively inexpensively. Peter Quinlan explains: 'Adshel are extremely good at this and very fast and they do our maintenance as well. They tend to respond, their first call is a sensitive issue – so is there broken glass, get it cleaned, get it safe, get the damaged product removed from site; that's their real urgency and they've got a guarantee that they'll do it within 24 hours.'

- Installation: Ease of installation was another key issue that arose during the briefing stages. Specially designed 'combined feed power units' were developed whereby engineers could quickly connect the information units to both regional electricity supplies and the BT network. Connecting the unit to the supply networks reduces aggressive behaviour through frustration, when it is in operation almost immediately. 'So that, when we install the kiosk, we can turn it on the day it goes in. That again massively reduces the amount of aggro. The odd kiosk where that hasn't happened has had far, far more vandalism, so it definitely, definitely works. Get it in and turn it on, on the same day' (P. Quinlan).

- Positioning: This issue was largely communicated through the tacit know-ledge of Peter Quinlan. Information units were positioned under the surveillance of CCTV cameras whereby if the units were vandalised or some-one was attacked the likelihood of arrest would be increased, which in essence is deterrence. Safety to the user was also a great concern. 'I was always a little bit concerned that somebody could be typing up an email or something, and they could have a dog or a child and they could run across the road. A child standing round there, away from their parents and across the road and someone knocks them over. And if you are focusing on the kiosk, you're not really seeing what they're doing. So I try to encourage them to install the kiosk where there's a natural barrier behind the road to prevent that. So that's built into the survey and it's little things like that which are just . . . not really design against crime, but they're public responsibility' (P. Quinlan).

- Lighting: The information units emit low levels of lighting; as a result users feel safe and secure using the unit, which provides a sense of security and safety after dark. This insight came particularly from a female colleague (project manager) who from a woman's perspective ensured the issue of lighting was addressed within the modified unit. 'In a lot of instances this will be single women late at night using that kiosk. So she feels that the lighting for the kiosk is very important, under street lights and so on. But where we'll be sitting these will be within a close vicinity of the tube station. We won't necessarily have the same control. So she, by saying that, has changed this brief. I will now make sure that we get lighting for this. So, any source. I've already established that lighting is important, but not necessarily on the kiosk. We have got lights in the kiosk, more to give people a feeling of security and enclosure' (P. Quinlan).

- Robustness: This was about reducing the number of 'prise' points on the unit. Maintenance engineers noticed that many units suffered from vandals attempting to open the rear door to gain access to the interior and steal valuable component parts. As a result, this knowledge gained from the 'field' was made explicit in the design brief, and consequently design modifications were made. 'Part of our design requirement is that there are no prise points, so there is nowhere where somebody can shove in a lever or whatever to open it. But by default you're also preventing anyone from putting in flyers. There are some areas around the screen box where you could put a flyer, so what we have tried to do is engineer it so as all the joints are extremely tight. And that's something that we do' (P. Quinlan).

Discussion

This case example has discussed two key issues in the successful development of the I+ information terminal. The first is that the design manager (Peter Quinlan) had an intuitive and deep understanding of the relationship between the unit and its users. This knowledge (both tacit and explicit) was communicated through-out all the main stages of the briefing process, providing the design team with clear guidance to develop and detail the initial concepts. The second key issue is related to purpose. Crime against vending machines is often related to frustration at the machine failing to deliver the product (in this case the product was infor-mation). Failure of the I+, essentially just providing information, would not invoke the same response. Emergent issues in crime such as credit card fraud are currently being considered for future generations of the I+ family, which should ensure its success as a crime-reduced service provider. Cityspace/Adshel and their customers are continuing to monitor crime resistance throughout the product life, capturing feedback from the users to inform future design amendments.

CASE STUDY 2: PARKSAFE CAR PARK, DERBY, UK

This case example investigates a highly practical and successful series of inter-ventions of design against crime thinking within the briefing and design stages of the car park's redevelopment. As a consequence it is regarded as 'one of the most secure places in the world' (BBC News 2004b). Parksafe car park is located at Bold Lane, Derby, and has been fully operational since 1998. Since its reopening, the car park has reduced criminal activity by 100 per cent and has brought considerable savings to both the local police force and the local council's site maintenance expenditure (Parksafesystems 2004).

Background to Parksafe

Parksafe is a 24-hour multi-storey car park on Bold Lane, near the shopping centre in Derby. It was developed in partnership with Derby City Council, and its 440 parking bays, covering ten floors, are targeted at short-stay shoppers and people who want to park overnight. Customers pay an extra 20p per hour for an 'assured' car park, where the cost of theft of a vehicle or from a vehicle is covered by Parksafe, as long as the vehicle is properly secured (Davey *et al.* 2002).

The Parksafe security system was invented by Ken Wigley after he became a victim of car crime when returning to his parked car in the airport car park from an overseas holiday in 1990. Consequently, he developed the Parksafe concept in an attempt to redress this injustice. 'As a result, Parksafe was born. The Bold Lane car park which is run in partnership with Derby City Council, officially opened on January 18, 1998' (*Derby Evening Telegraph* 2004a).

Bold Lane car park prior to design against crime intervention

Wigley incrementally developed the Parksafe concept over a duration of two years prior to formally classifying the car park as a 'Secured by Design' one. At the time Wigley was an agricultural engineer who was currently working on sensors for use in machinery that harvested grass into silage. The presence of rogue pieces of metal in the machine's blades potentially cause significant damage to the expensive machinery, so he developed a sensor system that can effectively detect foreign bodies within the system. With this in mind, he adapted the technology for use by cars within the car park, whereby vehicles stationed within a parking bay would trigger the sensors if moved from the bay by an unauthorised user. The Bold Lane car park has the facility to securely accommodate 440 parked cars, and it is this core concept that the Parksafe system is based upon.

Wigley (*Derby Evening Telegraph* 2004b) argues that:

> It was terrible. There were 167 incidents of theft in the year prior to us opening, but, not only that, you had urinating in the stairwells, graffiti, and beggars and tramps. It had got to the stage where you took your car's life in your own hands if you left it at Bold Lane. In one night I counted just six cars. If Parksafe was to be anywhere's saviour, it would be Bold Lane's.

The Parksafe system

The security system encompasses individual motion sensors in each of the 440 parking bays; panic buttons in case of alarm are positioned at 15-metre intervals on the parking decks and landings; 200 automated CCTV cameras are constantly monitored by a centrally manned control system; pedestrian access is limited to car park users only, with vehicle entry and exit gates; and there is separate ticket-only pedestrian access. This confidence means that Parksafe can guarantee followers of the four-steps system (valuables in the boot; vehicle locked; bay secured; ticket kept with the owner) against theft of or theft from the car.

The business case for design against crime

In the initial stages of developing the design brief for the car park, Ken Wigley undertook extensive market research to establish who would use the car park, how much they were prepared to pay and who the main competitors were likely to be. However, to offer this added-value service, the Bold Lane car park is slightly more expensive than its nearest rivals.

Wigley (interview, 2004) justifies this expense by arguing that:

> My car park started off by being 10p dearer, now it's 20p and it's still 20p dearer than the neighbouring Assembly Rooms or Chapel Street car parks. If the council puts up prices by 10p there's an outcry; we put our prices up by 20p and all we got was support. The users could see the benefits of parking here – they felt safe. They are prepared to pay a lot more than that, just for peace of mind. I suppose you can say we are charging slightly more but in return you can say that you are offering a far safer and secure environment to park your car.

However, in return for the higher expense the car park guarantees the safety of its customers' cars and their contents and has taken out full public liability insurance through Lloyd's of London to underwrite this guarantee.

Wigley (interview, 2004) adds:

> I visited many car parks, probably over 100 within an 18-month period, from one end of the country to another. I went as far as Glasgow in Scotland in fact. They all seemed the same; some were slightly better, cleaner, better lit, but at the end of the day a clean, well-lit car park doesn't stop crime.

The initial briefing phases

At the early developmental stages of creating the Parksafe concept, Ken Wigley began by drafting core principles of the scheme on paper. Wigley (interview, 2004) comments that:

> to start with, I didn't know what to do. I did realise that we had to have something in every bay. The crux of Parksafe is security within each bay.

Figure 7.3 Parksafe guarantee

Permission obtained from Caroline Davey, University of Salford

> I felt it was important by protecting a spot. I have got so many fag
> packets with drawings on. I did actually put it down over a period of time
> and I kept altering things, thinking that's not going to work.

This aspect of development accords with findings from a major report compiled by Frank Duffy (Construction Industry Board 1997) whereby the process
of developing a brief could 'inform others of his or her needs, aspirations and
desires, either formally or informally'. Confident of a commercially viable
solution to reducing criminal activity in the car park, Wigley contacted the local
police architectural liaison officer in Derby, Keith Halford. Through entering
into a dialogue investigating potential causes of crime and possible solutions, the
brief underwent significant change and development. However, the key input that
greatly enriched the briefing process, and consequently moved the possible concept nearer to implementation, was the involvement of key stakeholders.

Ken Wigley was unaware of a major report (Holden McAllister Partnership
2004) investigating the development of safer public environments and the provision of guidelines into the successful planning and design of public spaces; his
'intuitive' actions closely accord with the report's major recommendations,
which argue that:

158

good design is a consideration from the outset, and that the different professionals work together to develop solutions that encompass the broad objectives of sustainable communities. Where designers gain an early understanding of the problems, it will be possible that working closely with ALOs they will be able to work up solutions that encompass the broad range of attributes that combine to make up safer public environments.

Stakeholder involvement

The design brief acts as a central point of reference from which dialogue and the sharing of values can depart, and to provide a firm basis for all subsequent design decisions within and throughout the design programme. The design brief is to get everyone started with a common understanding of what is to be accomplished. Ken Wigley (interview, 2004) comments:

> I consulted heavily with the car park users. At the time, everybody seems a little bit like they don't really know what they want, so I had to instigate some things. Like how would you feel if you got a panic button and does it matter if we carry a guarantee or not? If they are paying a premium, of course it matters.

By soliciting a broad and varied range of views from all stakeholders of the car park, Ken Wigley was able to understand the needs and wants of all its potential users. This approach to understanding user needs and minimising potential crime 'hotspots' accords with research findings from a pilot research study into Designing against Crime (Design Policy Partnership 2001) for the UK Home Office:

> also the 'payer' of different crimes varies: sometimes it might be the producer of the product or service, sometimes the consumer, sometimes an insurance company, sometimes the government; this may be significant in thinking about the way a product or service is designed, so again it would seem valuable to study sectors where design issues related to different crime 'payers' can be explored.

Design Strategist Peter Philips is a firm advocate of the inclusion of key stakeholders in the early phases of the design project. He argues that to ensure 'buy-in' of the end users it is critical to engage them in a meaningful manner whereby their views can be 'invested' within the design brief and subsequent design proposals. Philips (2004) argues:

I have found that involving many stakeholders in the early phases is a good idea. There really isn't much harm anyone can do to a design project in its early phases. Stakeholders involved early on tend to feel more included, and are therefore less likely to raise significant objections later, as the project is coming to a conclusion. Let them see where you are, being careful to explain in very clear, non-subjective, businesslike language just what you are doing and why. You will also find some truly helpful input at times.

Philips argues further that the task of identifying key stakeholders is more difficult than expected. He goes on to say that 'the list is often longer than you would think. Identifying these people up front will allow the designer to develop key strategies and plan their involvement into the phase process of the project at the most appropriate time' (Philips 2004).

Ken Wigley undertook extensive research to fully understand what users of the car park would value most. Crime-free parking and the ability to return to parked cars late in the evening without the fear or threat of violence were the main concerns of users. One response to this issue was the installation of a comprehensive CCTV system that is manned 24 hours a day, which made a significant contribution to reducing anti-social behaviour and theft from the vehicles.

Quantifying the benefits of Parksafe

To constantly ensure the zero crime figures within Parksafe and provide a value-added service to its users, Ken Wigley continually conducts customer surveys with a particular emphasis on crime. He adds that 'the biggest thing I found was

Figure 7.4 The control room at Bold Lane car park

Permission obtained from Ken Wigley, Parksafe Systems

to listen to what people wanted; this really informed and continues to inform my thinking' (interview, 2004). Table 7.3 shows the results of a customer survey conducted on 18 and 21 November 1998.

A user survey conducted by the city council in 2000 (cited in Smith *et al.* 2003) showed that 97 per cent of users felt personally safe using the car park and 100 per cent felt that their car and contents were secure in the car park.

Owing to the success of Parksafe in Derby, Ken Wigley entered into an agreement with Lancaster City Council to operate a car park in partnership, which opened in 2002. When asked about the success of the car park he argues that 'it's just a copy book of Derby. Usage is increasing; we've got zero crime, no vandalism, perfect parking' (interview, 2004).

Table 7.3 *Parksafe, Bold Lane car park – customer survey*

372 questionnaires were completed on Wednesday 18 and Saturday 21 November 1998. Those surveyed were asked a series of questions and asked to rate their reply on a score of 1 to 5, with 1 being very good, 2 good, 3 average, 4 poor and 5 very poor. The answers to those questions are summarised below.

83 per cent of people considered the car park very easy to find, 10 per cent easy, 5 per cent average, 1 per cent poor and 1 per cent very poor.

80 per cent of people thought the car park was very easy to use, 13 per cent easy, 5 per cent average, and 2 per cent poor.

86 per cent of people thought the car park was very well lit and laid out, 10 per cent thought it was well lit and laid out, 3 per cent considered it to be average, while 1 per cent considered it to be poor.

93 per cent of people thought the car park was very clean, 6 per cent thought it clean and 1 per cent considered it to be average.

81 per cent of people thought the car park was very convenient for the places they wanted to visit.

94 per cent of people felt that their car and property were very safe within the car park, 4 per cent thought their car and property were safe and 1 per cent considered it to be average, with a further 1 per cent thinking it less than average.

95 per cent of people using the car park felt very safe when using the car park.

80 per cent of people considered the fact that the car park was open 24 hours very useful.

89 per cent of people felt that the fact that the pay machines accepted notes was very important.

71 per cent of people thought that Parksafe, Bold Lane car park was very good value for money in comparison to other car parks that they had used, 18 per cent thought the car park was good value for money, 8 per cent thought it average, 1 per cent thought it compared poorly and 1 per cent felt it compared very poorly.

100 per cent of those surveyed said they would use the car park again. 100 per cent of those surveyed said they would recommend the car park to their friends and family.

Source: Parksafesystems.com/benefits/survey

Summary

The director of Parksafe car park has taken a direct and user-centred approach to crime reduction through the extensive use of stakeholder involvement within the early stages of brief development. Firstly, Wigley enlisted the expertise of the local police architectural liaison officer, who identified the primary causes of criminal activity within the existing car park, notably anti-social behaviour (aggressive begging, vandalism and street drinking) and nuisance crime. Through extensive iteration of the initial brief and consultation with the car park users, design solutions were implemented that offered a highly innovative approach to reducing crime. The installation of CCTV (which formed a major part of the security system, coupled with the bay sensors) was widely welcomed by all stakeholders. Continual customer surveys revealed a belief amongst respondents that the combined security measures make the car park safer from criminal activity and, as a consequence, also significantly impact on the fear of crime itself. These findings are consistent with those of other Secured by Design car park evaluations that have been conducted (Poyner 1997; Tilley 1993). The use of good lighting within Bold Street car park was also considered important for reducing the fear of crime (with over 86 per cent of respondents from the 1998 customer survey saying improved lighting was a key contributor to reducing the fear of crime). As a side note, the effect of lighting has also been shown to have positive crime prevention effects in other settings (Painter and Farrington 1997; Welsh and Farrington 2002).

CONCLUSION

In the development of crime-resistant products, services and built environments, the task of design briefing is an important and highly complex part of the whole design process. Failure to effectively execute this process can often lead to incorrect, incomplete or ambiguous expression of the design requirement, which in turn leads to a designed solution that fails to prevent or reduce criminal activity or actually increases it. In essence, the solution fails.

The process of arriving at a design brief that encapsulates design against crime thinking and attributes is a complex one, characterised by the application of (often external) expertise in circumstances that vary about a multitude of sometimes conflicting tensions. This in turn makes the whole process of effectively managing the briefing process and anticipating criminal activity difficult. As increasing demands upon the organisation and design function become increasingly more complex and the penalties for failure in design increase, so too does the need to ensure that the crime-focused design brief is developed more effectively.

The account has considered a number of different aspects of design briefing, design against crime and design management, in order to achieve a better under-standing of this emergent area. This investigation has resulted in a deeper understanding of the influences and factors that impact upon the design against crime briefing process, and an analysis of the different types of approaches to reducing crime within different contextual environments.

The principal purpose of this has been to provide a better basis for the designer, design manager or project sponsor to provide an enhanced basis for design support in eliciting, evolving and communicating design against crime require-ments within the briefing process.

REVIEW QUESTIONS

1 How do you think the designer can help in the struggle to reduce criminal behaviour?

2 Why is it important for the design team to consider crime issues during and throughout the initial briefing stages?

3 It is commonly agreed that the fear of crime is disproportionate to the actual occurrence of crime; how can designers significantly reduce the 'perception' of crime in the products and environments that they develop?

4 Why does crime prevention through environmental design principles (CPTED) rely heavily upon stakeholder involvement to be successful?

5 What are the key elements of Secured by Design (SBD) and why do you think they are vital in ensuring its success?

6 Why is the design briefing phase so important to the successful outcome of any design project?

7 Designing against crime offers many and diverse business advantages; can you identify these?

8 What techniques would you suggest to a design team to 'creatively' envision crime 'misuse' scenarios in the initial briefing stages?

9 Can you suggest other ways to quantify the benefits of designing against crime, other than financial metrics?

10 Designing against crime is just one aspect of emergent design; can you identify other emergent issues or themes that are important to both design and design management?

PROJECT QUESTIONS

1 Why was it important to Cityspace that they adopt a design against crime strategy to reinforce their brand identity?

2   Cityspace have developed a briefing pro forma (V4) to assist in the early briefing stages; what other key considerations do you think should be included within it?

3   Peter Quinlan (the design manager within Cityspace) has considerable tacit knowledge regarding designing against crime; how could this knowledge be formalised within the organisation?

4   Ken Wigley (owner and manager of Parksafe, Derby) managed to identify and include key stakeholders in the briefing process almost by accident; what formalised mechanisms would you implement to aid and facilitate this process?

5   How can user feedback, knowledge and comments be incorporated into subsequent design against crime projects? How would you validate the integrity and success of this knowledge?

REFERENCES

Adshel (2004) Proven i-plus partnerships around the world. Available at http://www.adshel.co.uk/deploy/adshelinternet (accessed 12 July 2004)

AIGA (2001) A client's guide to design: how to get the most out of the process. Available at http://www.aiga.org (accessed 28 November 2002)

Allinson, K. (1998) *Getting there by design: an architect's guide to project and design management.* (London: Architectural Press)

Armitage, R. (2000) *An evaluation of Secured by Design housing within West Yorkshire.* Briefing Note 7/00 to the Home Office (London: Home Office) p. 1

BBC News (2004a) The UK's crime hotspots. Available at http://news.bbc.co.uk/hi/english/uk/ (accessed 16 January 2004)

BBC News (2004b) Car park makes top ten for safety. Available at http://newsvote.bbc.co.uk/mpapp/pagetools/print/news.bbc.co.uk/ (accessed 18 February 2004)

Brand, S. and Price, R. (2000) *The economic and social costs of crime.* Home Office Research Study 217. (London: Home Office)

Construction Industry Board (1997) *Briefing the team: Working Group 1.* (London: Thomas Telford)

Cooper, R. and Press, M. (1995) *The design agenda: a guide to successful design management.* (Chichester: John Wiley) pp. 51–97

Crowe, T. (1991) *Crime prevention through environmental design: applications of architectural design and space management concepts.* (Stoneham, MA: Butterworth)

Davey, C. L., Cooper, R. and Press, M. (2002) Design against crime case studies. University of Salford. Available at http://www.designagainstcrime.org

Derby Evening Telegraph (2004a) Think of the most secure places on Earth. Now add . . ., 17 February: 3

Derby Evening Telegraph (2004b) A busy day in Ken's park life, 19 February: 10

Design against Crime (2000) *Design against crime report.* (Cambridge, Sheffield and Salford: University of Cambridge, Sheffield Hallam University and University of Salford)

Design Council (2002) Frequently asked questions: how to brief a designer. Available at http://www.design-council.org.uk (accessed 28 November 2002)

Design Policy Partnership (2001) *Off the shelf: design and retail crime.* (London: Design Council)

Design Policy Partnership (2002) *Design against crime: guidance for professional designers.* (Salford: University of Salford)

Ekblom, P. (1991) Talking to offenders: practical lessons for local crime prevention. In: *Conference proceedings of 'Urban Crime: Statistical Approaches and Analyses'.* (Barcelona: Institiut d'Estudis Metropoitans de Barcelona) p. 1

Ekblom, P. and Tilley, N. (1998) *What works database for community safety/crime reduction practitioners: towards a specification for an ideal template.* (London: Policing and Reducing Crime Unit, Home Office RDS and Nottingham Trent University)

Ekblom, P. and Tilley, N. (2000) Going equipped: criminology, situational crime prevention and the resourceful offender. *British Journal of Criminology,* 40: 376–398

HOCD (2001) Car Theft Index 2001. Available at www.secureyourmotor.gov.uk

Holden McAllister Partnership (2004) *Safer places: the planning system and crime prevention.* (London: Home Office, HMSO)

Home Office (2000) *The 2000 British Crime Survey, England and Wales 1999.* (London: HMSO)

Home Office (2002) *The 2002 British Crime Survey, England and Wales 2001–02.* (London: HMSO)

Hymans, D. (2001) *Construction companion: briefing.* (London: RIBA Publications)

ICPC (International Centre for the Prevention of Crime) (1997) *Crime prevention digest.* (Montreal: ICPC)

Learmount, S. (1999) Design against crime: a review of relevant literature and selection of sectors to be studied. Unpublished report. September. Judge Institute of Management Studies, University of Cambridge

McKay, T. (1996) The right design for securing crime. *Security Management,* 40(4): 30–37

Maguire, M. (1997) Crime statistics, patterns, and trends: changing perceptions and their implications. In: R. Morgan and P. Reiner (ed.) *The Oxford handbook of criminology.* (Oxford: Clarendon Press)

Olson, E., Slater, S. and Cooper, R. (2000) Managing design for competitive advantage: a process approach. *Design Management Journal,* 11(3): 10–17

Painter, K. A. and Farrington, D. P. (1997) The crime reducing effect of improved street lighting: the Dudley project. In: R. V. Clarke (ed.) *Situational crime prevention: successful case studies*, 2nd edn. (New York: Harrow and Heston) pp. 209–266

Parksafesystems (2004) Available at http://www.parksafesystems.com/casestudy/ (accessed 14 April 2004)

Philips, P. L. (2004) *Creating the perfect design brief.* (Boston, MA: Design Management Institute)

Poyner, B. (1997) Situational crime prevention in two parking facilities. In: R. V. Clarke (ed.) *Situational crime prevention: successful case studies*, 2nd edn. (New York: Harrow and Heston) pp. 157–166

Press, M., Cooper, R. and Erol, R. (2001) Design as a tool for social policy: the case of design against crime. In: 'd3 desire designum design', 4th European Academy of Design conference proceedings, 10–12 April, Universidade de Aveiro

Slade, M. (1990) Understanding the brief. *Engineering*, March: 21

Smith, D. G., Gregson, M. and Morgan, J. (2003) *Between the lines: an evaluation of the Secured Car Park Award Scheme*. Home Office Research Study 266. (London: Home Office Research, Development and Statistics Directorate)

Tilley, N. (1993) *Understanding car parks, crime and CCTV: evaluation lessons from safer cities*. Police Research Group, Crime Prevention Unit Paper 42. (London: Home Office)

Topalian, A. (1994) *The Alto Design Management workbook.* (London)

Welsh, B. C. and Farrington, D. P. (2002) *Crime prevention effects of closed circuit television: a systematic review.* (London: Home Office)

FURTHER READING

Barrett, P. (1995) *Facilities management: towards best practice.* (Oxford: Blackwell Science)

Barrett, P. and Stanley, C. (1999) *Better construction briefing.* (Oxford: Blackwell Science)

Bruce, M. and Cooper, R. (2000) *Creative product design: a practical guide to requirement capture management.* (Chichester: John Wiley)

Bruce, M. and Bessant, J. (2002) *Design in business: strategic innovation through design.* (Harlow: Pearson Education)

Ekblom, P. (1999) Can we make crime prevention adaptive by learning from other evolutionary struggles? *Studies on Crime and Crime Prevention*, 8(1). (National Council for Crime Prevention)

Lawson, B. (1997) *How designers think: the design process demystified*, 3rd edn. (Oxford: Architectural Press)

Newman, O. (1972) *Defensible space.* (New York: Macmillan)

Town, S., Davey, C. L. and Wootton, A. B. (2003) *Design against crime: secure urban environments by design – guidance for the design of residential areas.* (Manchester: Pelican Press)

Worthington, J. (1994) Effective project management results from establishing the optimum brief. *Property Review,* November: 182–185

Chapter 8

Customer experience-based brand strategy at the Lenovo Group – exploring the potential for Lenovo in the UK PC market

Ray Holland, Yuanyuan Yin and Shengfeng Qin

INTRODUCTION

Personal computers (PCs) have infiltrated our daily lives and are increasingly indispensable in meeting various aspects of our professional and personal needs. This trend means that the PC industry is facing the question of how to sustain growth in the business environment. Research data from IDC indicate over 9.7 per cent growth registered in PC sales globally in quarter 2, 2006, with no obvious signs of growth slowdown in the next few years (http://blogs.zdnet. com/ITFacts/index.php?cat=7). In China, this growth is even faster compared to the global figures, and brand internationalisation has become an inevitable trend for Chinese PC producers. Lenovo is the best Chinese corporation example of internationalisation.

Lenovo is an innovative international technology company formed as a result of the acquisition of IBM's Personal Computing Division (PCD) by the mainland China-based Lenovo Group (www.lenovo.com). After the purchase, Lenovo planned to explore the European PC market as a part of its internationalisation programme. In seeking opportunities in the UK, it is competing with many established strong brands in the PC market (Figure 8.1).

The most successful brands by sales revenue are Dell and HP, and the fastest-growing brands are Acer and Dell; these leading companies use design and branding by designing new customer purchasing styles and better service. Therefore it is difficult for a new brand such as Lenovo to gain a share in the mature UK market even though Lenovo has powerful strength in the PC industry from its strong base in China. Building a brand image and gaining market share in the UK have become a major priority for Lenovo when exploring the European market.

In order to build up a brand identity in the UK PC market, Lenovo needs a new brand strategy to transfer its successful brand strategy from China to the UK based on differences in culture, user behaviour and customer experience between

Figure 8.1 *PC brands map in the UK PC market*

China and the UK. In order to measure the differences and develop a set of new brand strategy guidelines, a customer experience-based brand strategy exercise was conducted based on customer behaviour analysis (Cope 2003) and brand customer experience development analysis (Schmitt 2002). The case study begins with a literature review to set the context. Methodologies for formulating and evaluating the case study are then presented. Findings from the case study analysis are shown next. The discussion and results of this study follow. Finally strategic directions for Lenovo design and branding in addressing the UK market are offered.

THE LENOVO GROUP

Lenovo's head office is in Purchase, New York, USA, with principal operations in Beijing, China, and Raleigh, North Carolina, USA, and an enterprise sales organisation worldwide. The company employs more than 19,000 people worldwide.

ORIGINS OF IBM PCD AND LENOVO

In 1981, IBM PCD saw the future of computing at a new level – a personal level – with synergy power switching and extending the productivity of information technology from the mainframe to the individual, at home and at work. That vision led to the founding of a new unit within IBM, the Personal Computing Division (PCD). So having long been leaders in mainframe computing, the new department advanced the state of the art with a series of innovations in personal computing ranging from the very first laptop computers to the latest high-security technologies, such as the built-in 'air-bag' that protects data, and biometric identification that protects user identity. IBM PCD created the icon of notebook computing, the ThinkPad, and the unique software tools, known as ThinkVantage Technologies, aimed at increasing user productivity.

In 1984, not long after PCD was founded, 11 computer scientists in Beijing, China, also had a vision – to create a company that would bring the advantages of information technology to the Chinese people. With RMB200,000 (US$25,000) in seed investment money and the determination to turn their research into successful products, the 11 engineers and researchers set up business in a loaned space – a small, one-storey bungalow in Beijing. The company they founded, which was called Legend, opened the new era of consumer PCs in China.

Since it was established, the Legend company has affected the lives of millions of Chinese. It began by introducing PCs to households and then promoted PC usage in China by establishing retail shops nationwide. It also developed the pioneering Legend Chinese character card that translated English operating software into Chinese characters, and achieved breakthroughs like PCs with one-button access to the internet.

By 1994 Legend was trading on the Hong Kong Stock Exchange; four years later, it produced its one-millionth personal computer. In 2003, Legend changed its brand name to Lenovo, taking the 'Le' from Legend, in deference to its heritage, and adding 'novo', the Latin word for 'new', to reflect the spirit of innovation at the core of the company. The company changed its name from Legend to Lenovo a year later.

In 2003 Lenovo introduced a self-developed collaborative application technology, which was planned to establish the important role Lenovo intended to play in the 3C era (computer, communications and consumer electronics). These and other market-leading personal computing products catapulted Lenovo to a leadership position in China for eight consecutive years, with over 36 per cent market share in 2005.

LENOVO AND IBM PCD

Today Lenovo and IBM PCD are united under the Lenovo name. With Lenovo's landmark acquisition of IBM's Personal Computing Division in May 2005, the new Lenovo became a leader in the global PC market, with approximately $13 billion in annual revenue and products serving enterprises and consumers all over the world.

The entrepreneurial spirit of Lenovo and IBM PCD's track record of break-throughs live on in today's Lenovo, an IT giant with global reach, competing worldwide in a growing market.

Globally, Lenovo offers customers the award-winning ThinkPad notebooks and

ThinkCentre desktops, featuring the ThinkVantage Technologies software tools, as well as ThinkVision monitors and a full line of PC accessories and options. The Think family is consistently ranked as the premium-brand leader in the global PC industry, with products rated 'best in class' and 'number one' in survey after survey. No other family of personal computers has won as much recognition.

In China, Lenovo commands more than one-third of the PC market, covering all segments. Its leading-edge PCs are well regarded for their user-friendly, tailor-made designs and customised solutions for various customer needs, including the Tianjiao and Fengxing consumer desktops and Yangtian and Kaitian enterprise desktops. Lenovo also has a broad and expanding product line encompassing mobile handsets, servers, peripherals and digital entertainment products for the Chinese market.

LENOVO AND THE OLYMPIC GAMES

Lenovo has been a major supporter of sports and physical fitness in China. In 1999, the company sponsored the Chinese national women's soccer team and two years later sponsored Beijing's successful bid to host the 2008 Olympic Games. A tradition of social responsibility and corporate philanthropy is another shared value common to both IBM PCD and Lenovo. IBM PCD has donated ThinkPad notebooks and ThinkCentre desktops to a wide variety of non-profit organisations around the world, and its employees have also donated thousands of volunteer hours to local causes. Thinking globally, in 2004 Lenovo became the first Chinese company to join the Olympic Partner Programme. As a worldwide sponsor with the International Olympic Committee, the company will be a major supplier of computing equipment – such as desktop and notebook computers and servers – and funding in support of the 2006 winter games in Turin, Italy, and the 2008 summer games in Beijing, China. This major sports marketing initiative is intended to introduce the Lenovo brand around the globe and reflect its wish to be seen as socially responsible.

LENOVO TAKEOVER OF IBM PCD

Following the takeover of the IBM PCD, the new Lenovo became a leader in the global PC market, producing products serving enterprises and consumers the world over. Lenovo and IBM PCD formed a strategic alliance designed to provide a best-in-class experience for enterprise customers. Their customer companies have entered into significant long-term agreements that give businesses preferred access to IBM's world-class customer service organisation and global financing offerings and have enabled Lenovo to take advantage of IBM's powerful worldwide

171

distribution and sales network. Lenovo's customers are able to count on the entire IBM PCD team – including sales, services and financing – for access to IBM's well-established end-to-end IT solutions. As part of a five-year commitment, IBM will also provide Lenovo with warranty services and offer Lenovo customers leasing and financing arrangements. This long-term relationship is the base by which customers can receive the best products with the lowest total cost of ownership.

The question arises, why did IBM need to sell its PC Division? IBM entered the personal computer market in 1981 and became a leader in the PC revolution. But after the emergence of competitors Dell and HP and their rising sales, IBM computer PC sales fell continuously. In 1998, the deficit of the IBM PC section was US$992,000,000. The IBM PC division had become a serious obstacle to the overall profitability of the whole company. For IBM, PC manufacturing had lost its predominance in a tough competitive market environment, as compared to its other high-end information technology products. IBM currently focuses on high-end equipment, such as computer service, software, servers and the computer calculator chip, in order to increase its overall profitability. So IBM traded its PC division to Lenovo to get financial support for its high-profit products to keep its leadership position in the high-end information technology market.

THE LENOVO CHALLENGE

From Lenovo's point of view, there was not enough potential development space within the local national market. Because of a continually damaging price war, the profit margin has already been squeezed more and more in the PC industry. If Lenovo wants to acquire a larger share of the business of the PC industry and grasp the new profits growth point, internationalisation will be the necessary and essential strategy.

Before procuring the PC department of IBM, only 3 per cent of Lenovo's income came from the overseas market, primarily from South-East Asia. Undoubtedly, depending only on its personal strength in establishing the Lenovo brand and exploring new markets represented a high risk for Lenovo in the European and the global markets. However, after purchasing the PC division of IBM, Lenovo can utilise the reputation of the IBM PCD brand to promote its international position and image. Consequently, how to combine the brand value of IBM PCD to contribute to the Lenovo Group brand and to achieve the faith and loyalty of IBM personal computer customers in the Lenovo brand are the critical problems facing the company. Therefore, this case study addresses why and how Lenovo should use customer experience-based branding strategy to explore the UK PC market and find a new direction.

THEORETICAL FOUNDATIONS

In order to evaluate the Lenovo IBM PCD challenge there are many potentially valuable papers and books which provide the theoretical foundation on which to build the new brand strategy. In the design management arena, there are almost as many definitions of branding as there are books on the subject. Armstrong (2004) said that 'Brand is more than just name and symbols.' Brand represents everything that the product or service means to consumers, such as consumers' perceptions and feelings about a product and its performance. As Kotler (2003) suggests, 'Ultimately, brands reside in the minds of consumers.' Therefore, the real value of a strong brand is its power to capture consumer preference and loyalty (Armstrong 2004). Gobé (2001) has said that 'Brand is brought to life for consumers first and foremost by the personality of the company behind it and that company's commitment to reaching people on an emotional level.'

Branding carries benefits for all parties involved in the exchange process and in theory at least makes it easier to buy or sell products. As illustrated in Figure 8.2, Brassington and Pettit (2003) concluded that branding has three main benefits: consumer, retailer and manufacturer.

One of the most useful definitions of brand for the case study comes from Neumeier (2003), who says 'Brand is a person's gut feeling about a product, service, or company.' Neumeier goes on to point out that brand is a gut felling because customers are all emotional, intuitive beings, despite their best efforts to be rational. It's a person's feeling, because in the end the brand is defined by individuals, not by companies, markets or the so-called general public. Every

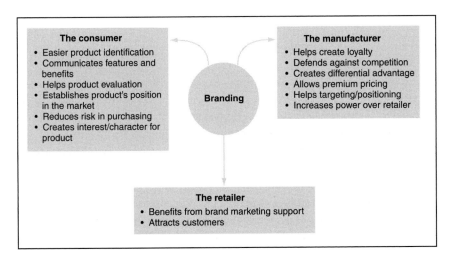

Figure 8.2 *The benefits of branding*
Source: Brassington and Pettit (2003): 283

customer creates his or her own version of brand. While companies cannot control this process, they can influence it by communicating the qualities that make the product and service different from the others. When enough individuals arrive at the same gut feeling, a company can be said to have a brand. In other words, a brand is not what a company says it is. It is what customers say it is. So brand is a bridge between customers and the company.

The customer is the most important business element for every company which wants to win in the global market. How to attract and keep customers has become a popular topic in both industrial and academic areas. Schmitt (2002) indicated that designing customer experience is the most direct and effective method to obtain customers' eyes and hearts. Customer experience brand strategy is a plan for the systematic development of a brand to enable it to meet its agreed objectives based on designing the customer experience. The strategy should be rooted in the brand's vision and operated by the principles of differentiation of customer experience and sustained consumer appeal. The strategy should influence the total implementation of a business to ensure consistent brand behaviours and brand experiences.

Creating a customer experience that becomes synonymous with a brand is increasingly recognised as a vital driver of corporate performance. Companies create loyal customers by delivering *branded customer experiences* that create value for customers beyond the products or services the companies happen to sell (Schmitt 2002). There is evidence that companies are listening. Hewlett-Packard, for example, now has two large customer enterprises: one for consumers and one for business customers. Each one has a president, and reporting directly to that president is a vice-president responsible for the total customer experience. Scott Livengood, CEO of Krispy Kreme, says: 'Instead of a customer service department – words are important and what things are called is very important – so we developed and implemented a customer experience group.'

The PC is a special product. Compared with daily necessities it is a complex and expensive product, so customers should consider it more carefully when they want to buy it. Compared with a car or a flight it has more flexibility to be operated as a customised product, so customers will have more choices to buy their favourite one. Although many products and services are moving towards a more customised approach, during the PC purchasing process customers will be more involved than with other electronic products. Consequently, customer experience design for PC products may be more important and significant than with other products. Customer experience is about more than semantics. Long (2004) formulated a hierarchy of customer experience which divides the process of customer loyalty development into four levels: trust, competence, autonomy and creativity/relatedness. Similarly, Schmitt's research indicated the principal elements of the brand development process as random experience, predictable experience, branded experience and customer loyalty. In this case study the customer experience brand development process will be analysed based on the PC industry practices to create a brand strategy for Lenovo to explore the UK PC market. The aim of this case study is to identify the requirements to create a branding strategy centred on customer experience, which will help Lenovo to better explore and exploit the UK market in an efficient way. This may be expressed as a key question: how can Lenovo use customer experience design as a basis for creating an effective brand strategy to fully understand its customers and gain a significant share of the UK PC market?

THE LENOVO AGENDA

In order to justify the takeover of IBM PCD, Lenovo has a limited time horizon to prove it can make a satisfactory return on capital invested. Inevitably the financiers will wish to see Lenovo making rapid progress. This means generating profitable sales in new markets.

Lenovo urgently needs to formulate a branding strategy centred on customer experience, which will help it to rapidly penetrate the UK PC market.

In order to achieve this it will have to address the following issues:

■ Clarify the important role that branding strategy plays in the development and growth of major companies and organisations.
■ Identify differing interpretations of the 'customer experience' and the relationship to total sensory branding in the UK PC market.
■ Evaluate customer behaviour and their requirements in the UK PC market.
■ Manage the introduction of the Lenovo Group to the UK, considering carefully how the existing brand may be received and interpreted.
■ Compare and contrast the differences and similarities in purchasing behaviour in the Chinese and UK PC markets.
■ Seek new design-led ways to attract UK customers.
■ Develop a new design and branding strategy to support the venture.

CASE STUDY METHODS

To address the Lenovo 'agenda' the following methods were employed.

First, the basic brand strategy and customer experience design principles were established through a literature review. Then the issues concerning the UK PC market environment survey and the UK PC customer survey were connected and integrated through questionnaire, interview and observation research.

A UK PC market survey was conducted in order to understand the UK market environment, so some good examples could be learned from the champions against which to benchmark Lenovo. The target questionnaire group was staff in the PC industry and PC customers. Results of the questionnaire were used to identify and explain which is a top PC brand in the current UK market and why. A PC customer experience survey was used to identify customers' satisfaction, customers' acceptance and customers' requirements in the UK market. Interviews were conducted in parallel to the survey in order to get the latest and most reliable information about PC brand strategy development from the industrial perspective, especially to gain greater insights into the Lenovo brand strategy; they also aimed to get a deeper understanding of PC customers' requirements and relevant and interesting trends. All the companies selected for examination have operated in highly competitive marketplaces, and most of them have a proven record of innovation through both product and service solutions. There were eight interviews conducted in seven PC companies, and most of the interviews lasted between 45 minutes and one hour. All interviews, where possible, were carried out in person. Where this was not possible, interviews were conducted over the telephone. Observation research was operated around different PC shops, which included mixed-brand PC shops and brand store shops. The objective of this observation research was to find customer requirements and good examples of environment design and customer service from the PC shops.

Finally, several brand strategy and customer experience principles were chosen to create the customer experience-based design strategy model for Lenovo to better explore the UK PC market. Customer behaviour analysis (Cope 2003) was used to evaluate PC customers' behaviour during the purchasing process. Then the brand customer experience development model (Schmitt 2002) was adopted to analyse how the brand development was proceeding based on PC customers' purchasing process. The proposed customer experience-based design strategy model was interpreted from a horizontal direction and a vertical direction, which are customer behaviour analysis during PC purchasing and PC brand development analysis.

FINDINGS FROM THE UK SURVEY

From the UK PC market survey, the favourite PC brand in the customers' mind was shown to be Apple. Table 8.1 shows that for design, brand personality and innovation aspects Apple got the highest mark. Apple epitomises the most successful example of design evolution in the PC industry and highlights success rooted in design, derived from human innovation. How does Apple keep its top position in the PC market? There must be many reasons; however, the result from observation research indicated that customer experience design is clearly a major part of the success.

In the Apple shop there are different customer experience areas where the

Table 8.1 Results of the UK PC market survey

PC Brand	Design	Brand Personality	Innovation	Service	Price	Attached Software	Total Quality
Acer	6.5%	5%	5%	2.5%	27.5%	2.5%	8.16%
Apple	62.5%	37%	62.5%	12.5%	1%	25%	33.4%
Dell	4.3%	2.5%	2.5%	22.5%	32.5%	15%	13.2%
IBM	15%	33%	15%	40%	15%	22.5%	23.4%
Toshiba	7.5%	2.5%	5%	7.5%	9%	5%	6%
SONY	12.5%	12.5%	7.5%	5%	2.5%	12.5%	8.75%
Other	1.7%	7.5%	2.5%	10%	12.5%	12.5%	7.78%

customer can experimentally try the latest Apple products (Figure 8.3). Apple has created a successful Macintosh practice ground and brand personality for its customer. No matter whether they are buyers or just visitors, most Apple shop customers expressed their good impression of the Apple brand and said they would like to buy its products. From a purchasing process aspect, the salesperson in Apple is friendly and professional in answering all questions from every customer. The indoor environment design makes the customer really comfortable and relaxed. The new user can get free training on how to use the Macintosh system and software produced by Apple. Apple's customer service has more counters than other PC brand shops, so customers do not waste their time in queuing. Apple customer services have considered more details than other brands for their customers in an effort to maintain the Apple brand quality. Customers can have excellent experiences in Apple shops, which not only allow the customers to buy Apple products, but also build up trust and Apple loyalty. That may be expected to bring intangible but positive benefits to Apple in the future.

In terms of design and brand delivery Apple emulates the total sensory experience approach.

Further survey findings

The other key results from the UK PC customer experience survey were revealed as:

- Pre-sales thinking:

  - Almost half the people surveyed believed that the PC is a normal (to lifestyle) and necessary product for all people, which means there is big potential in the UK PC market.
  - 35.9 per cent of people would like to collect PC purchase information

Figure 8.3 *Apple shop*

from the internet, but only 17.9 per cent of people trusted this information.

■ Almost half the people would like to ask for professional suggestions before purchasing.

■ Almost 80 per cent of people would like to buy a PC product in a mixed-brand shop.

■ Purchasing process:

■ In general customers are not satisfied with their existing PC purchasing

178

service. They are looking for better service and a 'fun' purchasing experience.

- Most of the customers need professional advice during the purchasing process.
- The majority of PC customers prefer a customised purchasing style.
- Customers thought that the current PC salespeople are not professional enough to give them good advice while purchasing PC products.
- 74.4 per cent of people would like to try some new purchasing and service methods for purchasing a PC and for after-sales service.
- Most customers want to have more efficient and more convenient after-sales service.

In response to identified social needs reflecting the changing lifestyles of customers, there are three main kinds of PC distribution in the UK market. One is the brand PC shop such as Apple, Sony, etc. Another is the mixed-brand PC shop, such as PC World, Dixons, and Micro Anvika. The third way is to purchase from the internet.

The distribution of PCs, both desktops and laptops, is evolving gradually, with the internet currently the area of most activity. It would appear that consumers have finally gained confidence in the use of this channel when making a high-price purchase, with Mintel estimating that a third (33 per cent) of retail sales were made using the internet during 2004. This was up by 26 per cent since 2002, with every prospect that further growth can be achieved.

Much of the growth on the internet has come from the development of retailer and manufacturer websites. They are increasingly easy and attractive to use, and the growing confidence of many shoppers in using the internet is also helpful. The success of direct sellers in their own right is also boosting the channel, with Dell the clear victor in this area. Other players here, such as Time Group and the large number of smaller direct sellers, should not be forgotten, as they have modernised their approach towards the internet, making it increasingly consumer-friendly.

A breakdown of retail sales for all PCs in 2002 and 2004 is shown in Figure 8.4, which highlights the performance for the main areas of the market. These figures show that the share of the market for specialist retailers fell back between 2002 and 2004. While specialist retailers still commanded the largest share of sales at 41 per cent in 2004, this was down from 44 per cent in 2002. Specialist electrical retailers claimed 14.5 per cent of sales in 2004, which was also down, from 15.8 per cent in 2002 (Figure 8.5).

The main explanation for this decline is the rise in sales over the internet. Such sales, which include sales made at specialist and non-specialist electrical retailers' sites, were credited with 33 per cent of the market in 2004 as compared to 26 per cent in 2002 (Figure 8.6). Sales from non-specialist retailers, typified by grocery multiples and the likes of Toys 'R' Us, are also up, with an estimated 3 per cent of

179

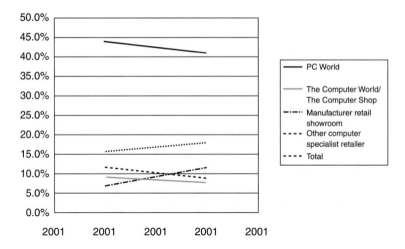

Figure 8.4 *Estimated retailer value shares for UK total home PC market, 2002 and 2004 – specialist PC retailers*

Source: Mintel

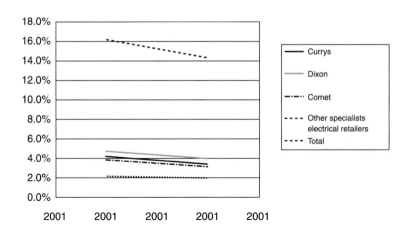

Figure 8.5 *Estimated retailer value shares for UK total home PC market, 2002 and 2004 – specialist electrical retailers*

Source: Mintel

sales in 2004 (Figure 8.6). Traditional direct-sales methods are the main casualty of the changing patterns of distribution within the market, down from 12.9 per cent in 2002 to 8 per cent of sales in 2004 (Figure 8.6).

The largest and most important route for PC sales is the PC World outlet, part of Dixons Stores Group, which is believed to hold 18 per cent of value sales in 2004, up from 16 per cent in 2002 (Figure 8.4). The other notable high street outlet is The Computer Shop, formerly The Computer World, which is owned by

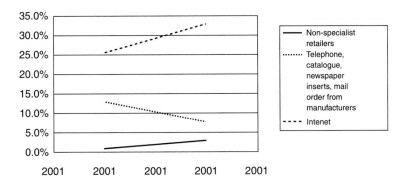

Figure 8.6 *Estimated retailer value shares for UK total home PC market, 2002 and 2004 – other PC retailers*

Source: Mintel

Time Group and was credited with 8 per cent of sales in 2004 (Figure 8.4). Other specialist retailers are also notable, with 9 per cent of sales in 2004 (Figure 8.4), although their share was down partly because of competition from the likes of PC World and partly because of the growth in their own sales via the internet.

Specialist electrical retailers are also active in the market, although there is no clear leader, with most of the major names seeing their share of the market using traditional shopping methods fall back in recent years. Currys is believed to be the largest player here, followed by Dixons and Comet.

CONCLUSIONS

The discussion will address the key issues posed at the outset of the case study research. Initially it will explore the differences between theory and practice. The latter stage will evaluate the benefits of customer experience-based brand strategy for Lenovo and future directions. After 20 years' development, Lenovo has created great brand credits and has retained these credits for many years:

- It is dedicated to the satisfaction and success of every customer.
- Innovation that matters to its customers, and its company, is created and delivered with speed and efficiency.
- It manages its business and makes decisions based on carefully understood facts.
- It has trust and personal responsibility in all its relationships.

The case study research indicates that these core brand values are relevant and applicable to the UK PC market. Thus Lenovo needs to maintain its brand credits

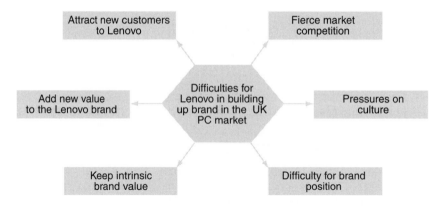

Figure 8.7 *Difficulties for Lenovo in the UK PC market*

shown above in addressing its new UK customers and try to add new value based on UK culture and living habits for the UK market.

However, Lenovo has to face many problems in building up the Lenovo brand in the UK PC market (Figure 8.7). Firstly, the UK PC market is a mature and competitive PC battlefield, made up of strong PC brands occupying the market. Therefore, it is very difficult for Lenovo to gain a market share in the UK. Secondly, since Lenovo is a Chinese brand there are some established Chinese characteristics and styles which characterise its products and brand. For the UK PC market, the question arises as to whether Lenovo should modify its brand characteristics and add more British culture into its brand in order to attract UK customers – or should it stay as it is? Does Lenovo adapt to the customer or does the customer adapt to Lenovo? Of course it is probably unrealistic to expect any major corporation to shed its identity and the powerful influences of nationality.

These questions can be addressed using customer experience design methods.

CUSTOMER BEHAVIOUR ANALYSIS

This analysis focuses on customer behaviours to understand how customers make decisions. The customer behaviours system is complex, involving the interaction of behaviours, emotions and thoughts. There are three elements or domains (Figure 8.8):

- behavioural: having to do with activity and doing – the hand
- affective: having to do with feelings, emotions, values and motivation – the heart
- cognitive: having to do with thinking and believing – the head.

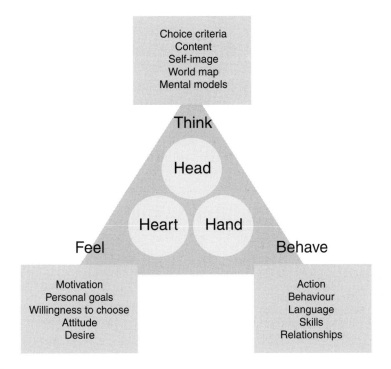

Choice criteria
Content
Self-image
World map
Mental models

Think

Head

Heart   Hand

Feel   Behave

Motivation   Action
Personal goals   Behaviour
Willingness to choose   Language
Attitude   Skills
Desire   Relationships

Figure 8.8 *Three interdependent processes*
Source: Cope (2003)

This model is the basic psychological view of humankind that goes back to Ancient Greek and probably Egyptian philosophy. It views a human as composed of three interdependent processes. All are interdependent, and no one part can change without the other parts also changing.

According to this research, during the thinking phase the British PC customer purchasing process would consider price, brand, functionality, product usability, quality and so on to make decisions. According to the result of surveys the most considered factor was functionality. It is not an easy factor to explain to PC customers, so customer experience design can allow customers to use the product and feel new functions of the product before they buy it. Customer experience design is the best way of explaining to customers to help them understand better about the product (Figure 8.9). From a feeling aspect, improving purchasing design and after-sales service design will give customers a deeper impression. This would not decrease the feeling during first sight of a well-designed product but rather maintain it at a high level. From a behavioural point of view, 88 per cent of British customers preferred a customised purchase style; thus customised sales design can be used as a main method to increase customer satisfaction in the UK PC market.

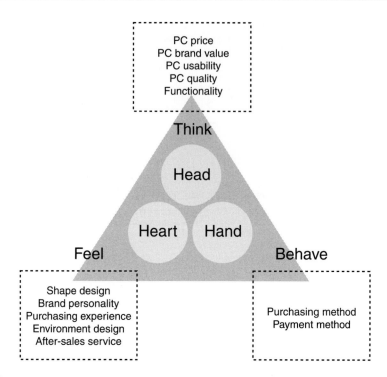

Figure 8.9 *Three interdependent processes analysis*

BRAND DEVELOPMENT PROCESS

For internationalisation purposes, the Lenovo group changed its original logo from 'Legend' to 'Lenovo', as depicted in Figures 8.10 to 8.12.

For the mainland China market Lenovo plan to use an 'English plus Chinese'-style logo (Figure 8.11); for the overseas market they will use 'Lenovo' only. 'Le' is from the original logo 'Legend', to continue the meaning of myth; 'novo' means 'innovation'. From the PC customer survey questionnaire it was revealed that 16 per cent of UK customers think that Lenovo is a brand for PCs, 10 per cent of customers think that Lenovo is an IT brand, 9 per cent of customers think that it is a brand for cars and 7 per cent of customers think that it is for shoes. The remaining UK customers think that Lenovo may be a brand of food, clothes or other product. Obviously, Lenovo really needs to highlight the characteristics and values of its brand. It is clear that Lenovo has much work to do to achieve even basic recognition. But since IBM is universally known in the UK, perhaps Lenovo needs to consider the need for care not to undermine the IBM PC brand in promoting the Lenovo brand.

There are many examples of successful sub-brands where customers are usually

Figure 8.10 *The old Legend logo*

Figure 8.11 *The new logo for the Chinese market*

Figure 8.12 *The new logo for the global market*

unaware of the brand owner and many industrial holding companies which own a range of brands and frequently buy and sell them.

If Lenovo opts to develop its own brand based on Schmitt's model (2002) in which customer experience drives customer loyalty and profits, Lenovo should develop its brand from consistent to valuable (Figure 8.13) – maintaining and protecting the core and adding value.

To achieve consistency Lenovo should have consistent mind identity (MI), behaviour identity (BI) and visual identity (VI). When comparing the three interdependent processes featured, MI can be associated with the head, BI with the hand and VI with the heart. Customers will accumulate brand purchasing experience when they are influenced by the same brand identity. BI and VI are more relevant to customers within the whole brand identity system than MI. BI relates to all the behaviours in the company in order to arrive at the final business aim. As part of the customer experience brand strategy, behaviours relevant to customers must be emphasised. Also from a consistency angle, all behaviours from the staff of Lenovo to their customers should have the same standard and quality. This means that a customer should always get the same high-quality service from every Lenovo shop. As long as customers have been consistently influenced by the same quality service experience, then the experience will turn into a brand impression. If Lenovo's service standard keeps changing all the time, it will be difficult for customers to build up a steady and good brand impression. VI is also a very important factor for Lenovo in creating a brand impression in the customers' mind. It is an identity factor for people; each company should have one VI system

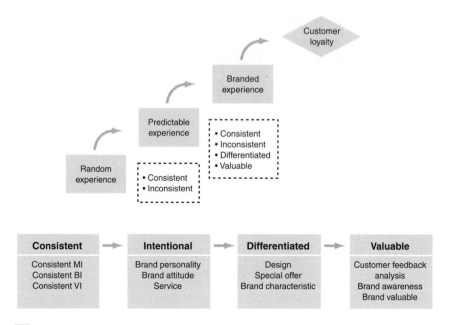

Figure 8.13 *Customer loyalty*

to promote its brand image. Consistent BI and VI can encapsulate how professional Lenovo is and make such brand features vivid.

To establish clear intent, the brand personality, brand attributes and service can
help Lenovo to support these brand characteristics and value in order to maintain
its brand position in customers' minds.

Differentiation in the company can be achieved by unique product and brand
features which should be used to distinguish Lenovo from other PC brands.
Creating a well-designed customer experience and consistently delivering
'special' customer services are the best way to distinguish Lenovo from other
competing brands.

Adding value can be featured by offering customers a value proposition based
on a timely and insightful understanding of customer needs. This requires an
ongoing measurement of customers' changing needs and emotional responses to
the products offered.

THREE PHASES FOR THE PC PURCHASE PROCESS

By examining the PC purchasing process (Figure 8.14), it is possible to gain a
deeper understanding of the thinking and decision processes.

The exercise begins by dividing the PC customer experience of the purchasing
process into three phases: pre-sales thinking, purchasing process and after-sales

Pre-sales thinking	Purchasing process	After-sales service
• Information selection	• Shop environment design	• After-sales repair guarantee
• Information evaluation	• Product display design	• Product delivery
• Personality	• Sales service	• Hardware upgrade
• Perception	• Product choice	• Software upgrade
• Brand awareness	• Brand choice	• After-sales social activity
• Socio-cultural	• Dealer choice	• Special service
• Technological	• Purchase timing	
• Economic	• Purchase amount	
• Political		

Figure 8.14 *Pre-sales thinking, the purchasing process and after-sales service*

service. In researching and building this case study an analysis of the PC purchasing process was conducted based on brand customer experience development analysis. This was previously introduced in relation to the way customers think (Figure 8.8) and must be interpreted in order to fully understand PC customers' requirements. During the pre-sales thinking phase, customers collect information in different ways, such as internet searching, advertisements or asking friends, etc. No matter what the customer has done before the purchasing behaviour, all of this is included in the pre-sales thinking phase. After customers have got enough information about the PC products they want, they will start the purchasing behaviour. From the time customers start to purchase until they get the product, this phase is defined as the purchasing process phase. This period includes remaking decisions, the in-shop purchasing experience, the sales service experience, the environment design experience and so on. After-sales service means all the service offered after the customers have bought their PC product. This period consists of after-sales delivery, the after-sales maintenance guarantee, hardware and software upgrades and so on.

LENOVO CUSTOMER EXPERIENCE BRAND STRATEGY MODEL

Based on the brand customer experience development analysis and PC purchasing process analysis, a new Lenovo customer experience brand strategy model was established, as shown in Figure 8.15. The three stages of the PC purchasing process are analysed with different criteria, as there were different customer actions or behaviours in each section. *Pre-sales thinking* should be derived from personality, attitude influences, perception, search conditions and active or passive information aspects. Through these aspects of 'designed' customer experience, the brand strategy will help British customers to understand Lenovo more easily and better before purchasing. Lenovo needs to design the customer

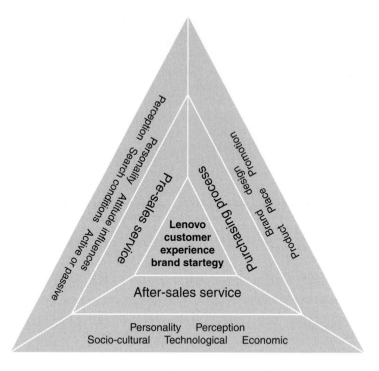

Figure 8.15 *Lenovo customer experience brand strategy*

purchasing process experience based on design, brand, price, place, product and promotion. This may be referred to as 'packaging' the total experience. The purchasing process is the process by which to feel Lenovo's brand characteristics and values. From personality, perception, socio-cultural, technological and economic aspects, design of the customer *after-sales service* can completely satisfy customers' physical and mental requirements. Customers will feel that they have 'got more than they paid for' in a delightful purchasing environment. Thus the design and branding strategy uses high-quality customer knowledge management to deliver a competitive advantage.

LENOVO'S CUSTOMER EXPERIENCE-BASED DESIGN

Lenovo was a pioneer of the home PC concept, and the Lenovo '1 + 1' home PC succeeded in the Chinese marketplace. But the PC was not very common in China at that time; it was regarded as expensive, very professional equipment which could only be used in some special science field. Lenovo created a new 'selling proposition' concept which recommended personal computer utilisation for education and the family. It created a good opportunity for customers to experience what a personal computer is and how it can improve their lives. In 1999, the internet was becoming influential, but only a few people in China knew how to use the internet, and connecting to the internet was a complex process for most PC users. To address these difficulties of internet operation, Lenovo designed an intelligent internet keyboard which had some special functions to help PC users to gain access to the internet (Figure 8.16). On the top right corner of the keyboard it designed and built an extra internet area, which included an internet button, a channel wheel and a row of information category buttons. The

a)

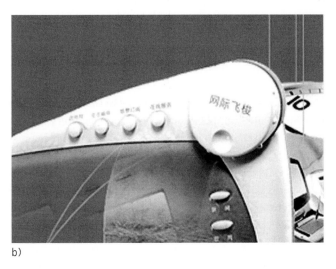

b)

Figure 8.16 *(a) The Lenovo PC and (b) the internet keyboard*

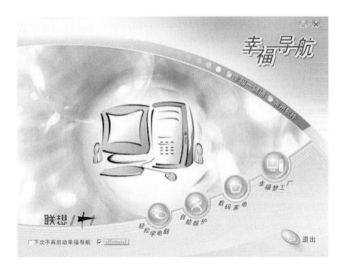

Figure 8.17 Happyhome

internet button can connect to the internet with just one press, the channel wheel can lead the user to different websites, just as with radio and TV, and the information category buttons can assist users to go directly to different websites with specific information, such as news, music, education, entertainment, life, and stocks and shares. Lenovo gained a lot of profit based on operating this customer experience-led design approach in their product design development.

Happyhome is another good example of customer experience design strategy which helped Lenovo to 'strike gold' in the PC market in 1996 (Figure 8.17). Happyhome is application software which builds up a virtual home environment in the PC interface. The objective is that, after opening the Happyhome, the customer will feel free and relaxed, as at home. The Happyhome makes computer operation easy and 'happy'. If customers want to watch TV, they can just click a TV set in the virtual home; if they want music, they can click a speaker in the virtual home. Lenovo utilised simple symbols to indicate different kinds of application software, and a simple double click will open every software function which customers want. There is a lot of 'furniture' in the Happyhome, such as TV, radio, photo albums, a movie maker, entertainment and so on.

After the IBM PCD acquisition in 2005, Lenovo extended the emphasis from its customer experience-based design strategy from product design development into the new Lenovo brand development. Since the core of the brand is the product range, it is clear that Lenovo has a valuable design strategy on which to build the new brand.

LENOVO IDENTITY SURVEY

To further evaluate the current progress in developing the Lenovo brand identity in the UK market a further survey was conducted in July 2006 to compare the brand recognition with the 2005 results.

The survey asked the following questions:

- Do you know the Lenovo brand and its products?
- From which media channel did you know Lenovo?
- What is your feeling about Lenovo brand attributes?
- Do you know the relationship between Lenovo and IBM PCD?

Survey results

Based on a statistically significant sample survey analysis, the questionnaire results indicated that 37.6 per cent of UK potential customers knew Lenovo as an international PC brand. Compared with 16 per cent from the 2005 survey which asked the same question, Lenovo has progressed very well in building up the Lenovo brand visual identity in the UK market although the non-recognition by 62.4 per cent may indicate a long way to go.

Almost 50 per cent of potential customers who knew the Lenovo brand had got Lenovo information from internet, newspaper and TV advertisement: this represents approximately one in five UK potential customers. Only 6.7 per cent of potential customers had got to know Lenovo from outdoor advertisement. So outdoor advertising may be a less effective communication channel or it may represent a new possible channel for Lenovo to extend its brand identity.

Of UK potential customers who identified Lenovo, 43.7 per cent think the biggest brand value from Lenovo is technical, followed by service and innovation. Nearly half of the UK potential customers who knew the Lenovo brand understand the relationship between Lenovo and IBM PCD.

Lenovo clearly needs more time to develop the Lenovo brand in order to match the position which IBM occupies in the UK PC market. However, the growth in recognition may be considered significant given the highly competitive UK PC market.

STRATEGIC DIRECTIONS

Through the customer experience survey and case study research, Lenovo can design a brand strategy model based on a deep understanding of cultural influences and customer experience. It could implement the customer experience-based branding model in the UK PC market by:

- Pre-sales thinking:

- Offer customers a different information search service for their different requirements and for different segments of customers.
- Design a PC information learning centre to help customers gain more IT knowledge and confidence through the Lenovo customer experience service.
- Design a free PC information search area in the Lenovo store brand shop.
- Design internet purchase and multimedia publicity channels.
- Create more opportunities to make contact with customers and build up faith in the Lenovo brand.

- Purchasing process:

  - Extend Lenovo's brand awareness during the purchasing process by interior environment design and visual communication design.
  - Optimise the brand's visual identity to make a deeper impression on the customers: consider choice of colours, font and tone of voice.
  - Design a retailing strategy through mixed-brand PC offices and an attractive service point.
  - Train sales assistants to a high standard to offer professional advice for customers who need help.
  - Bring out Lenovo's brand characteristics and brand values during the purchasing process through visual communication design.
  - Develop a customised purchase style which can be used as a key method with professional sales assistants.

- After-sales service:

  - Develop a special 'humanistic' design service and surprise 'added-value' feature.
  - Offer hardware and software upgrades to keep advanced technology available to customers.
  - Offer different after-sales service to different target customer groups.
  - Offer trade-in sales or discounts on relevant PC products for loyal customers.
  - Organise social activities to increase Lenovo's impression and reputation.
  - Improve product design and service based on customer feedback.

CONCLUSIONS

The proposed customer experience-based brand strategy model has been evaluated by a number of key people, including the design manager and designers in Lenovo, PC retailers and PC customers. Interviewees who work in Lenovo confirmed that the proposed model would be useful to help them better understand the UK PC market and UK customers. Other people thought this model could help them better understand their customers and improve the detailed design of the customer experience.

Each of the identified recommendations carries many creative implementation challenges. In this sense the recommendations may be regarded as a 'meta-strategy' and components as key elements for design development. All elements of the strategy are interdependent, and Lenovo must identify the priorities but also ensure it does not neglect important aspects, as even minor weaknesses can negate the advantages.

Once the strategic design and branding directions are established, future research can consider areas such as the following. Which kind of design practice can be used to effectively develop and add value to Lenovo? How can Lenovo design the total sensory customer experience to improve its brand impression? What are the best methods to gain a progressively deeper understanding of the culture, and influence UK customers to trust the brand and become loyal customers? What should be done following the strategy to maintain customer loyalty? Should Lenovo develop sub-brands or co-brand with another company? There are many other aspects which may be considered in future research to identify how Lenovo can use design and branding strategy for successful product development and branding.

REVIEW QUESTIONS

1 What are the advantages and disadvantages of branding?
2 There have been many definitions of branding; how would you define 'branding'?
3 It could be argued that successful branding requires the clear and consistent communication of visual messages to all stakeholders; why is this important?
4 Can you identify successful examples of sub-branding where the customer is unaware of the parent company?
5 What significant external forces in the European marketplace influence present and potential client needs?
6 What are the potential benefits for Lenovo as major supporter to the 2008 Olympic Games in Beijing?
7 What are the many benefits for organisations in developing close strategic alliances?
8 Apple has developed a sophisticated approach to providing a branded

customer experience in both its products and its services — can you provide examples of these?

9   How can consumer knowledge and feedback be captured and incorporated into the design and development process?

10   In the PC market, price is one key factor that influences purchasing decisions; can you identify and discuss other factors?

PROJECT QUESTIONS

1   The Lenovo case is complex and presented in such a way as to show the numerous factors involved in the brand development process; consider three questions and their results and provide research correlations between them which do not appear fully in the set of conclusions.

2   Referring to the text, devise a questionnaire pro forma for Lenovo in which to elicit customer purchasing considerations of which the results could be incorporated into the design development process.

3   What are the benefits for Lenovo that you can identify in terms of establishing a strategic alliance with IBM?

4   Lenovo wishes to develop a new design and branding strategy to gain a foothold in the competitive UK PC marketplace; referring to the text, can you identify and discuss other key considerations that may enable this strategy?

5   Can you identify other new market opportunities that Lenovo could exploit once it has gained strong market recognition in the UK?

REFERENCES

Armstrong, K. (2004) *Principles of marketing*, 10th edn. (London: Pearson Prentice Hall)

Brassington, F. and Pettit, S. (2003) *Principles of marketing*, 3rd edn. (Harlow: Prentice Hall)

Cope, M. (2003) *The seven Cs of consulting: the definitive guide to the consulting process.* (Harlow: Pearson Education)

Gobé, M. (2001) *Emotional branding: the new paradigm for connecting brands to people.* (New York: Allworth Press)

Kotler, P. (2003) *Marketing management*, 11th edn. (Upper Saddle River, NJ: Prentice Hall)

Long, K. (2004) Customer loyalty and experience design in e-business. *Design Management Review*, 15(2)

Neumeier, M. (2003) *The brand gap: how to bridge the distance between business strategy and design: a whiteboard overview.* (Indianapolis, IN: New Riders Publishing)

Schmitt, B. H. (2002) *Managing the customer experience.* (Harlow: Pearson Education)

FURTHER READING

Dicken, P. (1992) *Global shift.* (London: Paul Chapman)

Levitt, T. (1983) The globalisation of markets. *Harvard Business Review*, May–June: 10–27

Ohmae, K. (1994) *The borderless world.* (London: HarperCollins)

Porter, M. (1992) *The strategic role of international marketing: global marketing management.* (Boston, MA: Harvard Business School Press)

Williams, A., Hands, D. and O'Brien, M. (eds) (2006) Proceedings: D2B, the first International Design Management Symposium, Shanghai

Index